D1545847

The Texas Red River Country

NUMBER THIRTEEN:
Environmental History Series
Dan L. Flores, General Editor

The Texas Red River Country

THE OFFICIAL SURVEYS
OF THE HEADWATERS, 1876

Edited by T. Lindsay Baker

With Ornithological Notes by Kenneth D. Seyffert
Foreword by Dan L. Flores

Texas A&M University Press
College Station

The paper used in this book meets the minimum requirements
of the American National Standard for Permanence
of Paper for Printed Library Materials, Z39.48-1984.
Binding materials have been chosen for durability.

Library of Congress Cataloging-in-Publication Data

The Texas Red River country : the official surveys of the headwaters,
    1876 / edited by T. Lindsay Baker ; ornithological notes by Kenneth
D. Seyffert; foreword by Dan Flores.
        p.   cm. — (Environmental history series ; no.13)
    ISBN 0-89096-803-9
    1. Red River (Tex.-La.) 2. Red River Region (Tex.-La.)—
History. I. Baker, T. Lindsay. II. Series.
GB1227.R4T48   1988
508.764´8—dc21   98-4859
                                                                CIP

CONTENTS

ILLUSTRATIONS

MAPS

FOREWORD

In the year 1875 an observant military aide named Jacob Sturm got to do something few of us are ever privileged to experience in any kind of general way, and no one but Sturm ever got to do in this particular way. Sturm had been selected to accompany to the reservation from their secret redoubt in the recesses of the great Llano Estacado plateau what historians have called the last "wild band" of Comanches to surrender to the American military, a band that included not only Isatai, the famous shaman and Sun Dancer, but also Quanah Parker, the handsome young mixed-blood *nomnekaht* (war leader) who had attracted so much attention during the Red River War that finished Comanche tenure on the High Plains.

What Sturm got to see through the eyes of individuals like these was something of the Comanche conception of the core of a landscape—*La Comancheria*—they had held since seizing it from the Apaches 250 years before. The group Sturm accompanied were the last Comanche inhabitants of the vortex of what once had been a broader world they called their own. As inhabitants of the vast, flat, high plain and its canyon perimeter, these Comanches appropriately called themselves Kwahadis—antelopes. And as they moved in a northeasterly direction from the vicinity of Big Spring to Fort Sill, the Comanches pointed out to Sturm the landmarks of their countryside and their method of conceptualizing it.

To Comanche residents of the Llano Estacado of 125 years ago, the world was flat but its edges had been chewed upon. The sun, the first and principal cause of all life and the energy that pulsed through it, journeyed across this stationary world, bisected it, and radiated power into everything. As Sturm recorded for us, the names of particularized places were never given the common names of individuals but were most often named in a straightforward way from sensory apprehension (e.g. *Wah-we-ohr,* Blowing Mountain, *Acu-mah-cup,* Juniper-lined

Creek, or *Kit-a-kway,* Excrement Hill). Names often embedded valuable ecological information, as with *Sabe-Honovith,* literally a good-
place-to-camp-with-cottonwoods-and-springs, or the very frequent
suffixes *hono* (good-sized creek or river) or *honovit* (a little bit of water
most of the time), or *Tah-tem-a-reie* (Trader's Creek). Although Sturm
didn't record them (or the Comanches didn't tell him), we know some
of their most sacred places were associated with events from deep folk
memory. Bison herds were believed to be regenerated every spring in
the depths of Palo Duro Canyon, and the Medicine Mounds farther
down the Red River, sacred hills where a culture figure had anciently
been cured, are believed capable of healing even today.

The Kwahadis of the Llano Estacado said little to Sturm about
their sense of ecological relationships, but we know that they were
familiar with virtually every mammal species of the Llano Estacado,
and that for hunters they had a surprisingly complete botanical knowledge. Anthropologists have recorded detailed information on sixty-
seven medicinal and food plants among them, some of them
differentiated down to the level of the subspecies. Indians obviously
possessed not only a scientific method but a philosophy of intercon-
nections or systems in their world and probably saw ecological relationships in a way that involved energy flow between animals. The
Lakota, for example, linked moths, dragonflies, spiders, bears, elk, and
bison together as relatives.

It so happened that at almost the same historic moment that Jacob
Sturm recorded for us some Comanche thoughts about their world, a
military exploring expedition commanded by Lt. Ernest Ruffner and
assisted by ornithologist Charles MacCauley was examining that exact
country with the tools, techniques, and ideologies of the Western
scientific method. This Ruffner exploration of 1876 to the head of the
Red River in the Texas Panhandle was not the first time the American
government had attempted to probe this region for Western science.
President Thomas Jefferson, who regarded the Red River as "next to
the Missouri, the most interesting water of the Mississippi," had in
1806 initiated a remarkable string of failed attempts to get a scientific
party to map out the Red River of the Southwest. Spanish opposition
and an inability to conceptualize the Llano Estacado Plateau defeated
that attempt, Zebulon Pike's the following year, and Stephen Long's in
1820. The secrets of the Red River, in fact, proved almost as elusive to
nineteenth-century American science as the sources of the Nile were
to British imperialists.

This particular mystery seemed a little less mysterious in 1852 when
muttonchopped Capt. Randolph Marcy and Lt. George McClellan (*that*
McClellan, within a few years the source of Abraham Lincoln's vexa-
tion)—with naturalist-geologist George Shumard along—finally

claimed to have found the ultimate source of the Red River. But Marcy introduced still more head-scratching. Where, exactly, had he been when he described "the magnificence of . . . these grand and novel pictures . . . [of] unreclaimed sublimity and wilderness"? The best guess now is that Marcy actually decided to abandon the search one hundred miles short of his goal, in high-drama Tule Canyon, a stunning side gorge (as Ruffner would discover) of the main Red River canyon, Palo Duro.

Marcy in fact constituted the American government's fourth failure at penetrating the sources of the Red River. He had left one of the most intriguing regions of the Southwest, that unexpected canyon province on the eastern face of the Llano Estacado, barely explored and certainly unmapped. Which brings the story to the Ruffner Expedition, for even historians have realized only very recently that the real discovery and mapping of this colorful crimson canyonlands—a country "so washed and twisted shapen as to marvel the eye with its intricacy and daze it with its brilliancy," Ruffner said of it—fell to Ruffner, MacCauley, guide Billy Dixon, and their loquacious German-born artist-illustrator, Adolphus Hunnius, a full quarter century after Marcy. Setting up a base camp at Dreamland Falls in Palo Duro in late May, 1876, they spent the next five weeks immersed in a canyon country that even today is known intimately by only a handful of people. It was virtually the same country the Comanches had pointed out to Jacob Sturm the previous year. But what a difference the Ruffner party brought to its perception!

On a localized scale, this exploration bequeaths us the way of looking at nature and the kinds of knowledge that Meriwether Lewis and John Wesley Powell left us of nineteenth-century Montana or the Colorado Plateau. Rather than folk stories clinging to the landscape out of long association, places named for their ecological value to a nomadic life, or species linked together via energy flow, the Ruffner party brought the scientific worldview to bear on the Llano Estacado country. A geology refined on a world-wide scale allowed them to see different kinds of patterns in the landscape than the Comanches did. And MacCauley's specialty, the science of ornithology, enabled them to do a kind of baseline ecological examination of this canyon country, literally a time-machine snapshot of upper Red River nature as it existed in 1876.

Editor T. Lindsay Baker's splendid work in rescuing and bringing us this view of a lost world ought to be valued most in just that way, I think. The exploration of the West *was* high adventure, true enough, and one of the things readers of the Ruffner, MacCauley, and Hunnius journals get in this book is a wonderful backseat ticket on a journey into one of the last significant parts of the West that American explorers examined. But pay closest attention to the environmental history here. The ecological world the Ruffner party describes here—the "wilderness" at the sources of the upper Red River—is only superficially the same one that tourists and hikers in Palo Duro Canyon State Park see today. Books like this one are a fundamental way to understand history's most important lesson: How and why things change.

This is exactly the kind of book, then, to feed to the imagination on a winter night beside a fireplace popping with fragrant juniper. And then, later, slip into a backpack for a trip into the canyon country for a bit of walking and reflection on how fleeting is any one particular view of reality. And why.

—Dan L. Flores
Bitterroot Valley, Montana

INTRODUCTION

"I got commissioned to go out and catch as many butterflies as possible," penned War Department draftsman Adolph Hunnius on the evening of Friday, May 26, 1876, as he sat in camp near the head of the Red River in the Texas Panhandle.[1] Butterfly catching was not the government employee's regular activity, but the German-born Civil War veteran knew that whatever the commanding officer ordered was what he should do. Consequently he chased the winged insects across the Texas prairie from nine o'clock until twelve-thirty that morning.

Hunnius was a member of a combined topographic and scientific survey that recorded and mapped the land and its watercourses at the head of the Prairie Dog Town Fork (the main fork) of the Red River in 1876. The U.S. Army needed such maps and reports for planning military troop movements in the region, but its officers, men, and employees in the field recorded more than just the locations of water sources and the lay of the land. Perhaps even more important for us today, they also carefully made notes on the natural world they observed, even collecting botanical and faunal specimens for transfer to scientific institutions. The efforts by the members of the 1876 expedition to the headwaters of the Red River provided a verbal and visual portrait of the central Texas Panhandle at a pivotal time. The party recorded the region at the close of the commercial buffalo hunt but before the introduction of domestic cattle, after which livestock raising by Euro-Americans altered the vegetation and appearance of the regional landscape forever.[2]

The 1876 expedition to the head of the Red River, known as the Ruffner Expedition from the name of its commander, 1st Lt. Ernest Howard Ruffner, created detailed documentary records of the landscape, vegetation, and animal life of the central Panhandle of Texas. Not only did Ruffner himself make notes on the geology of the region, but the men under his supervision collected specimens and prepared written notes on botany, meteorology, ornithology, entomology, and herpetology. Lieutenant Ruffner forwarded at least some of the actual specimens to the Reading Society of Natural Sciences in Reading, Pennsylvania. The commander also made watercolor paintings along the route, while draftsman Adolph Hunnius prepared topographical sketches and survey field notes on which he later based maps. He also made pencil drawings for his own enjoyment that became known to scholars a century later.

On a survey line run north from the Red River to the Canadian, where it connected with known points on previous U.S. Army surveys, Lt. Thomas M. Woodruff of the 1876 party informally conducted what may be considered the first conscious "excavation" of an archaeological site in the Panhandle region. On May 25, 1876, atop a high hill overlooking the Canadian valley, he found "a space about 12 feet square, marked out by stones" that appeared to him to be a grave. There, he wrote, "after digging and scraping around with my sheath knife I found several arrowheads of flint."[3] Three-quarters of a century later archaeologist Jack T. Hughes identified the same site from aerial photographs, visited it, and recorded it, concluding that rather than being a burial it was instead the remains of a prehistoric Panhandle Aspect Indian slab house.[4]

Expedition members in their official reports painted word pictures of the southern Great Plains as they viewed the region during the late spring and early summer of 1876. The season had been drier than usual, Lieutenant Ruffner explained, noting that "the long steady view or the gentle swell, and long wave of the quiet parched plains has a strange fascination, and the slightest break to its vacuity has an alarming attraction." He elaborated, "A withered 'soap weed' may be a forest, its dead last year's stalk of bloom may be a painted warrior." In less romantic descriptions elsewhere, Ruffner chronicled in detail the landscapes he found, as he did for the playa lakes that dotted the plains: "Filled by the rain they sometimes are of a depth as great as ten feet, and many are seen filled every year to a depth of two, three, or four feet."

The party members also noted the effects wrought on the region by Euro-Americans since they had expelled the southern Plains Indians just over a year before. The cutting down of trees to be used as timber or fuel was one obvious change they made. Near Fort Elliott in the Texas Panhandle, Lieutenant Ruffner observed: "Not far off are fine groves on several of the adjacent streams which have been heavily drawn on for the construction of the post and for the necessary fuel." After traveling farther, Ruffner witnessed the work of the commercial buffalo hide hunters, commenting, "We were soon in the buffalo, but instead of the countless herds of five years before the bands were small and not numerous. Thousands ran where tens of thousands were found in 1872."

For the people who comprised the survey party, the 1876 expedition was first and foremost a topographic exercise. The army needed maps of the region, and the officers, men, and civilian employees in the field devoted the bulk of their time to the use of surveying instruments and equipment to record precisely the region so that detailed maps might later be drawn.

Two types of topographic surveys were undertaken concurrently. While some of the expedition personnel, including the teamsters with wagons, traveled as nearly directly as possible from campsite to campsite, soldiers measured the distances with an odometer attached to a wagon wheel. They also used a prismatic compass to measure the bearings from point to point along their routes. This group, led by a civilian scout and recorded by a sergeant, generally departed camp as early as sufficient light allowed them to read their compass, typically reaching their destinations by about midday. This party also carried a barometer, which was used for computing relative elevations of points along the survey line.

Another group of officers and enlisted men conducted the second type of survey using a theodolite. This instrument allowed its users not only to determine the bearings of each point from its preceding point, but also, when used with stadia rods, to compute distances traversed without having to measure them on the ground with chains. The soldiers holding the stadia rods adjusted movable targets or shields on the rods as signaled by the officer at the theodolite, who directed the placement of the targets to intercept two horizontal crosshairs he saw in the telescope of the instrument. The soldier then recorded the numerical positions on the scale of the stadia rod for the two targets. These relative numerical positions of the targets became the basis for mathematically computing the distances. Although this measurement system allowed for some error, it proved to be remarkably accurate, especially in rough country in which chaining of distances would have been difficult or even impossible. Heat waves from the surface of the ground impeded the efforts of the officers to see the targets on the stadia rods, so that much of the work on this part of the survey had to be conducted during the comparatively cool morning hours, leaving the afternoons for observation of the natural world and collecting of scientific specimens. At several camps along the route of the expedition, Lieutenant Ruffner set up a transit to establish true north-south meridians based on Polaris as a check on the bearings read by both surveying parties, while regular barometric readings provided the basis for calculating elevations of various points.

In time the survey crews learned how best to conduct their work. The men on the stadia line survey, for example, discovered that a person could carry the theodolite on horseback by placing the points of the tripod supporting the instrument into a carbine sling in front of a stirrup. They also learned to use two forward stadia rods so that the man at the instrument could choose which he could see better. The crews gradually increased their speed to two and a half to three miles an hour on the open prairie, measuring an average of about fifteen hundred feet from point to point.

Not all the survey work went smoothly. Deeply eroded country in and around the canyons of the Red River impeded progress, as did occasional stormy and windy conditions. Sometimes the difficulties involved human frailties, as Adolph Hunnius noted June 1, 1876: "Lt. Ruffner sent several messages up to me complaining about stations to[o] big, or Prairie Dog holes and ants' nests, and at least twice about my stooping down to watch his signals. I forwarded a rather uncivil note to him which he answered in a rather cutting and sharp way. I had stepped into a prairie dog hole and hurt my leg. Was in much pain. leg was swelling badly. Of all of which Lt. Ruffner did not know. Anyway, he wrote that he would discharge me on the spot, then and there. . . . But nothing was said by him afterwards."

Each afternoon or evening when practicable, the men "worked up" their field notes from the day's surveying. While they were making these computations and sometimes during the field work as well, draftsman Hunnius prepared topographic sketches of the landscape. He later would combine these sketches with the field notes he and others had made to prepare a series of large hand-drawn maps showing the route of the surveyors and the country through which they passed.

The survey of the headwaters of the Red River was the idea of its commander, Lieutenant Ruffner. In spring 1876 he was serving as the chief engineer for the Department of the Missouri at Fort Leavenworth, Kansas. Funds for the operation of his office had already been expended for the first months of 1876, so Ruffner on April 14 requested permission from the department to undertake the survey in the Texas Panhandle as an inexpensive yet worthwhile project for him and his small staff. He proposed temporarily closing his office at Fort Leavenworth, "the greater part of the office work having been completed." Approval came two days later, and immediately Ruffner set about making plans for the field work on the prairies.[5]

Members of Ruffner's Fort Leavenworth staff and other personnel traveled by rail in late April, 1876, to Dodge City, Kansas.[6] From that location they continued on to the nearby military garrison at Fort

Dodge. Next they went by wagon overland to Camp Supply, Indian Territory, and on to Fort Elliott, in the eastern Texas Panhandle, where they picked up needed supplies, additional wagons, draft animals, a military escort and working crew, and civilian guides. With all the preparations completed, the surveying expedition, consisting of fifty-two men and eighty-four horses and mules, departed Fort Elliott on May 11, 1876.

The surveyors traveled first around the north sides of streams flowing into the Red River, establishing a base camp from which they surveyed the northwestern headwaters. From this camp one contingent also ran a stadia line survey up to the Canadian River to connect with earlier army topographic surveys conducted there and to determine once and for all the actual distance between the two rivers. In the course of their survey work at the true head of the Red River, the juncture of Tierra Blanca and Palo Duro Creeks, the expedition crossed the route of Col. John Irvin Gregg and more than two hundred men from Fort Bascom, New Mexico, who on August 15, 1872, engaged a war party of Kiowas at that location. This tied their survey to known overland routes to New Mexico, giving their results further utility for the army. The party then proceeded southward as a single group down the right side of the Prairie Dog Town Fork of the Red River past Cañoncito Blanco and Tule Canyon before turning northward to reconnect with its earlier line. This "closed" the survey and permitted a check on the previous measurements and mathematical computations. The surveyors returned to Fort Elliott on June 21, 1876, at which time the members of the escort went back to their units and other expedition members started to make their way back to Fort Leavenworth.

Ernest Howard Ruffner, commander of the expedition and chief engineer for the Department of the Missouri, was a Kentucky native who had entered the United States Military Academy in 1863, graduating first in his class in 1867. During his military career, he advanced in rank to captain in 1879, major in 1889, and lieutenant colonel in 1903.[7]

Several other regular officers accompanied the expedition. Lt. Charles Adam Hoke McCauley, 3rd Artillery, and Lt. Thomas Mayhew Woodruff, 5th Infantry, assisted Ruffner in undertaking the stadia line survey. McCauley was on sick leave and participated in the expedition as a volunteer. A native of Maryland, he was appointed from Pennsylvania to West Point in 1866. Graduating twenty-second in his class, he became a second lieutenant in the 3rd Artillery on June 15, 1870. He was still serving at this rank when he traveled to the Texas Panhandle in the spring and summer of 1876. He later advanced to the rank of colonel and became Assistant Quartermaster General on February 24, 1903. McCauley also assumed responsibility for the ornithological portion of the scientific studies, collecting multiple bird skins and eggs and writing a detailed report on the birds that he observed.[8]

Thomas M. Woodruff, a New York State native, was appointed from Washington, D.C., to the U.S. Military Academy on September 1, 1867. Fifteenth in his graduating class, he was appointed a second lieutenant in the 5th Infantry. He received a breveted rank of first lieutenant in recognition of bravery in a fight against hostile Indians at Bear Paw Mountain, Montana, on September 30, 1877. Advancing in rank to major in 1890, he remained in the army until 1899, the year of his death.[9]

Lt. Frank Dwight Baldwin joined the party on its arrival at Fort Elliott in the Texas Panhandle. He commanded the detachment of thirty-two soldiers from the 4th Cavalry and 19th Infantry who escorted the expedition and who provided much of the labor required in undertaking the actual survey. A native of Michigan, Baldwin twice received the Congressional Medal of Honor for valor in service of the United States. He entered the army as a second lieutenant in the Michigan Horse Guards during the Civil War on September 19, 1861. Baldwin received his first medal of honor for distinguished bravery in fighting at Peach Tree Creek, Georgia, on July 20, 1864, and he won his second for gallantry in action against hostile Indians near McClellan Creek in the Texas Panhandle on November 8, 1874.[10]

A notable personage in Western history associated with the expedition was William Dixon, a former commercial buffalo hunter, who served as one of the three War Department guides for the surveyors. He was best known for a notable long gunshot in the Battle of Adobe Walls between white hunters and traders and a force of Comanche, Kiowa, and Southern Cheyenne warriors in June, 1874. Born in West Virginia in 1850, he moved west as an adolescent, became a teamster and later professional hunter, and after leaving the buffalo hide trade became a civilian scout for the army.[11]

On return to Fort Leavenworth at the close of the survey, Lieutenant Ruffner had expected the officers who had accompanied him in May and June to assist him in preparing the official report. He was surprised and disappointed to learn that Lieutenant Woodruff was ordered to return to his regiment, while Lieutenant McCauley, his sick leave ended, was ordered to return to duty and sent to Washington, D.C. Woodruff did prepare the entomological portion of the report and McCauley did write an ornithological report, but with these exceptions, Ruffner and his civilian draftsman, Adolph Hunnius, were left to complete the remainder of the paperwork and maps on their own. Ruffner wrote the report, while back at Fort Leavenworth Hunnius prepared seventeen sheets of beautifully drawn maps recording the route of the surveyors.

Ruffner and Hunnius worked on their report and maps through the autumn, winter, and spring of 1876–77. Finally in July and September, 1877, Ruffner sent the manuscript of his report in three installments to the chief of engineers of the army in Washington for publication in the annual report of the Department of War.[12] Ruffner was chagrined to learn that after Lieutenant McCauley returned to regular duty, he did indeed prepare an ornithological report for the Red River survey, but he did not give it to Ruffner. The commander complained, "By an unfortunate error of judgment . . . without mentioning the matter to me," McCauley sent a copy of his report to Dr. Ferdinand V. Hayden, a geologist working under the direction of the Secretary of the Interior. Hayden saw to it that McCauley's ornithological report appeared in the *Bulletin of the United States Geological and Geographical Survey of the Territories* in 1877.[13] Undaunted by the loss of McCauley's ornithological notes, Ruffner proceeded with final changes and corrections of printer's proofs for his report, which appeared in the annual report of the Department of War for 1877.[14] Adolph Hunnius's seventeen sheets of detailed maps went to Washington with the manuscript of Ruffner's report, but they were never published. Both the maps and the official report remained in army hands until well into the twentieth century, at which time the department transferred them to the National Archives, where they remain preserved today. There they lay virtually unknown and overlooked by historians until the 1980s.

Draftsman Hunnius returned to Leavenworth at the close of the expedition. In 1877 he left the War Department to open a combined newsstand and toy store in Leavenworth, where he lived with his wife and children. Occasionally supplementing his income by drafting, he remained in the city. Hunnius's sons became successful jewelers in Leavenworth, where Adolph lived until his death in 1923. Forty years later, one of his descendants transcribed his diary from the 1876 Red River survey and sent a copy of the transcript and reproductions of its pencil sketches to the Panhandle-Plains Historical Museum in Canyon, Texas. Then in the 1970s, half a century after Hunnius's death, his granddaughter transferred many of his personal papers to the Kenneth Spencer Research Library at the University of Kansas. Among those materials were the cloth-bound engineer's field book containing the immigrant draftsman's handwritten and beautifully illustrated diary of his experiences on the survey of the headwaters of the Red River.[15]

During research for the preparation of a co-authored study of the 1874 Adobe Walls Trading Post, I came across the typewritten transcript of Adolph Hunnius's diary in the manuscript files in the Research Center at the Panhandle-Plains Historical Museum. Stimulated by the lively text and striking illustrations, I then sought out the official report of the 1876 Red River survey in the National Archives, where I also discovered the long-forgotten detailed maps. Further investigation, assisted by Robert L. Knecht of Topeka, led me to the manuscript diary kept by Adolph Hunnius while on the survey. The good fortune of finding both the official report and Hunnius's diary prompted me to edit and combine the two to form an issue of the *Panhandle-Plains Historical Review* published in 1985.[16] At this time I had not found Lieutenant Charles A. H. McCauley's ornithological notes, which in 1876 had been separated from the official report. Dan L. Flores, then teaching at Texas Tech University, kindly informed me of its location in its obscure 1877 published version. Ornithologist Kenneth D. Seyffert then joined with me in co-editing this "missing" report for the 1988 volume of the *Panhandle-Plains Historical Review.*[17] This new edition for the first time combines in one volume the official report, the maps and diary of Adolph Hunnius, and Charles A. H. McCauley's ornithological report all from the 1876 survey of the headwaters of the Red River.

NOTES

1. Unless otherwise noted, quotations from Adolph Hunnius in this introduction are drawn from his manuscript diary. Carl Julius Adolph Hunnius, "Survey of the Sources of the Red River April 25th to June 30th[,] 1876," MS, Carl Julius Adolph Hunnius Collection, Kansas Collection, Kenneth Spencer Research Library, University of Kansas, Lawrence, Kansas; also available on microfilm and in typewritten transcription (ca. 1960s) in Research Center, Panhandle-Plains Historical Museum, Canyon, Texas.

2. For a general overview of this survey, see T. Lindsay Baker, "Surveying the Headwaters of the Red River in 1876," *P.O.B. Point of Beginning* 13, no. 1 (October–November 1987): 10–12, 14, 16, 18.

3. Unless otherwise noted, all quotations from U.S. military officers in this introduction are drawn from E.H. Ruffner, "Survey of the Headwaters of Red River[,] Tex.," MS, U.S., Department of War, Army, Department of the Missouri, Correspondence of General Records Division Exclusive of Accounts and Returns, Letters Received 1871–86, General Records File 2187 (1877), Record Group 77, National Archives, cited hereafter as General Records File 2187 (1877).

4. Archeologist Jack T. Hughes in 1954 documented this site as Panhandle-Plains Historical Museum site number A-133. Jack T. Hughes, "Field Trip Record Jan. 2, 1954," TS, in Jack T. Hughes Field Notes (1954), 1–2, in Archeology Department, Panhandle-Plains Historical Museum.

5. E. R. Platt, Fort Leavenworth, K[ansa]s, to E. H. Ruffner, Fort Leavenworth, Kansas, 17 Apr[il] 1876; E. H. Ruffner, Fort Leavenworth, Kan[sa]s, to Assistant Adjutant General, Department of the Missouri, [Fort

Leavenworth, Kansas], 15 Apr[il] 1876; E. H. Ruffner, Fort Leavenworth, Kan[sa]s, to Chief of Engineers, [Washington, D.C.], 19 April 1876, all of these letters in U.S., Department of War, Army, Division of the Missouri, Office of the Chief of Engineers, Correspondence of General Record Division Exclusive of Accounts and Returns, Letters Received 1871–86, General Records File 1254 (1876), Record Group 77, National Archives, Washington, D.C.; E. H. Ruffner, "Annual Report of Lieutenant E. H. Ruffner, Corps of Engineers, for the Fiscal Year Ending June 30, 1876," U.S., Department of War, *Report of the Secretary of War*, vol. 2, part 2, in U.S., Congress, House Executive Document 1, part 2, 44th Cong., 2d Sess. (Washington: Government Printing Office, 1876), 718–49.

6. The Leavenworth press reported to its readers that on the morning of 25 April 1876, "a Government surveying party under command of Lieut. Ruffner, left Fort Leavenworth for Texas." *The Leavenworth Daily Times*, (Leavenworth, Kans.) 26 April 1876, 3.

7. Francis B. Heitman, *Historical Register and Dictionary of the United States Army, from Its Organization, September 29, 1789, to March 2, 1903*, 2 vols. (Washington, D.C.: Government Printing Office, 1903), 1: 850.

8. Heitman, *Historical Register*, 1: 655.

9. Heitman, *Historical Register*, 1: 1058.

10. Alice Blackwood Baldwin, *Memoirs of the Late Frank D. Baldwin, Major General, U.S.A.* (Los Angeles: Wetzel Publishing Co., 1929); Heitman, *Historical Register*, 1: 185–86.

11. Olive King Dixon, "Early Days in Hutchinson County," *Frontier Times* 5 (April, 1928): 316–17; Olive King Dixon, *Life and Adventures of "Billy" Dixon of Adobe Walls, Texas Panhandle*, ed. Frederick S. Barde (Guthrie, Okla.: Co-Operative Publishing Company, 1914); Mrs. Sam Isaacs, "Billy Dixon: Pioneer Plainsman," *Frontier Times* 15 (June, 1939): 372–74.

12. E. H. Ruffner, Fort Leavenworth, Kan[sa]s, to Chief of Engineers, [Washington, D.C.], 18 July 1877, 23 July 1877, and 27 Sept[ember] 1877, all three letters in General Records File 2187 (1877).

13. For McCauley's ornithological report in original published edition, see C. A. H. McCauley, "Notes on the Ornithology of the Region about the Source of the Red River of Texas, from Observations Made during the Exploration Conducted by Lieut. E. H. Ruffner, Corps of Engineers, U.S.A.," *Bulletin of the United States Geological and Geographical Survey of the Territories* 3, no. 2 (Washington, D.C.: Government Printing Office, 1877), 655–95.

14. For Ruffner's report as originally published by the War Department in 1877, including some typographical errors and changes of meaning, see E. H. Ruffner, "Annual Report of Lieutenant E. H. Ruffner, Corps of Engineers, for the Fiscal Year Ending June 30, 1877," U.S., Department of War, *Report of the Secretary of War*, vol. 2, part 2, in U.S., Congress, House Executive Document No. 1, part 2, 45th Cong., 2d Sess. (Washington: Government Printing Office, 1877), 1399–1438.

15. For a study of Adolph Hunnius's life and examination of his contributions to the cartography of the American West, see Robert L. Knecht, "Ado Hunnius, Great Plains Cartographer," Master's thesis, Emporia State University, Emporia, Kansas, 1987.

16. T. Lindsay Baker, comp. and ed., "Survey of the Headwaters of the Red River, 1876," *Panhandle-Plains Historical Review* 58 (1985): 1–124.

17. T. Lindsay Baker and Kenneth D. Seyffert, eds., "Notes on the Ornithology of the Region about the Source of the Red River of Texas, from Observations Made during the Exploration Conducted by Lieut. E. H. Ruffner, Corps of Engineers, U.S.A., by C. A. H. McCauley," *Panhandle-Plains Historical Review* 61 (1988): 25–88.

The Texas Red River Country

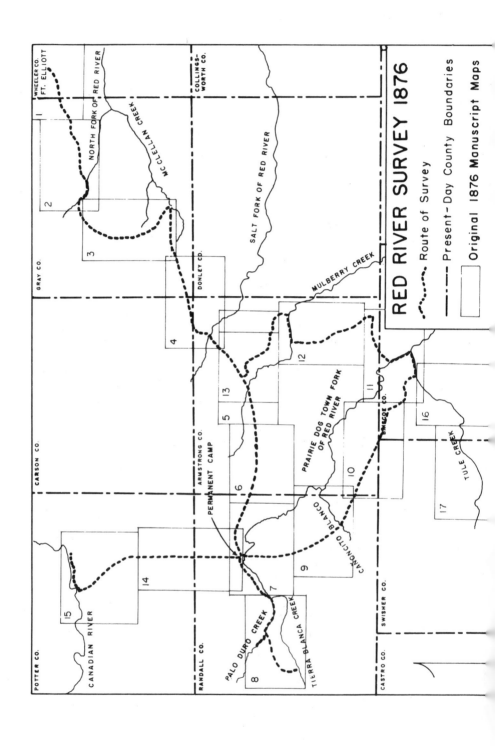

RED RIVER SURVEY 1876

••••••• Route of Survey

—•— Present-Day County Boundaries

☐ Original 1876 Manuscript Maps

WHEELER CO.
FT. ELLIOTT
NORTH FORK OF RED RIVER
McCLELLAN CREEK
COLLINGS-WORTH CO.
GRAY CO.
DONLEY CO.
SALT FORK OF RED RIVER
MULBERRY CREEK
CARSON CO.
ARMSTRONG CO.
PERMANENT CAMP
PRAIRIE DOG TOWN FORK OF RED RIVER
BRISCOE CO.
TULE CREEK
POTTER CO.
CANADIAN RIVER
RANDALL CO.
PALO DURO CREEK
TIERRA BLANCA CREEK
CANONCITO BLANCO
CASTRO CO.
SWISHER CO.

OFFICIAL REPORT

Lt. E. H. Ruffner
Chief Engineer, Department of the Missouri

Survey of the Headwaters of Red River[,] Tex.

In accordance with verbal instructions from the Department Commander, and with a schedule of written instructions prepared by myself and approved by Gen. Pope[,][10] I left this Post on April 25th, 1876, to make a Prismatic Compass and Theodolite and Stadia Line Survey of the head of permanent water of the Red River of Texas.[11]

The party took wagon transportation from Dodge City to Camp Supply and having obtained the necessary transportation at the latter point for the whole trip, went on to Fort Elliott, Tex. Here a suitable Cavalry and Infantry escort was obtained to do the necessary labor and give proper protection during the work. Fort Elliott was reached May 6th. The preliminaries of preparation were made and some work necessary to secure a good start was done so that the party was able to leave on the 11th.

The plan of work was as follows. The escort and train proceeded from camp to camp by the most direct line or trail and this route was recorded by Sergeant G. A. Lichtenberg[,] Co[.] "D" Engineers[,] by means of the usual Prismatic Compass and Odometer readings. The start was made as early in the morning as it was light enough to read the instruments by, and except in case of an unusually long march, the new camp was reached by noon.

The stadia line was run by myself. The meridian was determined by an astronomical portable transit at each camp where practicable, and from the line so established the azimuth of the course was taken by a theodolite, and was preserved throughout the march by back sights from each station to the preceeding one.

The distances were obtained by use of the cross hairs of the telescope bisecting the two shields of an ordinary leveling rod, which were separated as directed by signal from the person at the theodolite, until the interval between the shields marked the angular distance of the two parallel horizontal wires of the reticle. The two readings of the shields were recorded and the difference gave the interval in feet to the decimal of thousandths. The coefficient of distance was obtained by carefully chaining off on the ground a thousand feet, and then by repeated measurements getting the angular distance as given by the difference between the readings. The value in decimals of a foot for the stadia interval was thus given for one foot, one hundred feet, &c on the ground on horizontal distance.

This coefficient was afterwards tested by measurements at different times. The method is not intended for the most accurate of work, but under the circumstances the results were good.

It was found that ordinary spider lines were apt to sag in the early morning when the air was damp, and when the "mirage" became excessive with heat of the day, difficulty was found in getting an exact bisection of the shields from their "dancing."

The rate of work depended upon the facility with which the arrangements were carried out. The theodolite was carried on horseback, at a walk, the points of the tripod being inserted at the stirrup into a carbine sling, as a guidon would be carried on the other side. It was found best to use two stadia rods, alternately; so much depended upon judicious selection of stations. When the best conditions prevailed between 2½ and 3 miles an hour could be run upon the open prairie. As high as 22 miles were made during a day's march. The distances were best maintained at about 1500 feet though one particular advantage of the system was well displayed in the crossing of Cañons and wide valleys where chaining would have been difficult or impossible. Indeed the best results of this method are found in rough country.

The records when reduced were platted by latitudes and departures and the error in closing from Mulberry Creek Camp to return to the same was about 1 per cent.

Errors of azimuth were detected upon reaching the following camp and establishing the meridian again, and after a due allowance for convergence the remaining errors were not found to be material.

The details of topography were recorded by the recorders of the stadia rods as well as on the Prismatic Compass Line which latter was the longer as the stadia line went direct across obstacles which caused the wagons to make a detour.

Lieut. C. A. H. McCauley[,] 3d Artillery[,][12] and Lieut. T. M. Woodruff[,] 5th Inf.[,][13] assisted in the selection of the stadia line and its stations, and enlisted men were soon taught to read the verniers of the level rods correctly and kept good records.

When passing through country where it seemed advisable[,] Ado Hunnius, draughtsman in this office, made topographical sketches at suitable points to catch the shape of the land. At other times he assisted on the stadia line and Lieut. McCauley took the necessary sketches.

Sergeant G. A. Lichtenberg[,] Co. "D" Batt. of Engineers[,] in addition to his other work kept the meteorological record and the manner in which the observations were taken will be found specified in the Meterological Report annexed.

During the march my own attention was given entirely to the stadia line, but during our stay in camp I endeavored to take such Geological Notes as I could and a brief resume will be found under that head.

At night I established the meridian when practicable, and for this and other reasons I carried with me a Wardeman Portable Transit and as an experiment a framework which could be sunk into the earth and after being made solid by ramming the soil back again around the legs could be used as the pier for the instrument.

It was my intention to attempt to determine the latitude by the prime vertical and the longitude by lunar culminations in addition to using the transit for meridian lines and for time. I found however that I did not stay long enough in any one place and at this writing I am disappointed in the results. The latitude of two points were attempted. One may be considered well determined. Observations for lunar culminations were made at two points and the reductions are not satisfactory to me, whether from lack of skill in the reduction or from inherent fault of the observations themselves I am unable to state. Possibly I expected to do too much myself and I should have succeeded better by taking sun time and being more at ease.

Lieut. C. A. H. McCauley[,] 3d Art.[,] joined the party as a volunteer and gave me great assistance in everything where intelligence, industry, and enthusiasm were expected. Although in bad health he was always willing, cheerful, and efficient. He made a collection illustrating the ornithology of the region, and brought back an interesting series of bird skins, nests, and eggs. Besides this work he rendered as stated above services on the stadia line and in taking sketches of the topography. Upon returning to this point he rendered me a full and interesting report on the ornithology of the region. By an unfortunate error of judgement, he afterwards furnished to the Survey conducted by Dr. Hayden a copy of his report without mentioning the matter to me, and requested its publication. This was done and the report will now be found among the publications of that Survey, to which it does not in any manner belong.[14]

Lieut. Thos. M. Woodruff[,] 5th Inf.[,] was engaged in his leisure moments in making such a collection of botanical and other Natural History specimens as his facilities allowed him to do and his unwearied attention to this and his faithfulness in executing all duties entrusted to him are worthy of special mention. His reports on the specific duties performed by him will be found appended.

Lieut. F. D. Baldwin[,] 5th Inf.[,][15] was in command of the escort which consisted of eighteen enlisted men of the 4th Cavalry and fourteen of the 19th Infantry, and by his activity, energy, and attention to details caused the utmost smoothness to exist in all the work, and the surveying parties were always found ready for work, and uninterrupted by any annoyance or drawbacks.

Acting Assistant Surgeon W. E. Sabin completed the personnel of the party.

The first camp was made at Cottonwood Creek 12½ miles west from Fort Elliott and a delay of a day enabled the party and escort to be suitably organized for work. The next day[']s march was 9½ miles west to Big Springs on the North Fork of Red River.

Fort Elliott is beautifully situated on a high level between two of the heads of the Sweetwater, a branch of the North Fork. An abundance of fine fresh water and a heavy grove of cottonwoods led to its selection. Not far off are fine groves on several of the adjacent streams which have been heavily drawn on for the construction of the post and for the necessary fuel. On the north and west the edges of the upper level of the Staked Plains appear, and outlying buttes similarly capped with the hard white limestone which preserves the upper layers, and until washed away all that may be covered by it, are met with from the Canadian down. Rolling country well grassed in the spring extends to the east and south[,] and the lower levels and valleys have as fine grazing as need be wished.

The advent of the new Post and the removal of the Indians have brought many settlers into the vicinity, and milk and butter and eggs are sold in ranches where three years ago a single company of cavalry was not too great an escort.

Cottonwood Creek runs into the North Fork some eight miles down below our crossing. A ranche was found on the creek and growing corn. A particularly large grove of cottonwoods fills the bottom, and was the subject of the first watercolor sketch submitted with this report. The country of the North Fork is much the same as the rest described except that more sand is found than at any other point since leaving the Canadian.

Upon leaving the Big Springs we entered directly upon the general surface of the Staked Plains. From this point to the Camp on McClellan Creek and (excepting the slightly rolling drainage of the Salt Fork) from that point until we came down the mesa with the Tule Cañon we were on the upper level.

A description of monotony may be tiresome and monotonous but the reality need not be. The long steady view or the gentle swell, and long long wave of the quiet parched plains has a strange fascination, and the slightest break to its vacuity has an alarming attraction. A withered "soap weed" may be a forest, its dead last year's stalk of bloom may be a painted warrior. The wide shallow ponds may have water in them or not according as pleases the Spirits of the desert. The white swells of the canvas wagon covers or tents may loom up and waver as though a mountain of sand in the distance, and the dancing, quivering heat and flame between you and them may be those of adventurous souls who have tried to reach the cool breath.

The rabbit or the startled antelope may be the sudden vision that all eyes see, and the bleaching bones may seem to be herds of antelope, deer, elk, or what not animal known or unknown. The first low swell ahead of you a hundred yards may magnify its short dried herbs to a distant forest in the misty morning, and the cliffs of the breaks eight miles away may really be twice that.

The short grass–the famed buffalo grass–grows everywhere and the sad signs of many bleaching carcasses, and later in our journey the occasional tent and wagon of the buffalo hunters, and the scattered bands, and their many halt, lame, & blind show that the buffalo have no longer here a home.

As there had been little or no rain during the early spring, and as we had very little during our trip, the ponds or drain basins that are everywhere on the plains had no water in them, though they were evidently wet during some part of each year. The hard firm road made traveling easy everywhere for man and beast.

The point at which we crossed McClellan Creek was near the head of its water and we had passed around the head of its North Fork entirely. The creek was at that place in a cañon some 100 or more feet below the general level.

Upon our return we first struck the creek some five miles below this point and here we met the finest grove of cottonwoods encountered on the trip. It was three or four miles long and the valley was pretty with rolling hills and a bottom in places a quarter of a mile wide.

The Salt Fork and Mulberry Cr[eek] were both pretty much alike with a scant supply of good water, a few trees, and rolling ground at the upper breaks. Mulberry Creek[,] however[,] cañons soon and very deeply.

The next march brought us to the main Cañon of Red River,[16] and a gorgeous sight the first view of it was. Down one of its side cañons we looked on the strange scene. Cliffs of brilliant red sandstone were the main walls of the Cañon and the cap stone the usual white limestone of the country. Lower down in the valley the sandstones are seen to be supplanted by clays and the gypseous mixtures of lime- and sandstone and clays. The whole so washed and twisted shapen as to marvel the eye with its intricacy and daze it with its brilliancy, formed a wild and enchanting scene. So vivid are the colors that I have in vain tried to secure from one, who has not seen such, the recognition due some of my copies of the tints. Nay, though I have specimens of the colored clays and stones placed beneath the pictures themselves[,] they seem not to acknowledge them truthful.

Our camp occupied near the head of the Cañon was called a Permanent Camp[17] and I submit a view of the Cañon here. At this point, I halted the party and devoted a week to running a line to the head of water on the Paloduro, the northern of the two streams which form the Red River. It had been said that this stream was many miles in length[,] but I traced it to its head with no trouble and then crossed south to the other stream, called the Tierra Blanca.[18] The route made by Col. J. I. Gregg of the 8th Cav. in 1872 was down this stream[19] and as he had been to the head of water there it was not necessary to go farther.

The heads of these streams and of the Tule[,] which was afterwards ascended to a similar point[,] presented at these three a very lovely picture. We were above the cañons and the low rolling banks of the courses were not enough to call hills. The fringes of bushes and low trees near the water opened into one or two groves on the Palo Duro, and the grass and foliage bore its brightest spring green.

The birds swarmed in the untouched wilderness and sang and twittered without ceasing. Antelope in great quantity and an occasional herd of mustangs gave life to the scene. The upper course of the Tierra Blanca lay through marshes and low flat meadows, and the whole evidently formed a choice grazing ground for a limited number of suitable animals. Doubtless we saw it at its best but it must always be of value as a stock range.

I have endeavored to represent accurately and without any exaggeration the vivid tints of this region in two sketches on the Palo Duro and the Tierra Blanca. The water of the first stream contained small catfish within two miles of the head of water. The upper course of the Tule has an exactly similar country to this and I went to the head of water there also.

During my trip to the Palo Duro[,] Lieut. Woodruff ran a line to the Canadian as described by him and of which the two sheets[,] 14 and 15[,] give the result. This was done to connect the work with the various Surveys up that river.

At the Permanent Camp I took a sketch which exhibits the character of the cañon there exactly. It is about 250' deep and about 2½ miles below this point are the falls of the River. Here the stream breaks through the lower sandstone, the second hard rock of the series, perhaps 250' below the top of the cañon. The falls are about 30' high and just below them the gorge may be 100 feet across and

50' high besides the cañon above it which may be 300' higher and at the the top 1/3 mile wide.

Down this gorge I rode[,] having soon found a way to get down into it. At about five miles below I found it gradually widening and becoming more like the cañon in other places. When I came within sight of our first camp on the Cañon wall, given in Sheet No. 6, I rode up onto the prairie and back to camp. At this point the cañon walls may have been 450 feet high and half a mile wide. I am confident this is the place so vividly described in Marcy and McClellan's Red River Report,[20] p. 55, as I have traced up or down every cañon which could fit their descriptions and this comes the nearest to doing it. I concluded that their sufferings disordered their imaginations.

The narrowest and deepest cañon met by us in a month's steady search of them is that pictured by me as Tule Cañon[,] which is 500 feet deep by the barometer and about ¼ mile wide from top to top. The steepest and highest cliff seen is that painted in the center of the picture and it is 125 feet by the barometer.

During our stay in this region the closest search of the members of the party failed to detect or find any signs of fossils in the main cañon or above it in the two creeks forming the main stream. I except from this statement the petrified trunks of trees which were occasionally seen and petrified rootlets which were found in the upper clay just under the white or reddish white limestone which has been so often referred to as the capping stone of the region.

We remained five days in camp at the head of Cañoncito Blanco.[21] This enabled me to take astronomical observations for longitude and latitude, and to run a stadia line down the cañon, and to make investigations into geology. Here we were rewarded for the first time by the discovery of waterworn lamellibranchiata ostroea, gryphoea, and others so worn as to be unrecognizable.[22] The place where found and a more particular description will be given farther on. This cañon is sharply cut, narrow, and soon very deep, reaching in about 2½ miles, the same depth acquired by the main stream in 10½. There is found in the course of the stream, which contains fresh sweet water in a running brook, a narrow falls some fifteen feet high.

At the last point reached by the stadia line as shown on Sheet No. 9, the view of the distant cañon of the main stream was very fine and the wild masses of weatherworn rocks seemed in their strangest confusion and brightest colors. The channel of the river was about four miles distant from the last point reached on the mesa.

The narrow cañon, as is the same case below the falls of the Red River, had a choice covering of deciduous trees, where the protection from storms and fires was perfect and the water in abundance.

Birds found the cañon a natural abiding place and there were tracks of bears and perhaps a "mountain lion" though we saw neither.

An unfortunate buffalo straggled to the stream during our stay, and though despised by his comrades seemed to be welcomed by our escort "with bloody hands to a hospitable grave." A heavy hailstorm on June 6th gave unexpected and unnecessary animation to our stay.

As we left this point on the 7th June a caravan of New Mexicans, with women and children, flocks and herds came into camp, having taken the night for their march, as is preferred by them. They were going as settlers to the Quita Que country to the south of us and as we were traveling over the field traversed in 1872, 3 & 4 by the cavalry in chase of renegade Indians, the sudden appearance of this peaceful hegira was an evidence of the improved state of affairs.[23]

We found good water at our next camp, which was at the head of a small cañon as it broke through the mesa.[24] Indeed from what the guides reported and from what I deduced from the geological relations of the region[,] good water may be found near the head of any side cañon to the west or north and west of the main cañon at points where the two water bearing rocks, the upper or limestone near the surface, and the lower conglomerate some 350' below the upper level, crop out into the section. I say may be found and an inspection will soon show whether or not a search would be worthwhile; because the highest point or line on the plains is directly west of the main cañon and the water flowing eastward is in general following a direct course, or at most is gathered by gentle slopes into troughs which empty into these side cañons. Any water flowing into the streams from any source below the conglomerate may be tainted from the gypseous formation and its concomitants. So the streams to the north, Mulberry Creek and Battle Creek have only a limited source of supply and that from the north, while the side cañons of the main cañon to the south and east of the great bend need not be searched for good water.

In traveling up the bed of the main river from the mouth of the Tule, each side cañon to the left may be explored in the confident belief of finding good water in a distance of a mile at least, while the streams from the north and east containing a much larger flow of water are inexpressibly nasty to the taste; worse than the main stream in fact, and upon examination the sources of these side affluents may be found within a mile or so of the main bed.

The descent from the edge of the mesa into the cañon of Tule Cr. was made with difficulty by wagons, and the fall of about 1000 feet was effected in three miles. The topography of this region is well illustrated by Sheet No. 11. We were now fairly in the alkali region and the water of the Tule was serviceable without the addendum of soap. The valley was verdant with rank vegetation and through part of its course had good groves of deciduous trees. The camp was established at the mouth of the stream,[25] and I went to the head of the creek, and found it of the same characteristics as described for the Paloduro and the Tierra Blanca. The creek is known of good length and volume of water and where it broke into the cañon I saw the finest exhibition met with during the trip of the perpendicular walled cañon. It was impossible to descend with the horses and only after some two hours of hard climbing did we reach the bottom. The barometer showed a fall of 500 feet.

While making this trip we saw another New Mexican emigrant with two wagons at the crossing of the stream above the head of the cañon. My return to camp found the party amply satisfied with four days of epsom salts and we were ready to move the next day. The sketch showing the mouth of Tule Creek is made from its south bank and looking north. The river bed may be half a mile wide and as it glitters in the sun is as dazzling almost as snow. The quivering heat and the disagreeable odor make the passage up its bed even for three miles at five o'clock in the morning anything but pleasant.

Our camp on Battle Creek was on the scene of an encounter between Col. N. A. Miles[,] 5th Inf.[,] and the hostile Indians on August 30th[,] 1874.[26] Between Tule Creek and "D" Co[mpany] Creek[27] we made two marches along the rolling plains and hillocks at the foot and along the edge of the Staked Plains. Just before reaching "D" Co[mpany,] we crossed the Mulberry Creek. These streams have a limited supply of brackish water and although they may furnish a limited area for stock purposes[,] they will not I fear ever be of much value. The scrubby cedars which enjoy a growth in all situations where sand and drought make their existence pleasant, are here found, as well as scattering on the sides of the cañons anywhere and everywhere. We killed at "D" Co[mpany] Creek a black bear[,][28] the only one seen on the trip, and a scrubby fellow at that. During the camp at the mouth of the Tule the party feasted on deer, antelope, buffalo young and old to their hearts contents and until pork again grew to be a luxury.

We were soon in the buffalo, but instead of the countless herds of five years before the bands were small and not numerous. Thousands ran where tens of thousand were found in 1872 and the great numbers of animals who had though wounded escaped the knife of the buffalo hunters testified to the approaching doom. We encountered these herds from this time until our arrival at Camp Supply and we met occasional parties of hunters hanging on the flanks of the herd.

The buffalo are already so few in number that the pursuit is not very remunerative and I doubt if any who were out made much more than a fair living by their campaign. Indeed one of our scouts told me "it didn't pay" and as he himself was engaged in this work when most attractive and had made with one partner $975 in two weeks, from skins obtained in the Arkansas Valley in 1873, he probably knew. He gave me this as the best he had done.

From "D" Co[mpany] Creek we again ascended to the plains and connected our line with that of the outgoing party at the camp at Mulberry Creek.[29] Leaving the party in camp here[,] I rode south west to the cañon again and down and across it to a point not far from our Camp Cent. Lieut. McCauley had made a reconnaissance from the camp on Tule Creek up to this point and I connected my line with his. A part of the topography thus given is found on the sheets but the whole can not be put down until a general map is made; but I have not as yet been able to commence this. The cañon there has magnificent proportions. At the point where I descended the walls it may be eight miles wide though it spreads as the lower course of the stream turns southwardly. The upper walls may be 300' high, and a plateau then stretches to the river proper. The plateau is seamed with water courses, and the main walls are indented by "breaks." The river bed has immediate enclosing hills of 300 or more feet in height and on the west the mesa walls rise nearer the river and are more sharp. The short water courses of the plateau are the aff[l]uents from the north quoted by Marcy and McClellan. During this ride I found a few shells in conglomerate about 200 feet or more above the river and at the place we camped. Perhaps the spot was three or four miles from Camp Cent.

During my absence Lt. Woodruff ran a short line down Mulberry Creek and the evening of my return to camp was celebrated by a brief hailstorm and an attempt at stampede of the mules.

From this point we returned directly to Fort Elliott. The line of march was to the east of that taken on the outward march. The Prismatic Compass line was the only one recorded on the return.

We camped on McClellan Creek, at the junction of its two forks, and in the fine grove of cottonwoods already spoken of. Reaching Fort Elliott on June 21st the escort was returned to duty at its post and it gave me pleasure to express to the Commanding Officer the entire satisfaction felt at the willingness, interest, and soldierly bearing of the escort during their performance of the duty expected of them. We arrived at Dodge City on June 28th.

The general mileage was as follows:

Stadia line complete	260 miles
Prismatic Compass line	450 miles
Horseback reconnaissance	175 miles
Total	885 miles
Fort Dodge to Fort Elliot and return	370 miles
Total mileage surveyed & by wagon	1255 miles

The general results were gratifying in showing that the Map of the Indian Territory[30] was quite correct and my survey but confirmed my deductions and conclusions from prismatic compass lines already on hand.

In working up the report I have met with much difficulty. Soon after coming back Lieut. Woodruff was detailed in the office to work up his own notes but was soon relieved and went with his regiment to Dakota. Lieut. McCauley was afterwards on duty but to be relieved and ordered to Washington. I myself was absent two months and a half, and I had no funds to hire a draughtsman.

I have made some remarks in my geological notes which may be of interest as to the features of the country. As it is economical value it will be recollected that my notes commence and end on or near the Staked Plains and that whatever may be the future of the country the needs for it are not apparent as yet, and with the miles and miles of fair grazing land in the Indian Territory and in Kansas as yet unflocked with peaceful herds[,] I see no reason for speculating on the use of the Staked Plains. For the present it will suffice us to know where we may go and how we shall best travel, and where the best roads, wood, water, and grass may be found.

Stadia Line Connecting Red and Canadian Rivers

Fort Leavenworth Kansas
February 1st, 1877

1st Lieut. E. H. Ruffner Corps of Engrs.
Chief Engineer Dept. Mo.
Fort Leavenworth Kansas.

Sir

I have the honor to submit the following report upon my trip from the Permanent Camp on Red River[31] to the Canadian River.

In accordance with your instructions to run the Stadia Line up to the Canadian River, I organized my party, consisting of Sergt. G. A. Lichtenberg Co. D Engineers, Scout Dixon with 1 Corpl. and 8 men, one wagon and 7 days rations and forage, as follows: To Sergt. Lichtenberg I entrusted the keeping of the Prismatic Compass and Odometer readings. The Scout Dixon and Corpl. Merriam of Co. "M" 4th Cavalry rode some distance in advance and chose stations. Private Replogle had the Stadia Rod, and Pvts Hall, Kirch, & Hope assisted me as flagmen. I myself took Aloe Theodolite #93.

Scout Dixon informed me that it was quite a long distance from the Permanent Camp to the next water, therefore in order to gain time, and run the line more quickly, I left the Camp at 1 o'clock on the 23rd. of May, taking only the working party, and ran the line out about five miles. I returned to the Camp about 6 P.M. The afternoon had been cloudy, but very cool and pleasant.

At 5 o'clock on the morning of the 24th. of May, I left the Camp with my whole party and reached the last station of the previous day about 6:30 o'clock. The morning was cold and cloudy, with a heavy mist; cool northerly wind. Everything however was favorable for taking readings, & I made rapid progress until 9:30 o'clock when the sun came out very bright driving away the mist. Soon after this and during the remainder of the day the mirage troubled me a great deal, and the heat was intense.

About 11:30 o'clock, a troupe of about a dozen wild horses came very near my party, so near in fact as almost to stampede our horses. The wild horses were very fleet and were not at all curious for they kept on their course without stopping. They presented a beautiful sight as they galloped swiftly past.

Scout Dixon had conducted the wagon & the portion of the detachment not working with me, to a point near the head of the "Rio Piedroso"[32] where we camped, reaching this place about 3:15 in the afternoon. The distance from the Permanent Camp was 17 miles 1137 yards.

The country over which we had passed during the first part of the day, for about 14 miles presented all the characteristics of the Staked Plain, the remainder was gently rolling indicating the proximity of a stream. At our Camp we found a series of pools of good clear water, apparently permanent springs. There were a few cottonwood trees, and the grazing for the animals was good.

Whilst my dinner was being prepared I made collections of botanical and entomological specimens, which were about the same as those that I had collected at the permanent camp.

On the 25th. I broke camp at daylight, and left at 5:20 taking nearly a north westerly direction; the country became more and more hilly, and finally very much cut up with deep arroyas. We reached Camp about midday, having made 10 miles 881 yards. The day was cool & pleasant, and fine for working. Our Camp was located about a mile above the mouth of May Creek,[33] which runs into the Canadian. As we neared the Canadian, I noticed that the hills were composed largely of Drift, with out-croppings of Limestone, & Red & Yellow Sandstone. Our Camp on May Creek was in a very pretty little grove of Cottonwoods. The water here was not very good, being slightly alkaline.

After dinner I walked down the creek to the River, which I found contained a large flow of water & the bed was about 300 yards wide. On the north side of the Canadian the bluffs were more abrupt, and higher than on the south. On the west bank of May Creek right at its mouth, there is a hill about 60 feet in height, on the top of which I found a space of about 12 feet square, marked out by stones, it seemed to be a grave & after digging and scraping around with my sheath knife I found several arrowheads of flint.[34] I should like to have investigated this further but I had to return to Camp before darkness set in. On this same day Sergt. Lichtenberg & Scout Dixon went some five miles up the River; the Sergeant making a very accurate topographical sketch accompanying his notes.

On the 26th. I broke Camp at daylight; I sent Sergt. Lichtenberg with a small guard & the wagon back to our Camp of the 24th. I ran the Stadia Line about five miles and a half down the River, it consumed a great deal of time owing to the very rough nature of the ground. My last station was on a very high hill near the mouth of Muster Creek or the Arroya Bonita,[35] in the valley of which some three or four miles distant were several large cottonwood groves. On the hills that I this day passed over, I remarked the frequency of Cedar trees of a rather stunted growth; there were some however, that attained considerable height. I suppose that the general level of the tops of these hills, which were largely composed of gravel, was about 150 feet above the valley of the Canadian. A little below the mouth of the Arroya Bonita, the Canadian makes a sharp turn toward the north, forming I suppose the Great Bend. From our Camp of the previous night to this point our course had been mainly east.

After making a topographic sketch I assembled my party, and taking about a southerly course, over country similar to that, that we had just passed over, we arrived at our Camp of the 24th. inst. about 2 o'clock, having had a very hard days work.

On the 27th. I broke Camp at 5 o'clock and reached the Permanent Camp on Red River at 10:30 A.M.

It is a curious fact that during the three nights, while I was on this Reconnaissance we had very heavy rains, accompanied by thunder and lightning; and this in a region that had always been thought to be very dry.

I am Sir very respectfully

Your obedient servant

Thos. M. Woodruff

Lieut. 5th Infantry

TABLE GIVING ALTITUDES AND BAROMETRICAL READINGS AT POINTS OCCUPIED IN THE SURVEY OF THE SOURCES OF RED RIVER, TEXAS.

Dates when observations were made.	Station.	Difference in altitude [between] Dodge City and station occupied. (Feet.)	Number [of] observations used in Determin'n	Altitude. (Feet.)	Probable Error of— Single result.	Probable Error of— Final result.	Mean Barometrical Reading— Observed.	Deduced from Diff. Alt. and Dodge City	Mean. Dodge City Mean.
April 27 and June 27	Dodge City	—	3	2,479	...	...	27.325*		27.325
April 27	Bluff Creek	− 75.1	1	2,404	...	...	27.439		27.399
April 28 and June 26	Bear Creek Redoubt	− 471.4	1	2,008	...	...	.616		.820
April 28 and June 26	Redoubt Creek, Cimarron River	− 676.0	3	1,803	...	...	28.088		28.038
April 29	Kansas boundary	− 517.0	1	1,962	...	...	27.906		27.869
April 29	Gypsum Creek	− 960.4	1	1,519	...	...	28.096		28.346
April 29	Dog Soldier Creek	− 825.8	1	1,653	...	...	28.006		28.200
April 29 and 30	Sand Creek	− 825.8	2	1,653	...	...	27.971		28.200
April 30	Summit divide between Sand Creek and Beaver Creek	− 386.5		2,092	...	...	27.496		27.808
April 30 to May 3 and June 25	Camp Supply	− 577.7	11	1,901	± 51.2	± 15.5	27.463		27.934
May 3 and 4	Crossing Wolf Creek	− 533.3	3	1,946	...	...	.496		.886
May 4	Willow Spring	− 387.7	2	2,091	...	...	.456		.732
May 4	South Commission Creek	− 237.7	1	2,241	...	...	.241		.574
May 5 and June 23	Canadian River	− 66.7	2	2,402	...	...	.136		.494
May 5	Washita River	+ 30.3	1	2,509	...	...	.219		.294
May 5 till and June 21 and 22	Fort Elliot, Tex	+ 115.6	18	2,595	± 22.2	± 5.2	.282		.205
May 12	Old Cantonment Creek	+ 218.2	3	2,697	...	...	.051		.099
May 13	Big Springs, North Fork	+ 269.0	1	2,748	...	...	26.599		.046
May 14	Level of Staked Plains, between North Fork and McClellan Creek	+ 550.7	1	3,030	...	...	.775		26.757
May 14 and 15	McClellan Creek	+ 380.2	4	2,859	44.8	22.4	26.859		26.932
May 16	Level plain between McClellan Creek and Salt Fork	+ 692.6	1	3,172	...	...	.883		26.613
May 16	Salt Fork	+ 467.8	2	2,947	...	...	.714		.842
May 16 and June 16 and 17	Mulberry Creek	+ 626.8	7	3,106	29.5	13.2	26.314		.680
May 18 and 19	First camp on Red River	+ 955.0	5	3,434	42.8	19.2	.153		26.348
May 20,22,23,28, to June 1	Permanent Camp	+ 1,088.7	21	3,568	37.2	8.1	.455		.214
June 3 to 6	Cañoncito Blanco	+ 1,012.4	12	3,491	58.0	16.7	.278		.290
June 7	Camp Cent	+ 946.5	2	3,426	...	...	27.518		.357
June 8 to 13	Mouth Tule Creek	+ 189.1	14	2,290	37.2	10.0	.334		27.523
June 13	Battle Creek	+ 131.0	2	2,610	...	...	.140		.189
June 14 and 15	D Company Creek	+ 298.2	4	2,777	26.8	13.4	26.862		.016
June 19	Whitefish Creek	+ 548.6	1	3,028	...	...	26.985		26.759
June 20	McClellan Creek at the forks	+ 304.3	2	2,783	...	...			27.010
	Determined by comparison with permanent camp on Red River:								
May 24 and 29	First camp on Palo Duro	+ 1,131.7	3	3,611	32.8	18.9	26.416		26.171
May 25 and 26	Second Camp on Palo Duro	+ 1,273.2	2	3,752	...	...	.340		.030
May 24	Rio Piedroso	+ 1,039.2	2	3,518	...	...	.543		.263
May 25	Canadian River	+ 755.4	2	3,234	...	...	.888		.549
May 27 and 28	Tierra Blanca Cañon	+ 1,162.1	5	3,641	57.0	38.4	.216		.139
	Determined by comparison with camp at mouth Tule Creek:								
June 9 and 10	Camp Scare Spring	+ 905.5	12	3,384	31.8	9.2	26.321		26.397
June 10	Head of water, Tule Creek	+ 1,053.8	1	3,532	...	...	.187		.259
June 11	Camp Sunday Spring	+ 830.0	9	3,309	15.0	5.0	.622		.474
June 10	Prairie west of Scare Spring	+ 995.3	8	3,474	44.9	15.8	.200		.307
June 9, 11, and 12	Between Scare Spring and cañon	+ 923.9	11	3,403	38.5	11.6	.440		.379

Meteorological Report

As the country to be traversed was but a rolling prairie and the differences in altitude were not expected to be very great it was thought a constant reference could be made to a barometrical base at Dodge City, one of the Stations of the Signal Service of the Army, a point at no time more than 225 miles distant from the working parties.

Any inaccuracies arising from the necessary assumption that abnormal changes of pressure at the one station were probably equally experienced at the other were believed to be less than would be errors in the determination of a mean barometrical reading for a station occupied for the short time which could at best be devoted to this purpose. Two or three points were to be determined by several days barometrical observations and the differences of altitude between these points and Dodge City being determined by this the relative altitudes of neighboring points would probably be fairly accurate.

In conducting the Survey these points in the field were reoccupied long enough to enable parties to make surveys in various directions, thus determining at the same time with other work profiles of the lines surveyed.

The instruments used were a mountain Barometer No 392 made by P Green of New York and two aneroids made by Casella and marked B & C. The tube of the mountain barometer was broken twice on the trip but the frequent comparisons between the aneroids and the mercurial during the survey and the comparisons between all of these instruments and the barometers at the Dodge City station both going and coming gave satisfactory results and proved the instruments to be good.

I did not have a wet bulb thermometer and the observations for humidity are therefore wanting. As the general character of the country is very nearly the same as at the meterological base it is probable that but little difference in the condition of the atmosphere arose from this reason, and it is certain that the error arising from the omission of the humidity terms is less than that which necessarily was introduced by the starting assumption of comparing our observations with the distant base.

[There follows a detailed thirteen-page analysis of barometric readings made during the course of the survey, concluding with a general summary table giving estimated elevations for points on the survey.]

In preparing the following General Table of Altitudes the principal points occupied are referred to and in the determinations the probable errors are calculated from the range in the various results. The accuracy of such comparison is doubtful and the formula should be applied to weighted observations, wherein the distances between the stations should enter. Some function indicating the amount of abnormal atmospheric disturbance should also enter, as is plainly indicated in the results of the determination at Camp Supply.

As it is however the probable errors serve somewhat for comparisions of the accuracy of results. The altitude of Dodge City was taken from the Report of the Chief Signal Officer of the Army for 1876. The mean of the barometric observations at that point for this period in question gives a slightly different result. The column of the No. of observations used sometimes includes the mean of two Barometers and sometimes of three. The profile of Tule Cr. and of the Palo Duro and Tierra Blanca were obtained by using one Barometer on the road and comparing its record with that of the one left at one of the camps occupied for a longer period.

Botany

The following list of plants collected during the Survey is necessarily an imperfect catalogue of the flora of the country. The collection was made by persons unfamiliar with botany and generally at the close of a hard days work when the leisure hours of camp were utilized in part by gathering specimens of plants at that time in bloom. Besides the numbers of individuals not yet in bloom and therefore not reported, there was of necessity thus omitted in the list the names of all trees; ferns and all nonflowering plants. The list is therefore submitted merely for what it is worth itself.

Upon reaching Fort Leavenworth Kas. the collection was placed in the hands of Dr. T. E. Wilcox Assistant Surgeon U. S. A.[36] who kindly offered his services. The classification has been prepared by him, and through the kind assistance of Prof. Wood[37] to whom all specimens not recognized were submitted the list was completed and Prof Wood's name will be found as the authority in these cases.

The list may be considered as almost exclusively one of the Flora of the Staked Plains of Northern Texas.

Catalogue of Plants collected in N. W.

Texas (Head Waters of Red River) by

1st Lieut. E. H. Ruffner U. S. Engineers 1876[38]

Ranunculaceae
Anemone Caroliniana, Watt; Torr. and Gr. Fl. 1, p. 12.
Delphinium Azureum, Michx; Torr. and Gr. Fl. 1, p. 32.
Ramuculus aquatilis. Wood.

Papveraceae
Argemone Mexicana, Linn; Torr. and Gr. Fl. 1, p. 61.

Cruciferae
Vesicaria
V. Ludoviciana D. C.
V. Augustifolia, Nutt, in Torr. and Gr. Fl. 1, p. 101; Gray, Pl. Lindh. 2, p. 145.
Nasturtium sinuatum, Wood

Portulacaceae
Talimum Teretifolium, Pursh, Fl. 2, p. 365; Gray Gen. Ill. t. 98.

Malvaceae
Malvastrum Coccineum, Gray, Gen. Ill., t. 121. Pl. Feudl, p. 24.
Malva coccinea, Nutt.
Sida coccinea, D. C., Torr. and Gr. Fl. 1, p. 235.
Callirrhoe involucrato, Gray, Pl. Fendl., p. 15 and Genl. Ill., t. 117.
Malva involucrata, Torr. and Gr., Fl., p. 226.
C. Digitata, Nutt. in Jour. Acad. Phil., 2, p. 181; Gray, 1. c.
C. Pedata.

Linaceae
Linum Berlandieri, Hook. Brt. Mag., t. 3480; Engelm. in Gray, Pl.
Wright. 2, p. 25.

Oxalidaceae
Oxalis Violaceae, Linn; Torr. and Gr., Fl. 1, p. 211.
O. Stricta, Linn; Torr. and Gr. Fl. 1. c.

Anacardiaceae
Rhus Trilobata, Nutt in Torr. and Gr. Fl. 1, p. 218; Gray Fl. Fendl,
p. 28.
R. Toxicodendron, Linn; Torr. and Gr., 1. c.

Vitaceae
Vitis Rupertis, Sheele in Linnaea, 21, p. 591. Gray Pl. Lindh. 2, p.
165.

Sapindaceae
Sapindus Marginatus, Willd; Torr. and Gray, Fl. 1, 255, Gray, Gen.
Ill., 2, t. 180.

Polygalaceae
Polygala Alba, Nutt. Gen. 2, p. 87; Gray Pl. Wright, 1, p. 38.
P. Beyrichii, Torr. and Gr., Fl. 1, p. 670.

Krameriaceae
Krameria lanceolata   Wood

Leguminosae
Tephrosia Virginiana, Pers; Torr. and Gr. Fl., 1, p. 295.
Glycyrrhiza Lepidota, Nutt., Gen. 2, p. 196; Torr and Gr., Fl. 1, p.
298.
Psoralea
P. Tennifolia

Dalea
D. Formosa
D. laxiflora Ph.   Wood
Sophora sericea   Wood
Petalostemon Violaceus, Michx, Fl. 2, p. 50, t, 37, f. 2; Torr. and Gr.,
    Fl. 1, p. 310.
Petalostemon Gracile; Nutt. in Jour. Acad. Phil. 7, p. 92. Torr. and
    Gr., Fl. 1, p. 309.
Amorpha Canescens, Nutt, Gen. 2, p. 92, Torr. and Gr., Fl. 1, p. 306.
Astragalus Nuttallianus, D. C., Prodr. 2, p. 239; Torr. and Gr. 2, p.
    234.
A. Caryocarpus, Ker. Brt. Reg., t. 176; Torr. and Gr., Fl. 1, p. 331.
A. Gracilis.
Baptisia Australis, R. Br.; Torr. and Gr. Fl. 1, p. 385.
B. Leucophaea, Nutt., Gen. 1, p. 282; Torr. and Gr., 1, c.
Desmanthus brachylobus.
Mimosa fragrans.
Hoffmanseggia Jamesii, Torr. and Gr., Fl. 1, p. 293. Gray, Pl. Lindh.
    2, p. 178.

Rosaceae

Sanguisorba Annua, Nutt., in Torr. and Gr., Fl. 1 p. 429.
Poterium annum, Hook. Fl. Bot. Am., 1, p. 198.
Rosa blanda.   Wood

Onagraceae

Oenothera Rhombipetala, Nutt, in Torr. and Gr., Fl. 1, p. 493; Kunze
    in Linnaea, 20, p. 57.
Oe. Sinuata, Linn; Torr. and Gr., Fl. 1, p. 294.
Oe. Speciosa[,] Nutt. in Jour. Acad. Phil. 2, p. 119; Torr. and Gr., Fl.
    1, c.
Oe. Lavaudalaefolia, Torr. and Gr., Fl. 1, p. 501; Hooks. Lond. Jour.
    Bot. 6, p. 223[;] Gray, Pl. Wright. 1, p. 72.
Oe. Serrulata, Nutt. Gen. 1, p. 246; Torr. and Gr., Fl. 1, p. 501.
B. Oblongifolia   Wood
Gaura Coccinea, Nutt. Gen. 1, p. 249; Torr. and Gr., Fl. 1, p. 518.
G. Villosa, Torr. Ann. Lyc. N. York, 2, p. 200; Torr. and Gr., Fl. 1, p.
    518; Gray, Pl. Wright, 1, p. 73.
Oenothera canisceus Torr.   Wood
Oe. Missouriensis   Wood
Oe. Hartwegii   Bentle   Wood
Gaura sinuata   Nutt   Wood
G. parviflora   Wood

Compositae

Solidago Odora, Nutt; Torr. and Gr. Fl. 2, p. 219.

S. Missouriensis, Nutt. in Jour. Acad. Phil. 7, p. 32, and Trans. Amer. Phil. Soc. (n. ser) 7, p. 327; Torr. and Gr. Fl. 2, p. 222.

Artemistia Filifolia, Torr. in Ann. Lyc. N. York 2, p. 211; Torr. and Gr., Fl. 2, p. 417.

Achillea Millefolium, Linn; Torr. and Gr., Fl. 2, p. 409.

Riddellia Tagetina, Nutt, 1. c. p. 371; Torr. and Gr., Fl. 2, p. 362; Torr. in Emory's Rep., t. 5; Gray, Pl. Fendl., p. 93.

Rudbeckia Hirta, Linn; Torr. and Gr., Fl. 2, p. 304.

Echinacea Angustifolia, D. C., Prodr. 5, p. 554; Torr. and Gr., Fl. 2, p. 306.

Lepachys Columnaris, Torr. and Gr., Fl. 2, p. 315[.]

Rudebeckia columnaris, Pursh, Fl. 2, p. 575.

Helianthus Petiolaris, Nutt. in Jour. Phil. 2, p. 115; Sweet Bril. Fl. Gard. (n. ser) t. 75.

Gaillardia Pulchella, Foug., D. C., Prodr. 5, p. 652; Torr. and Gr., Fl. 2, p. 366.

Engelmannia Pinnatifida, Torr. and Gr., in Nutt, Trans. Am. Phil. Soc. (n. ser) 7, p. 443 & Fl. 2, p. 283.

Crepis Runcinata, T. & G.

Thelespirunum gracile, Gray

Cosmidium T. & G.

Hellinium Tennifolium, N. (but the lower leaves are not entire.)

Lygodesmia juncea.   Don.

Melampodium Cincreum, D. C. Prodr. 5, p. 518; Gray, Fl. Fendl. p. 78.

M. ramosissimum, D. C. 1, c.[;] Torr. and Gr., Fl. 2, p. 271.

M. leucanthum, Torr. & Gr., 1. c.

Centauria Americana, Nutt, in Jour. Acad. Phil. 2, p. 117[;] Bart. Fl. Amer. Sept. t. 50; Torr. and Gray, Fl. 2, p. 453.

Cirsium Undulatum, Spreng; Torr. and Gr., Fl. 2, p. 456.

Aplopappus Hookerianus	Wood
Aplopappus spinulosus	Wood
Hymenopappus tennifolius	Wood
Townsendia strigosa	Wood
Cosmidium gracile	Wood
Pyrrhopappus grandiflorus	Wood
Melampodium cinerium	Wood
Berlandiera incisa	Wood
Eclimacea angustifolia	Wood
Erigeron tume	Wood
E. radicatum Hooks	Wood
Actinella linuariifolia	Wood
Lygodesmia aphylla	Wood
Chrysopsis villosa	Wood

Aplopappus rubiginosus T. & G. This plant agrees well in all respects with descriptions, but the rays are tinged with *blue*. They should be yellow. What does it mean? Wood

Gentianaceae
Erythraca Beyrichi, Torr. and Gr., Fl. 2. ined.

Apocynaceae
Apocynum Canabinum, Linn; Hook. Fl. Bar. Amer. 2, p. 51, t. 139.
A. hypericifolium   Wood.

Asclepiadaceae
Asclepias Speciosa, Torr. in Ann. Lyc. 2, p. 218 and in Fremont's first Rep. p. 95.
Asclepias tuberosa   Wood

Chenopodiaceae
Monolepis chenopodioides   Mog.
B. trifida   Wood.

Convolvulaceae
Evolvulus Pilosus, Nutt. Gen. p. 174 (as a synonym); Trans. Amer. Phil. Soc. (n. ser.,) 5, p. 195.
Convolvulus Lobatus, Engelm., and Gray, Pl. Lindh. 1, p. 44 (in a note)
C. hastatus, Nutt, in Trans. Am. Phil. Soc. (n. ser.) 5, p. 194. not of Thumb.
C. Nuttallii, Torr. in Emory's Rep., p. 149.
Ipomea leptophylla Torr.   Wood.

Solanaceae
Physalis Pumila, Nutt. in Trans. Amer. Phil. Soc., (n. ser.) 5, p. 193.
Solanum Mexicanum   Wood.
Physalis lobata   Torr.   Wood.

Rhamneae
Ceanothus Americanus   Wood.
C. Ovalis   Wood.

Scrophulariaceae
Pentstemon acuminatus   Doug   Wood.
Veronica Peregina,   L.   Wood.
Pentstemon coeruleus   Wood.

Acanthaceae
Ruellia stripens　　　　　　Wood.

Labiatae
Monarda Aristata, Nutt, in Trans. Amer. Soc. (n. ser.) 5, p. 186[;]
　Benth, in D. C. Prodr. 12, p. 363.
Scutellaria Resinosa, Torr. in Ann. Lyc. N. York. 2, p. 232. Benth in
　D. C. Prodr. 12, p. 427.

Verbenaceae
Lippia Cuneifolia, Torr. in Ann. Lyc. N. York, 2, p. 234.
Lippia lanceolata　　　　　Wood.
Verbena Bipinnatifida, Engelm. and Gray, Pl. Lindh. 1, p. 49; Shauer
　in D. C. Prodr. 11, p. 553.
Verbena Erinoides　　　　　Wood.

Boraginaceae
Eretrichium Jamessii, Myosotis suffruticosa, Torr. in Ann. Lyc. N.
　York 2, p. 225[;] D. C. Prodr. 10, p. 114.
Phacelia integrifolia, Torr.
Echinospermum Lappula　　　Wood.
Lithospermum longiflorum　　Wood.

Cupuliferae
Quercus Undulata, Torr. in Ann. Lyc., 2, p. 248, t. 4.

Gnetaceae
Ephedra antisiphilitica Meyer (without fls. or fruit) Wood.

Coniferae
Juniperus Virginiana, Lin.; Michx, f. Sylv. 2, p. 353, t. 155; Torr. Fl.
　N. York, 2, p. 235.

Commelynaceae
Tradescantia Virginica, Linn. Brt. Mag. t. 105; Bart. 1, o. t. 144[;]
　Kunth, Enum. 4, p. 81[;] Torr. Fl. N. York, 2, p. 333.

Iridaceae
Sisyrinchium Bermudianum, Linn., Torr. Fl. N. York 2, p. 290.
Nemastylis Acuta.

Liliaceae
Allium reticulatum.

Cyperaceae

Carex Muhelberg, Sckt. Car. 2, p. 12 f. 178, Schwein and Torr. Car.
p. 304; Torr. Fl. N. York, 2, p. 374.

Carex lanuginosa	Wood.
Carex disjuncta	Wood. Allied to C. conjuncta Boott.
Scirpus pungens	Wood.
Eleocharis olivacea	Wood.

Equisetaceae

Equisetum Cyemale, Linn; Pursh, Fl. 2, p. 652[;] Torr. Fl. N. York,
2, p. 482.

Equisetum Levigatum   Wood.

Filices

Adiantum Capillus —— Veneris   Wood.

Gramineae

Uniola Latifolia, Michx. Fl. 1, p. 71; Ell. Sk. 1, p. 167; Kunth. Enum.
1, p. 425.

Poa Andina (an imperfect specimen)		Wood.
Poa Michauxii Kunth.		Wood.
Hordeum jubatum		Wood.
Triticum repeus L. (? no root or leaves.)		Wood.
Poa compressa		Wood.
Andropagon argenteum		Wood.
Festuca tenella		Wood.
Aristida purpurea		Wood.
Eatonia obtusada	Gr.	Wood.
Tricuspis acuminata	Monro.	Wood.
Elymus Sitanion	Schutt.	Wood.

Elymus Virginicus B. vaginatus —— a dwarf from 3 - 6' high spikes
sheathed.   Wood.

Nyctaginaceae

Allionia incarnata.	L.	
Oxybaphus angustifolius.	Sweet.	Wood.

Polmaniaceae

Gillia filefolia, Nutt.

Plantagenaceae

Plantago Patagonica, Torr.
Stenosiphon virgatus?

Entomological Report

Fort Leavenworth Kansas
February 1st, 1877

1st Lieut. E. H. Ruffner
Corps of Engineers U.S.A.
Chief Engineer Dept. Mo.
Fort Leavenworth Ks.

Sir

I have the honor to submit the following report on the Insects collected by me during the explorations & survey of the Headwaters of Red River of Texas in 1876.

My implements were very incomplete, and those I had were hurriedly constructed. They consisted of three nets which could be fastened to the end of a long pole; a couple of killing boxes, and two collecting boxes; these boxes were tin baking-powder boxes of different sizes. I also had two sets of trays, or drawers, 16 dozen pill boxes, in nests, raw cotton, long sharp pointed pins, some glass bottles and a pair of steel pliers.

For killing and preserving the specimens, I used Cyanide of Potassium, Chloroform, Arsenic in solution and Alcohol.

As far as my limited knowledge extended I arranged the specimens under their general classes; and in every case I gave date and locality of capture. In doing the former I was guided by Dr. A. B. Packard's Pamphlet on the directions for collecting & preserving Insects;[39] I regret[,] however, that I had so little knowledge of the subject, for I lost many interesting facts concerning the habits of many of the specimens, and also failed to note many well known species. In order to have the specimens properly classified they were sent to Mr. Herman Strecker,[40] of the Reading Society of Natural Sciences, to whose list I respectfully refer you. He finds about 126 different species.

I am greatly indebted to the officers and men of the exploration for collecting many interesting and valuable specimens.

I am Sir very respectfully

Your obedient servant

Thos. M. Woodruff

Lieut. 5th Infantry

Reading Society Nat. Sciences

Reading Penna. Nov. 9th 1876.

Lieut E. H. Ruffner

U. S. Engineers

Dear Sir

I herewith transmit a classified list of the insects,[41] forwarded to us in Sept. last, which were collected by the Expedition under your charge during the surveys and explorations of the region of the Headwaters of the Red River of Texas in May and June 1876.

The general area from which the collection was made, was that part of the "Llano estacado" or Staked Plains of Texas, embraced between Longitude 100° 30′W to 102° and Latitude 34° to 35° 30′.

My thanks are due to Messrs. Chas. A. Blake and E. T. Cresson[42] for aid in determining the Hymenoptera–to Mr. A. B. Fuller in the Coleoptera and to Dr. Dyrus Thomas[43] in the Orthoptera.

Very Respectfully yours truly

Herman Strecker.

HYMENOPTERA

	Chrysididae	
Chrysis Clara	Cress.	1 ♀
	Larridae	
Larrada semirufa	Cress.	1
Tachytes abdominalis	Say.	1
	Sphegidae	
Chlorion coeruleum	Dru.	1 ♂

Pompilidae

Pomilus Aethiops	Cress.	3 ♂	
" tenebrosus	Cress.	1 ♀	
Priocenemis validus	Cress.	1 ♀	
Pepsis marginata	Beau.	2 ♀	

Mutillidae

Mutilla californica	Rad.	3 ♀	
" fenestrata	St. Farg.	3 ♂	
" ferrugata	Cress.	2 ♀	
" fulvohirta	Cress.	1 ♂	
" gorgon	Blake	2 ♀	
" orcus	Cress.	1 ♀	
" oajaca	Blake	1 ♂	
" sayi	Blake	1 ♂ var.	
" simillima	Smith	2 ♀	
" zelaya	Blake	1 ♂	
Agama eastanea	Cress.	1 ♂	
" Tapajos	Blake	1 ♂ var.	

Vespidae

Polistes minor	Cress.	3 ♀
" texana	Cress.	11 ♀

Andreniade

Augochlora fervida	Smith	1 ♀
Eunomia marginipennis	Cress.	1 ♂

Apidae

Megachile gentilis	Cress.	1 ♀	
Melistodes australis	Cress.	1 ♂	
" menachus	Cress.	1 ♀	
Anthophora occidentalis	Cress.	1 ♀	
Bombus nevadensis	Cress.	1 ♀	
" pennsylvanicus	DeGeer	3 ♀	4 ☿

LEPIDOPTERA

Rhopalocera

Papilionidae

Papilio asterius	Cram.	1 ♀	Tule Creek.

Differs from the normal ♀ form in the total obsolesence of the submarginal row of yellow spots on both the upper and under surfaces of primaries.

Pieridae

Pieris protodice   Bdl. et. Lec.   2 ♂ , one from
  Tule Creek[,] the other from Salt Fork.
Colias eurytheme   Bdl.   1 ♂ from
  Cañoncito Blanco; 1 ♀ normal and 1 ♀ albino from Mulberry
  Creek.
Meganostoma caesonia   Stoll.   1 ♂ Cañoncito Blanco.
    These Pieridae present no points of difference from those found in
various other localities in the U. S. and territories.

Lycaenidae

Thecla mopsus   Hubn.   1♂1♀Tule Creek.
Lycaena melissa   W. H. Edwds.   1 ♀   Tule Creek

Nymphalidae

Euptoieta claudia   Cram.
Argynnis Columbina   Godt.   2♂1♀ Mulberry
  Creek, 1   Head of Red River, rather small, otherwise not peculiar.
Eresia Carlota   Reak.   1♀ Head of Red
                                                            River.

Eresia Tharos   Dru.   1♂Head of Red
                                                            River.

Apartura celtis   Bdl. & Lec.   2 ♀ var.   Tule
  Creek, both expand 2 1/8 inches. They are much the same reddish or
tawney hue as the variety described by W. H. Edwards under the
name of Alicia, but the outer half of the primaries is not blackish
brown as in that form, but is reddish with some light pale brown
shading differing but little from the ground color of rest of upper
surface; the most noteworthy point of distinction in the example is
however in the presence of another ocellus on primaries, situated in
cell 3 in a line with the one in cell 2, the two being of like size nor are
they larger than the largest one of the six on the inferiors; Both have
a large white pupil. Beneath they are larger and are ringed with
yellow and also pupilled with white. This description applies to both
examples except that the other has in cell 4 also an ocellus making a
submarginal row of four ocelli on superiors; this ocellus in cell 4 has a
much larger white pupil than either of the other three though on the
whole it is smaller than the two in cells 2 and 3 and the same size as
its partner in cell 5. The ocelli on upper surfaces of secondaries have
bluish white or gray pupils. These two examples are by far the most
interesting of the Lepidopterous insects taken.

Danaidae

Danais erippus   Cram.   4 ♂. This species
  in every locality visited by the expedition.
Danais Berenice   Cram.   1♀ Tule Creek.

Hesperidae

Pamphila	vitellius	Ab. et Bm.	4♂Tule Creek.
"	ottoe	W. H. Edwds.	1♂ 1♀ . Mulberry Creek.
Aegiale cofaqui		Streck.	1♀ Tule Creek.

Is of much greater size than the type from which the species was recently described (in Proc. Acad. Nat. Sc. Phila.) expanding fully three inches; it has also one more white spot (situated somewhat towards the apex) on under side of secondaries. The sub-apical marks in primaries are also larger than in the type. I have adopted Felder's generic name as having priority over Megathymus of Scudder.

HETEROCERA

Zygaenidae

Alypia octomaculata	Fabr.	1 ♀ Mulberry Creek.

Sphingidae

Deilephila lineata	Fabr.	1 larva.
Sphinx Lugeus	W lk.	1♂Salt Fork.

Noctuidae

Hadena inordinata	Morrison	1♂ Head of Red River.
Syneda ingeniculata	Morrison	1♀ Cañoncito Blanco.
Bolina deducta	Morrison	1♀ Salt Fork.

DIPTERA

Tabanus atratus	Fabr.
Sarcophaga carnaria	Lin.
Toshina ?	Figure 18 on plate V of Glover's

"Illustrations of Insects. Diptera" but without being named.

Lucilia Caesar	Lin.

COLEOPTERA

Cincindelidae

Amblycheila cylindriformis		Say.	2 examples.
Cincindela	pulchra	Say.	3
"	scutellaris	Say.	1
"	tranquebarica	Hubn.	1
"	punctulata	Fabr.	1

	Carabidae	
Pasimachus elongatus	Lec.	1
Ebarthus inscisus	Lec.	7
Harpalus calignosus	Fabr.	
" pennsylvanicus	Deg.	1
Chlaenius tomentosus	Say.	1
Cymindes abstrusa	Lec.	1
Helluomorpha texana	Lec.	1

	Hydrophilidae	
Hydrophilus triangularis	Say.	1

	Staphylinidae	
Creophilus villosus	Grav.	2

	Dermestidae	
Dermestes lardarius	Lin.	
" marmoratus	Say.	abundant

	Coccinellidae	
Hippodamia glacialis	Fabr.	
Ceclonida abdominalis	Say.	

	Histeridae	
Saprinus oregonensis	Lec.	

	Scarabaeidae	
Phunueus carnifex	Lin.	1♂
Trox suverosus	Fabr.	2
Canthon hudsonias	Forst	1
Lachnosterna glabricula	Lec.	1
Iostegoptera lanceolata	Lec.	1♂
Anomala binotata	Gyll.	2
Strigoderma arboricola	Fabr.	1
Euryomia Kernii	Hald.	very abundant and in many varieties.

	Buprestidae	
Melanophila miranda		1
Chrysobothris femorata	Fabr.	1

	Elateridae	
Lacon rectangularis	Say.	3

	Lampyridae	
Photuris pennsylvanicus	Deg.	1

	Cleridae	
Phanasomus Spinolai	Lec.	2

	Cerambycidae	
Batyle ignicollis	Say.	3
" suturalis	Say.	2
Typocerus cinnatus	Neum.	in great numbers
Mecas inornati	Say.	1
Moneilema anulatum	Say.	3

	Chrysomelidae	
Chrysomela exclaimationis	Rog.	1
Plagioera confluens	Rog.	2

	Tenebrionidae	
Eleodes sponsa	Lec.	2
" tricostata	Say.	3
" obsoleta	Say.	2
" extricata	Say.	2
" acuta	Say.	1

	Meloidae	
Macrobasis imaculata	Say.	6
" segmentata	Say.	3
Epicanta ferruginea	Say.	5
Nemognatha lurida	Lec.	many examples
" discolor	Lec.	3
Gnathium mimmum	Say.	1
Oxacis cauna	Lec.	1

	Curculionidae	
Sphenophorus 13 puncatus	Ill.	4

	HEMIPTERA	
Galgulus oculatus	Fabr.	1
Brochymena arborea	Say.	5
Strachia histrionicha	Hahn.	2
Leptoglossus phyllopus	Lin.	7
Apiomerus spissipes	Say.	2

ORTHOPTERA

Gryllidae

Gryllus abbreviatus	Serv.	1♀ 3 pupae

Locustrariae

Udeopsylla robusta	Scud.	3 ♂

Acrydii

Caloptenus bivittatus	Uhler.	1 pupa
Hesperotettix viridis	Thos.	2♂3♀1 pupa
Odeipoda corallipes	Hald.	2♂also pupa of either this or the allied
Oedipoda discoidea	Serv.	
Trimerotropis citrina?		1♂In reference

to this example, Dr. [Cyrus] Thomas says "I am not positive[;] it is possible that it belongs to T. vinculata[,] a very closely allied and scarcely distinct species."

Tragocephala pacifica		1♂
Acrolophitus hirtipes		2 larvae

Blattariae

Ischnoptera unicolor?		3♂2♀

NEUROPTERA

Libellulidae

Aeschna heros	Fabr.	3
Libellula trimaculata	DeG.	2

Geological Notes

The Staked Plains of Texas wherein are found the sources of the Red River present features favorable to geological research in the fine sections presented in the various cañons made by the different streams. To the student who visits these places, the first view seems fraught with promise of glorious results. Strata vivid in color and various in composition lie clear cut in sheer cliffs before his eyes and invite a study made easy. And as he passes from one cañon to another, and finds the whole country seamed by the network, the fortuitous labor of Nature appears almost supererogatory.

Standing on the brink he sees the solemn front of the huge mesa break down at the edges, and a jumble of rolling or abrupt and rough hills succeed the ceaseless long gentle swell of the plains surface proper, and the field for study increases and swells to vastness.

But the reality is a disappointment. The rolling swell of the general surface is participated in by the underlying rocks and cañon after cañon throughout this whole extent present in general but the same section, different only as the erosion has been greater, or from slight local causes. So the grand walls of the grand cañon, with their brilliant cliffs and spires, their castellated hills, and cathedral ruins, red and red; and red; are again encountered in the smaller tributaries, until the red sandstone goes under the surface, and the chalky tops of the cañon walls are found from one to the other until they too disappear, the very water courses cease to be and the unbroken prairie reigns supreme.

Again the series of strata which do form the field for study are vaguely coarse and unattractive, upon close inspection, and the absence of fossil life make their stony pages almost the blank leaves of nature's volume;–unless perhaps they are instead the highly decorated pages of her book illustrations only.

One thing however can be read everywhere, and that is the effects of aqueous power on a grand scale–commensurate with the boundless area at nature's disposal when forming these fields to her taste. The section which is here presented will describe the country between longitude 101° and 102° west from Greenwich and between latitude 34° 30′ N and lat. 35°, or about 60 miles east and west and 30 north and south. As I shall point out, the same or a similar section may be expected through the whole region from this to Dodge City or on a line running a little east of north. The thickness of the various strata varies at points but not to any great extent and within the region as given I have myself verified the general section at nearly every point, certainly at places within sight of one another and so situated that no serious difference could occur.

I shall commence at the top and describe the series in descending order.[44]

The general surface of the plains is gently undulating and sometimes in such great swells as to present all the appearance of distant hills or mountains even, where magnified by the mirage and with the heightened illusion of the level where with nothing to serve as a comparision the judgment often fails to locate the distance. A noticeable instance of this swell and depression; this wave and its trough; occurs at the head of the main cañon where a north and south wave has made a trough, and the swell of which is cut through in the minor cañons of the Paloduro and the Tierra Blanca ten miles west of this. Again the bluffs of the cañon of the southern stream rise up to the traveler from the north.

No. 1 Drift 75 feet.
[Pleistocene loess]

At the Permanent Camp eight miles east of the head of the main cañon the drift and alluvium may have been 75 ft in thickness, and at Cañoncito Blanco this thickness may have been equal or less. The drift is fine and gravelly, or at times sandy, though near enough so to make the roads troublesome, the surface is almost always hard. Near the Tule Cañon farther to the south the drift sometimes entirely disappears or is found only in the side arroyas or drainage channels, and the chalky limestone of No. 2 is found frequently exposed on the level surface of the plains, while the outcrop near the cañon almost precludes the existence of drift above.

No. 2 Chalky lime-
stone 75 to 100 ft.
[Pliocene caliche of
Ogallala Formation]

Number 2 is a chalky limestone, very friable and weathering into minute fragments with rectangular joints. No fossils were found and it was difficult at any time to get access to the limestone stratum so extensive was the disintegration. This member was seen at every place where the summit of the general level was met and was last seen at Bluff Creek near Fort Dodge and on the prairie between that point and the Arkansas River. It will be noted that the altitude of Dodge City is about that of Fort Elliott and the line joining the same may be considered a strike line of the section under description.

No. 3 Compact
limestone 5 to 10 ft.
[Pliocene Ogallala
chert]

Number 3 is a layer of compact limestone, almost marble, of smooth grain but conchoidal in fracture, and inclined to break into small rectangular fragments. This seems to contain no fossils though very carefully examined for such. It is very firm and porphyritic in appearance with whitish blots. The color is white or light gray, sometimes with a pinkish tinge in the sun light. It will be seen as the upper decided outcrop in the views given of all the cañons. It is the upper water bearing rock and when it disappears under the surface at the head of the Palo Duro, Tierra Blanca, Tule and Cañoncito Blanco, there will be found the head of water. It, and the member just above it, seem to be quite insoluble as the water of these springs is singularly sweet and fresh. This rock is used in the construction of Fort Elliott, where it is burnt for lime, and when its small and convenient size at the quarry make it suitable for the foundations of the light frame houses of that Post. At this point it is not far distant to the north in a spur of the plains which pushes to the east and is the divide between the Washita and the North Fork of Red River. This member was not noticed again unless perhaps in the high land between the heads of Bear Creek and Bluff Creek in Kansas.

No.4 clay sometimes sandy, sometimes gravelly 75 to 100 ft. [Triassic Trujillo Formation]

Number 4 is a clay sometimes sandy, sometimes gravelly but never stone although very compact. This presents curious features. On the Red River and the Paloduro and Tierra Blanca, on the margin of the cañon wall were found at places immense quantities of calcified and silicified (sometimes) roots which seemed the stratum in all directions. Trunks and butts of trees were found above in No. 3. So extensive was the calcified fibrous character at times that the appearance was almost that of a coral bed. In other cañons this feature seemed lacking in this number and from the fact that upon excavating into the bank the roots were thought to diminish in quantity and lessen in size as the bank was entered, it appeared likely that the trees were located there as now on the margin of a water course. No fossil leaves were found; nothing but the petrified wood so generally reported upon by every traveler in these parts. The formation of this member seems to have been quite rapid from the evenly smooth character and from the fact that pockets of sand and gravel were found in considerable quantity resting upon the next lower number. These pockets evidently belonged to the member under description, and were formed by the sifting and settling of their contents through the lighter mud of the upper part. In these pockets were discovered the first fossils.[45] At Cañoncito Blanco wherever exposed, shells could be found by a little search, but no shells were even found in this number except in these pockets. The shells were all Lamellibrachs, and were abundant in number but of few varieties. I have spoken more in detail of them in another place. All were more or less waterworn, and appeared in general to have been brought or washed there, rather than to have been left by their wearers. At no other place were the shells so abundant as in Cañoncito Blanco though a few were found in the Tule and in Mulberry Creek.

No. 5 Sandstone conglomerate 6 to 20 ft., [Triassic Trujillo Formation]

Number 5 is a sandstone conglomerate, compact in texture but easily worn by water or weather. The gravel found in it is small and is not very abundant. A few fossils were found and even occasional pockets. Generally however the conglomerate was quite free from shells.

No. 6 Red Sandstone shales and clays 75 to 100 feet [Triassic Trujillo Formation]

Number 6 consists of from 75 to 100 feet of red sandstones or clays sometimes passing with shales. Occasionally were beds of white shaly sandstones and sometimes almost clear sand or even partially conglomerate. Very few shells were found but these were believed different varieties than those of the upper number; the difference being perhaps in Ostroea.

This number varies very much running through all the varieties of sand and clay and their rocks. Shales are light colored or red or sometimes dark and in these shales are found springs at several points. The number also varies considerably in thickness, and in many places gives less than the minimum here quoted.

No. 7 Hard sandstone 15 to 50 ft. [Triassic Tecovas Sandstone]

Number 7 is a hard dark colored sandstone withstanding both water and weather. It is heavy and compact and by its resistance it forms the second check in the formation of the cañons, the upper limestone being the first. The main falls of the Red River are formed by this layer and the narrow gully or trench described as cut in the rock below the falls could have been possible only in this number. These falls 25 or 30 feet high are reproduced in the Cañoncito Blanco by the same stratum, and at a less height, and again in the Tule Cañon and found the same. Its firmness and dark color make it bold in relief and in appearance whenever the cañon walls are precipitous. Occasional pebbles and gravels are found but no fossils have been noted. This rock supports the last good water in descending order, and springs or running water found lower than this will be apt to be alkaline.

We have thus far described a section from 325 to 455 feet in depth and as yet the gypsum has not been encountered. Moreover the characteristics of the members already specified are quite distinct and are easily recognized. The main cañon cuts fully 12 miles of its course before these are passed through and our camping places on the Mulberry, the Salt Fork, the upper McClellan Creek, and the Big Spring on North Fork as well as Fort Elliott itself and the creek on which it is supplied with water are all found within the limits of so much of the section.

In ascending the divide from Bear Creek K[ansa]s; that is in passing out of the valley of the Cimarron, we also pass through the lower of these numbers; and there are outcrops of conglomerates and sandstones containing not only the same fossils already obtained and alluded to, but many others of similar varieties. Many specimens of the Ostraea Patnia are found in good condition, and very little waterworn.

It appeared to me that much the same varieties were obtained at Bear Creek that were collected on the divide between Beaver Cr[eek] and Sand Cr[eek] just north of Camp Supply, and that in addition thereto the small shells of Cañoncito Blanco were added, which were not found certainly in numbers, at the outcrop near Camp Supply.

It bore every appearance that the formation at Bear Creek was contemporaneous with that of the lower portion of the section as so far described; and that the more quickly communicated elements of the Staked Plains; the waterworn specimens; the less number of varieties and the smaller shells all indicated that Bear Creek was nearer the edge of the Cretaceous ocean at that time and that the Red River country was probably in deep and quiet water. I might add that no boulders or even large gravel are found in the Red River Country in the conglomerates of the whole section.

It is difficult to separate the lower number into distinct and definite individuals. A confused mass of red sandstone and clays, or shales are formed as low as the cañon walls extend. Where the sandstones predominate as in the Tule Cañon a massive and striking cliff of brilliant red 200 feet and more in height rises sheer from the stream. Where the clays are in excess or clays and shales or slates, the weird castles and churches, and brilliant mockeries of the Red River itself are seen. In this member the occasional or at times more numerous or thicker beds or layers of gypsum are found. The gypsum is not found above No. 7. The gypsum deposits are scattering and varied in importance as well as in colors. All water found flowing beneath the lower surface of No. 7 is apt to be tainted, and

No. 8 Sandstones Shales & clays 700 feet and more. [Triassic Tecovas Formation and Permian Quartermaster Formation Red Beds]

no exception of a fresh sweet spring was found. There may be light colored sandstones and at times limestone in beds or their layers may be seen. Occasionally a bluish tint is found in the shales. The gypsum is generally white or light colored, but all colors are overwhelmed with the general vivid red of the whole land. Beds of conglomerates are seen and from one such a few of the small shells of the same varieties as in Cañoncito Blanco were obtained. This was located not far from Camp Cent, and probably eight miles north of Tule Cañon. A few of the same were also seen in position not far from "D" Co. Creek Camp. It seems hardly necessary to dwell on the peculiarities of this region so often and well described.

It seemed worthy of remark however that the barometer confirmed my own conclusions while on the line of march. The mouth of Tule Creek and the camp on Sand Creek nine miles north of Camp Supply are about at the same altitude and they have nearly if not quite the same geological altitude. The water of Sand Creek is nearly if not quite as disagreeable as that of the Tule. Camp Supply is on a higher level and the water is somewhat better though I think quite disagreeable. In crossing the divide between the Beaver and Sand Cr. the top layer is a conglomerate with a great abundance of shells of various varieties. I think this is of the same age as the layer spoken of as near the Camp Cent Cañon. These shells were not much waterworn and were in very great abundance, more so than at any other points visited on the trip. The vivid gullies, and arroyas, and vistas seen from the summit of this divide, as one looks to the north down the washed slopes are as attractive as many views in the cañon one hundred and fifty miles to the south. Gypsum outcrops are met with between this and the Cimarron, which again exhibits the characteristics of the gypsum formation. The rise from this up the bluffs of Bear Cr. brings us out of the region again to more pleasant surroundings.

The profile shown by the barometer is one of general level to the north and south and a long easy slope from the west to east. The upper level is well preserved and reappears in detached portions as far as the Antelope Hills on the south of the Canadian and east of the 100th Meridian. The east & west streams have cut much the same kind of channels and the side streams are all constructed in the same fashion. So long as the upper limestone remained in situ the first difficulties were great but as is shown by the shapes of the denudation the climate has in general been mild and much the same as now, the rains moderate and only the effects of unusual powers are shown in the commencement of the formation of the cañons.

The easy roll of the ground gave inequalities of the surface which formed ponds and lakes. Today [there] are many basins of size enough to be called small lakes. Filled by the rain they sometimes are of a depth as great as ten feet, and many are seen filled every year to a depth of two, three or four feet. The largest of these lakes in times past found its outlet over its rim in a small stream which wore away the hard limestone by degrees. At length the time came when the stratum was entirely gone and the softer material below disappearing rapidly an extra rainfall perhaps carried the small fall of exit for the lake, back to its brim and the large mass of water was set in motion. Tearing down its outlet the sand, shales and clays were swept away; the unsupported upper layers caved into the channel and were also carried off by the rush; the wild torrent now with its great fall and huge volume tore its way through the harder sandstone below and the sharp cut heads of each cañon were made at one great effort. The lake disappeared, the cañon walls were gradually shaped by the rains but not very much, and the network of these watercourses extended backward toward the head of the stream, as the additional height given by the scouring out of the lower channels made the outbreak of the upper lakes more effective and more easily begun.

As each fresh torrent tore down the main stream it lent its effort to alter the shape of its bed. Sometimes it widened it, sometimes it cut a new channel leaving the bed of the former stream to one side and at a higher level to be cut up into valleys and gullies afterwards. As soon as the main work was done the power was exhausted. The light fall of rain was never enough to smooth down and round the sharp cut walls into gentle quiet hills, and the formation of soil was impossible from this reason. The absence of soil and rain prevented the accumulation of vegetable life, especially trees, and the whole past of the country since its elevation above the level of the cretaceous sea appears to have been that of a lake region with a scant neighboring flora; small outlets bordered by trees; a cataclysm–perhaps covering some few years–of cañon formation; and the same quiet life of today ever since that time. The small streams going down the main cañon has only cut a few hundred yards backward through the sandstone at the falls and this work might easily have been done in hundreds of years by the present stream. There are definite bounds now visible to the ancient lakes which formed the main cañon, that of Cañoncito Blanco, and the Tule. The evidences are also patent of a similar origin to the Mulberry Creek Cañon.[46]

In the Geological Report of Lieut. Whipple's Report, Vol III, Pacific Railroad Surveys, the Antelope Hills are described as having "white limestone" for some of the upper beds. To the west of this point between the Washita and the Canadian were found fossil ostracea in a limestone four feet thick, and of a whitish grey color. (P. 19) "The only representation of this formation found in the collection is the well known Cretaceous fossil Gryphoea Picheri."

The sections given on P. 24, and 25 represent the edges of the Staked Plains, and are all described as having "white limestone" for the upper rock in one case giving 10 feet for the thickness. Underneath this is given "calcareous conglomerate," "sandstones and marls" and "yellow limestone with bluish grey beds at the bottom containing ostroea–[?]"[47]

The last section quoted is of Mt[.] Tucumcari in the valley of the Canadian,[48] about longitude 103° 40' west or more than fifty miles beyond my farthest western point. These sections and descriptions are much more in accordance with my own those recorded in Marcy and McClellan's Report on the Red River,[49] and confirm me in my belief that the geology of the northern part of the pan handle of Texas and extending some distance north into the Indian Territory is one and the same.

The fossils which were brought back were sent to Prof. O. C. Marsh[50] for identification[,] he having kindly promised to do this as a labor of love. He has not as yet sent me the list but I hope it may be received in time to be printed with this report. I have endeavored myself with the slight sources of comparison at my disposal to classify or describe some of these brought back.

By far the greatest number of speciments obtained at the Cañoncito Blanco and in the Cañon wherever found consisted of Ostroea. The varieties figured in Meek's Report on Cretaceous invertebrates, U. S. Geological Survey of the Territories as the Ostroea Patina, Var. A, B, and C,[51] are well represented; in especial the latter named.

As I lay no claims to being an expert in Paleontology I may be pardoned if I state that these figures and those of the Gryphoea Pitcheri given in Vol III Pacific Railroad Reports[52] seem to me to run the one into the other and that it might be difficult to say at times whether an individual should belong to one or another of the four names quoted. At any rate whether right or wrong in this I am certain that I have specimens which exactly resemble all the plates and varieties given and drawn in the volumes cited.

The next most prominent fossil in point of numbers I have concluded to be the Ostroea glabora P. 509 Meek. The fossil so named occurs in great quantity and of all sizes from one to two inches in length. In addition to these I have found I think specimens of the Ostroea inornata, Meek P. 14[,] Mactra (Cymbophora) Alta P. 210 Meek, Callista Pellucida P. 187 Meek[,] Portocardia Rara P. 176 Meek. I have tried to make myself believe that among the specimens collected there were also exhibited ostroea congesta[,] Proceramus problematicus or indeed any variety of Invcerainus but I failed and at present I do not believe these varieties were found. It so happens that the fossils named so far are located in No. 4, No[.] 5 and upward of Hayden & Meek section of the Cretaceous rocks of the northwest.

I am not familiar with the appearance of this section as described nor have I seen the upper numbers as quoted in the various reports of the upper Missouri. It also happens that many of the fossils quoted in the general section as characteristic were not found by myself, and it is again worthy of remark, that if the Staked Plains section does not belong to the upper rocks of the cretaceous period the colors and general appearances of No[.] 4 & 5 will not fairly describe the southern rocks. Prof. Hayden described the northern lands as dark and somber and no mention of red is made above the Dakota Group. The fossils of the Fort Benton Group as figured are certainly *not* characteristic of the Staked Plains and without attempting to place these strata I merely desire to call attention to these points, and to note particularly the force of my observation that all the fossils so far named are much *waterworn*, and generally small in size, and must have been brought some distance.

The fossils found at Camp Supply are very abundant, and some portions of the rock seem entirely composed of them. The varieties of Ostroea quoted are found, and I thought I could safely call two or three specimens Inoceramus. Many and interesting individuals of Scaphites were noted and were all well marked and very little waterworn. Scaphites Conradii was noted and it is believed Scaphites Nodosus. Pholadourya (Procardia) Hodgii Meek P. 219 was marked as one example, though others were thought to have been possibly the same. Many specimens of scaphites of different varieties were recognized, and a much convoluted shell was thought to be a portion of an ammonite. A strongly marked bivalve, of beautiful shape and well preserved awaits recognition and there are many other varieties which it is hoped will be classified in time.

Perhaps it would be proper at this point to say that at the heads of the various streams, and sometimes in accumulated beds in the lower parts of their courses; and in the ponds on the prairie were found shells of land and freshwater varieties of Physoe, Lucinoea, Planorbis, and Unios. These were not found alive perhaps because no search was made for them, but I recollect that the head of the Paloduro was in especial marked by great quantities of these shells.

E. H. Ruffner

1st Lieut. Engineers.

Reptiles

Headquarters Department of the Missouri,
Office of the Chief Engineer,
Fort Leavenworth, Kas., Sept. 27th, 1877.

To the
Chief of Engineers
Wash. D.C.

Sir,

I send herewith a short addendum to my Report on the Survey of the headwaters of the Red River. This letter was mis-laid and should have been sent with my annual Report, but I trust it is not too late yet to have it inserted.

Very respectfully

Your obedient servant

E. H. Ruffner

1st Lieut Engrs

To be added to Lieut Ruffner's Report on the Survey of the headwaters of the Red River.

The party did not attempt to make a full collection of the Reptiles. The full and well illustrated report on this subject in Marcy and McClellan's Report[53] seems to have about covered the entire ground; at least, to one not a specialist. A few specimens collected were sent to the Reading Society of Natural Sciences and the accompanying letter gives the list of all specimens so sent. It may be said however that all specimens collected represent species which are abundantly represented everywhere along the line of the Survey.

Reading Society of Natural Sciences

Reading Pa.

Dec 22d 1876.

Lieut. E. H. Ruffner

Dear Sir,

I have the honor to transmit the following list of reptiles forwarded to the Society, which were collected by the expedition under your charge during the surveys of the region of the headwaters of the Red River of Texas in May and June 1876.

Very respectfully

M. D. Roads M. D.

Order Sauria

Genus Crotophytus
  Crotophytus Collaris   Holbrook

Genus Tapaya
  Tapaya Douglasii   G.

Order Ophidia

Genus Crotalus
  Crotalus Adamantus   Beauv.
  Crotalus Confluentus   Say.

Genus Heterodon
  Heterodon Nasicus

also along with the above *Mygale Hentzii*

Tintype photograph of Carl Julius Adolph Hunnius about 1876.

Carl Julius Adolph Hunnius

Survey of the Sources of the Red River
April 25th to June 30th[,] 1876

Tuesday, April, 25th 1876.
Train left from Leavenworth City, Kansas at 7:44 A.M. met on
board 1st Lt. E. H. Ruffner Corps of Engineers, Chief Engineer,
Dept. of the Missouri, 1st Lt. Frank D. Baldwin, 4th Infy., 2nd Lt.
Thos M. Woodruff 5th Infy., Dr. J. H. Mendenhall, a gentleman
accompanying our party, and Sergt. Gustav A. Lichtenberg, Comp.
D, Batt. Engineers. at Kansas City we changed trains for the Atchison,
Topeka and Santa Fe R. R. went over the Kansas Pacific Rails to
Topeka as the south track of the river has been partly swept away
by the last heavy rain storms. at Topeka Dinner 75 cts. saw a nice
little parrot. Supper at Florence, 75 cts. and arrive at Dodge City,
Kansas at

Wednesday, April 26th 1876.
4:15 A.M. did not sleep at the Hotel of which I took a sketch.
went to breakfast with Mr. Hermann and Bronnecker who are staying
at the Hotel. Lt. Ruffner ordered me to take hourly observations on
barometer and Aneroid barometer and compare with the U. S.
observer's instruments here. the party except me went in ambulance
to the fort. Had my boots re-heeled by Mr. John Miller formerly of
Ellsworth a relative of the Haeberlein family. it was very warm 88°
in the shade. a thunder storm was coming up slowly and at 4 o'clock
a few drops of rain fell, but farther south there must have been a
heavy shower. after dark the party except Sergt. Lichtenberg came
back from the Fort. Mr. Jerome J. Weinburg observer Sergt. at this
place lost his little grey kitten; he takes it pretty hard. about 9 o'clock
Mr. Bronnecker proposed to go once more up to the saloon,
(Kelleys)[54] so we went and Hermann [too,] but we were not in there
three minutes [before] in came through the back way 2 girls and from
the front a strange crowd of men and in less than no time there was
a swearing and cursing and obscene talk and words going on which
I had never dreamed of to hear. especially one fellow using croches
[crutches] and one tall powerfully built man did themselves credit.
it was evidently a put-up arrangement because we met that Kelley
the owner of the saloon on the street where he told Bronnecker that
he looked for him to give him [Kelley] another order for cigars.
Hermann was very much scared, Bronnecker too. I felt uneasy too,
but happening to look at the mans eyes I saw or thought at least I

saw, a merry twinkling in their eyes, but some one as they went for each other, might, in the long run, have seen it wrong and started the thing for earnest so I thought after all it would be better to go out of the house but with grace. Hermann was the first to run away and after the paying of our drinks, Bronnecker and me walked quietly out. the best thing of it was that they unkindly thought we would pay ourselves off. I was all the while afraid H. or B. would call drinks all hands around for they did not and the crowd had to stand it after all and Keep Dry. At 10:50 saw Broennecker leave here for Leavenworth, and I went to bed at 15 minutes past Midnight.

Thursday, April 27, 1876.

Going to bed I discovered a bed bug, so I laid on the quilt and at 3 o'clock I was awakened again for further hourly observation. the train going west being behind 2 hours so Hermann left this place at about 6 o'clock this morning. Old Cunningham, the father of one of the two men who were lynched on the 10th of the month on Saw log creek for stealing [a] horse, is in town and after the statements now coming to light he [his son] was not at all concerned in the stealing and he was hung innocently. We will have a nice to-day[.] barometer rising since 8:15 A.M. 76.5° in shade. I do not know but *think* the cows furnishing the milk for the tables at the Dodge House must have been drinking water pretty freely, after the looks of it. At about 9½ [the] Ambulance and wagons arrived for our partys transportation. every thing alright except the expressed instruments which Lt. Ruffner could not get as there were no orders to their transfer to him here. at ¼ before noon Sergt. Lichtenberg started with the first wagon and after we had another dinner at 1:25 A.M. [*sic*] our Ambulance started. The second wagon with part of the escort and some camping equipment left about ½ an hour earlier. it was very windy and after crossing the bridge a wooden one, over the Arkansas River we were in the sand hills and had plenty drifting sand, sometimes it was really bad. at 3 P.M. crossed Mulberry Cr. nearly dry. at 5:15 P.M. 3 prairie chickens were killed after some skirmish. they let the ambulance right up to them but as soon as [as] they saw a person they would take wing. saw a great number [of] antelopes. At 5:50 we stopped on the south side of Bluff Creek right near the water on a piece of elevated ground[.] at 6:20 the wagons arrived. Lt. Ruffner and Lt. Baldwin went down and Lt. Woodruff and Mr. Mendenhall up the creek to look for ducks. The Creek is quite dry at [the] crossing but the water being beautifully clear. there are sloping bluffs of [the] creek about 100 yds each way. a ranch and mail station in bottom. The tents were put up. I went to take a sketch. found the first violets; plenty mosquitos. The hunting parties had no success. Now if everything goes in the right[,] something will be forgotten. Lt. Baldwin has been thinking of everything, except of Sergt. Lichtenberg and me, no rations drawn. well, I went to the Ranch and bought me some stuff in cans to have something if it should come the worst. Had some eggs left from home. went into the tent about 10 P.M. and so there is another tenting life for me going on.

travelled 26 miles.

Friday April 28th 1876.

Got up about 5 o'clock this morning. Had a good wash in the cool morning air, pretty good and ample breakfast, which does not look like starvation. The wagons left at 6¾ and our ambulance followed at 7 A.M. There were several fine opportunities to shoot an antelope but all missed. it was rather chilly all the morning and it looked like rain very much at 8:15. several antelopes, but all escaped unhurt. At 9:15 there we had a fine view down the bluffs for miles. it was quite a picture to look at. 10:15 near the old Redoubt on Bear Creek. at 11:15 passed a ranche, and at 2 P.M. we stopped on south side of Cimarron River. Baggage arrived at[?] Our camping place is near the Redoubt and Redoubt Cr. there are many violets blooming. We met the stage this morning and every one took the opportunity to send some message per postal card. for supper we had tomatoes, very sweet because they were extra sweetened, and eggs & ham. At 7:27 went to bed, a splendid evening[.] no change in barometers since the last two observations, and so I think we may have good weather for tomorrows trip. it was very windy and we drove some extra tentpins.

travelled 30 miles

Saturday April 29th 1876.

The Guard woke us 4 o'clock this morning for an early start as we have 36 miles to make by very sandy roads, as they say. before breakfast, which consisted of Potatoes, Salmon etc., had a good wash in the Creek, the water of which is not so salty or alkali as I expected. At 6¾ we left. It was a very promising morning, the country is very hilly some very high; a good variety of blooming prairie flowers. about 8 o'clock we crossed the boundary between the State of Kansas and the Indian Territory; half a hour later we crossed Snake Cr. a thunderstorm came up from the west and now I felt very sorry that I did not had taken my raincoat out [of] the wagon into the ambulance but the driver, Wm. C. Hadder gave me part of his blanket and it was not so bad as it might have been. Lt. Baldwin shot a pretty large rattle snake which was in our road. saw some large land turtles. it is getting pretty stormy, at 10:15 as we crossed Buffalo Cr, a wide sandy bed with some water in it, pretty alkali. at 11:45 we stopped at Buffalo Springs. It is some water there to be found all the year round. Lt. Woodruff tried to shoot a duck but missed. at 12:15 P.M. we passed a place, known as Red Hole[.] it is a very steep [grade] going down and the road is very winding. the rain had now stopped but the wind is increasing. there are very large rocky banks at this place and everything looks red after the red clay which has a very bright color. shortly after this we came to Gypsum Cr. all this [way] to the next crossing are laying very deep and all are very rocky. the water not fit to drink, bitter alkali. about two miles further on we crossed Soldier Cr. there are a few trees scattered along its high banks, some running water in it. By this time it was 1:15 P.M. about 2 miles further on there came Dog Soldier Cr., it being dry and now we had to cross only one hill more to see Sand Cr. at which we arrived at 2 o'clock. it is awfull stormy and it is looking like rain tonight. we are only 9 miles off from Camp Supply. Sergt. Lichtenberg and I put up our tent on a place he, the Sergt. selected which was surely the best on this poor camping place. At 4 P.M. had a small slice of fat bacon and tomatoes and a cup of coffee which is rather not much till to-morrow. I tried to go up on a hill right north of our tent to sketch this unlucky place, but it was too stormy up there. Our trip was after all today the nicest we [have] had, scenery was always changing and very pleasing to the eye. saw from Buffalo Springs, which is by the way, about halfway between, the Cimarron River and Supply, it being called 13 miles either way from the Springs, the so-called "Taylors Indian" this being a monument on a cluster of hills to the South West, which some years ago Paymaster Taylor took for an Indian lookout and had the train corralled and every thing prepared for an attack. since that, it is known by that name. Made another attempt to take a sketch of this place and this time I succeeded. the storm was not so bad any more as it had been. after coming back from this expedition Lt. Ruffner called me up to the ambulance to look on his water color view of a part east of us, which was pretty nicely done, and another of the Mouth of Redoubt Cr. He showed it to everybody and as everybody admired his work, Lt. Ruffner was very much pleased. all at once Dr. Mendenhall rose in the back seat of the ambulance and said, "now, as every one has seen Lt. Ruffners work, I will show you mine"[;] by this he showed the back seat of a pair of red drawers, on which he had been patching for the last 2 or 3 hours. every body was laughing[.] it was too comical. about 7½ P.M. I felt so hungry that I asked the officers for something to eat, and I made a pretty good lunch out of it. As the Aneroid Barometers were still going down we prepared for rain[.] drove the tentpins tighter and made a ditch at the back of the tent, to keep the water from running into or through it. at 9:27 took the last reading and went to sleep.

travelled 26 miles

Sunday, April 30th 1876.

Woke at 5 o'clock. it looks like very fine weather. there was no rain last night. The water in Sand Cr. is not made for washing ones hand and face. it is very hard. Plenty mosquitoes. For breakfast at 6 this morning had coffee and dry bread. The sun is hot and as there is no wind it is not so nice as it could be. at 8 o'clock our outfit was in motion after the ascent of the bluff behind our camping place, we had a long level stretch of ground for about 2 miles and then we had to climb the hills. 9:05 we passed a place known as the Devils Gap, which was the finest view we had yet on our trip. it is a very narrow road and on both sides you look down into deep cañons, (red sand stone) and this was relieved by Cedar trees, the first we saw on the road. and all over this stretch was a long range of Hills in the distance. Thence traveling on over still more tops of elevations on a sudden the red sand stone changed into yellow. the next big high rise was 425 feet above our camping place from last night, [and] from this point we saw Camp Supply laying far off in the bottom. The descent was easy. it is in fact a long slope for about 2 miles on top of the hill. Lt. Baldwin killed 2 very large Otters. another big one got out of the way in good time. at 9:45 we came into the bottom and between the mosquitoes, which were very thick and large, drawing heavily on ones blood. at 10:27 A.M. we stopped for camp north of Post of Camp Supply. By the orders of Lt. Ruffner the greatest display of canvas was made. starting from the East was one A tent in which was quartered Hunnius and Sergt. Lichtenberg, next a Wall tent with Lt. Ruffner and Dr. Mendenhall, next Wall tent [with] Lts. Baldwin and Woodruff, next Wall tent [which served as] Kitchen, Dining room, etc. Our dinner was very short[,] coffee and cooked potatoes and bread. Paid a visit to Mr. Carl Moller, who is a clerk at the Quartermaster Office at this post. He was kind enough to invite me during my stay here to take my meals at their messhouse and I was only too glad to accept. About sundown the mosquitoes got rather thick and about 9 o'clock it was awful. I never saw them so thick and hungry. During the day wrote a letter to Mrs. Hunnius. North of us are signs of a thunderstorm, but Sergt. Lichtenberg did not think it necessary to drive extra tentpins. There were not so many mosquitoes in our tent. we went to sleep.

traveled 9 miles.

Monday, May 1st 1876.

About two this morning I woke from some noise and there sure came the thunder storm in full speed upon us, and as our tents were facing the north I expected to see them go. the fire near our tent to smoke away the mosquitoes had kindled and there was danger of

Camp Supply, Indian Territory, 1 May 1876.

being burnt. I got some water to put the fire out and the Sergt. did hold the tent. He then found the axe and drove more pins. At 5 o'clock this morning it was very chilly and plenty [of] rain clouds were coming from the north. Had breakfast at Mr. Mollers, Lt. Gardner & Lt. Bishop being there. about 11 o'clock Lt. Ruffner gave orders to strike all the tents and move to quarters No. 15, and a great improvement it was. it is getting pretty cold and very stormy. had dinner at Mollers, with whom I spoke about my board during my stay here, which may be several days as the expressed goods did not arrive. Lts. Woodruff & Bishop were at the table. Mrs. Moller is a treasure to Mr. Moller and I think in the long run he will be all right. But I poor fellow feel like an outcast in the[ir] society. this evening there was a big dress parade as the band of the 5th Cavalry is here for a visit.[55] Dr. Mendenhall had a very long and interesting talk with Sergt. Lichtenberg about the Staked Plains, and he heard at least the full truth of the stories the Officers have told him. he is not very well, and is anxious to avoid rain and getting cold or wet. at 10 P.M. went to sleep on an iron bedstead which was quite comfortable.

Tuesday May 2nd 1876.

At 6 o'clock took my first instrumental readings. There will be during our stay here only the principal readings taken at 6, 7, 10:27 A.M. and 2, 3:02, 9, 9:27 P.M. It is pretty cool but a clear sky [with] some light clouds. This forenoon it was made known that we might start, if our express goods came in[,] tomorrow early in the morning.

Asked Mr. Moller to let me have a box for at least one month supplies. At 10:30 this morning the Astronomical outfit arrived with Lt. A. H. McClousky, Arty. The Escort what brought the articles up to-day gave to Sergt. Lichtenberg a young Prairie dog. Had some running from Quartermaster to Commissary to and fro to do to get some of my and the parties things together. Arranged to mess with the ambulance driver, McCloughlin, and Team driver, Sullivan, and on their advice I bought from the Commissary for 45 days provisions[:]

12 cans Milk	@ 21 1/4	$2.55
24 cans #2 Tomatoes	@ 11 5/6	2.84
10 cans green corn	@ 18 1/3	1.83
5 cans Yeast Powder	@ 35	1.75
1 box Rasins	@ 1.15	1.15
10 lb Apples dry	@ 21	2.10
2 jars Jelly	@ 79	1.58
30 lb Ham	@ 13 1/2	4.05
10 lb Sugar	@ 10 18/100	1.02
5 lb Rio Coffee	@ 22 3/4	1.14
		$20.01

Sullivan and McCoughlin will turn their 45 days rations into flour, coffee, tea, Bacon, Rice, beans etc. And they will find the cooking utensils and do the cooking. I think it is very cheap for me. Mr. Moller got me a mess box made with a Pad lock. After supper Lt. Gardner showed me some of his drawings[,] his Hound, and his carbine with his own improvements. He is at any rate a very fine draughtsman and should go ahead and not let it lay. The weather is very promising and it is getting warmer. After dress parade took the readings of the Thermometer at the Post Hospital during our stay here. The Mail came in from the North and I felt very disappointed not finding any for me. There were some for the party. Bought a tin cup 15[cents], one pipe stem and crackers 50 cts, our former Escort took my tin cup with them. Lt. Ruffner handed me a package containing a mosquito bar for me. It was very nice and considerate of him. Lt. Gardner showed me the room in which there will be a ball given to-night. It is an oblong room about 18 x 36[.] the walls are posts, the cracks very roughly plastered[; on] the ceiling as decoration a Garrison flag, and for light 8 candles. Well out here anything will do. I told him why he did not make use at least of the Signal Flags; he said it was a good idea but too late to do now. Got my washing back and paid 40 cts. to Mr. _____ the cook to Lt. Ruffner and party. About 10 P.M. went to bed.

Wednesday May 3rd 1876.

As orders were given last evening for an early start I got out of bed at 5 o'clock, woke the cook. about ½ past 5 Lt. Ruffner came to our room in a long night gown (in which by the way he looks very well) and inquired about the Escort. There was much going on in loading the team and Escort wagon after which Sergt. Lichtenberg and myself went to Comp. G., 19th Inf. Quarters and had through the kindness of 1st Sergt. Fisher a cup of coffee and a slice of dry but fresh bread each, as a breakfast, and at 8¾ A.M. the two Wagons pulled out as it is expressed here. Sergt. Lichtenberg, myself and part of the Escort in one of the wagons. The Ambulance with the Officers to follow later. It was very windy from the S. S. East and the sand drifting so much that it was impossible to ride in an open wagon. We pulled the wagon cover over which was so far good to keep the most part of the sand away but it shut off the view of the country too. It is a very barren piece we traveled over to-day[,] grass very scant, but plenty timber along Wolf Cr. at 2 o'clock crossed the Creek and went right into Camp; a most lovely spot of an elm and cottonwood grove. Had a very good dinner prepared by Mr. Sullivan[:] ham, fried, green corn, good coffee and milk. After this was over I went to make a sketch of our camp. it was hardly possible to keep the eyes open for [blowing] sand. Lt. Ruffner had a better position for his water color sketch, he being covered by brush. Dr. Mendenhall asked me to put him on the sketch so he took position against a big cottonwood. He came just back from carbine practice. Lt. Baldwin told me he is no bad shot, of which I am very glad to hear. it would be just one more in case of necessity. The A tent behind the big Cottonwood on which Dr. Mendenhall leans is Sergt. Lichtenberg's and my quarters. After supper consisting of coffee, milk, bread and jelly, Mr. Sullivan said to me to be quiet and he would bring [in] a wild turkey. he was not more than ½ hour gone when he brought one. Several went to do the same but without success. He said they were only good to shoot at in a moon[light] night as they roost close on a tree and you have to get the turkey between the moon and the gun or else you will hit nothing. Went to bed about 10 P.M.

travelled 18 miles.

Thursday May 4th 1876.

Was called at 5 o'clock as there should be an early start. It looks very much like rain. The rain came from the North West and was sharp and the sand flying. After a good breakfast and much ado we started at 7 o'clock. It was a very disagreeable day[,] cloudy, stormy so that we most of the time rode under the wagon sheet. we were very crowded but one can not have everything for 5 cents as Lt.

Ruffner says. Saw some prairie chickens, antelopes. Mr. Sullivan had a shot on a turkey but missed. Lt. Baldwin killed one. The country was rolling, good grass very scarce, but some bunches here and there. about Noon saw far in the distance to our left the Antelope Hills which must look very pretty on a clear day. There was not much water on the road except on Willow Springs where there will be a Post Ranch built, and after the completion of which there will be 2 mails weekly between Camp Supply and Ft. Elliott. Willow Spring has his [*sic*] name from some willow bushes growing on it, and a very crooked Cottonwood is on the pond in which was found a year ago an Indian child buried. About noon the storm and drifting sand was bad. we all looked very dirty. It was pretty chilly too. after 2 P.M. crossed North Commission Creek where there is much and fine timber, a celebrated turkey roost as I was told[.] sometimes one can see them here by thousands. We expected to find the ambulance, which went ahead of us, there, but did not. They the officers were gone to South Commission Cr. about 2 miles farther. at 3 P.M. we arrived on our camping ground. it was blowing very hard but there was soon a good fire built and Mr. Sullivan had dinner in very short time ready[:] Ham, Green Corn and Coffee and we did it all honor and made a clean table. South Commission Creek is a small but very fast running stream of clear and good water. There is not so much timber as on the North Creek; but some tall cottonwoods. North West of our Camp are some very marked hills with rocky outcrops. for dinner Mr. Sullivan dished the wild turkey, which he had cooked the evening previous. it was delicious, so tender I was delighted with it. The first wild Turkey. after supper we sat around the camp fire, it being chilly and told stories all around. Sergt. Lichtenberg made flapjacks, but it did not agree with his mess. about 10 P.M. went to sleep. We had the tent right hand on the sketch. Sergt. Lichtenberg and Mr. Sullivan had been on a turkey hunt but without success. They found an old Indian saddle and brought it in for me. it was most considerate.

travelled 29 miles.

Friday, May 5th, 1876.

At 3 o'clock the camp guard woke me to ask the time. it was very dark and raining a little. At 4 o'clock we were called on to rise as there would be another long march to-day. At 6:15 A.M. we started. Mr. Sullivan found an Indian top, and gave it to me. The weather disagreeable and the wind bad, but it went down after a while. Walked 6 or 7 miles. At noon we crossed the Canadian River which has a very wide and sandy bed about 12-1500 feet [wide]. There was only a very small stream of water on and near the north bank. before we came there passed Springers Ranch, from there to the River about

2 miles, Codroy [corduroy] road awfull rough[;] it shook and jostled us fearfully. During the afternoon I found a grasshopper which went into the alcohol. at 4 P.M. crossed the Washita River and went into camp, all pretty well worn out and very hungry. Though we had about 10 A.M. a lunch, but as the party was large and only one loaf of bread and half a turkey, one did not get much. Washita is a very narrow affair here about 10 feet wide and 2 inches deep. I who walked the last three miles ahead of the wagons waded through it. on some places near Camp it is from 3 to 4 feet wide and about 12 inches deep. The timber is Willow and Willow bush, Cottonwood and a few Elm. at 5 o'clock we had dinner [of] ham and tomatoes[.] thence I went sketching. It is getting much warmer and from time to time [the sun] broke through the clouds. The Ranch of which I took a sketch is about 300 yds south of our camping ground on a little rise of ground. It started to rain and going out to our tent [I] found that Sergt. Lichtenberg put the inside of it out. What will do in good [weather], but not in wet weather, as he came back with Mr. Sullivan from an unsuccessful hunt after turkey, I argued with him to have it re-set but he would not do it. rather slept outside, and so he did, and I had the tent all to myself. by walking near our camp found three eggs laying on the ground, no nest, only a little hole scratched. took them to Lt. Ruffner, where I was informed that they were of the Whip-poor-will, so I carried them back from the place I took it. The eggs was very sharply pointed and the other end very rounded with irregular dark brown speckles [but] at [the] point nearly none. It being so disagreeable outside so I went into the tent and read Harper's Monthly, and at 9½ P.M. went to sleep. It was very chilly.

travelled 31 miles

Saturday, May 6th 1876. [Refer to Map No. 1]
Was called to breakfast at 5 o'clock. every thing very wet and started at ½ to 6 A.M. This was a very cold and windy morning. The country is broken and more or less hilly. about 9 A.M. crossed the Heads of Gageby Creek, no water, and crossing very steep. Mr. Sullivan caught two lizzards which went into the bottle, and one man of the escort gave me two Horned Toads. at 10:30 A.M. we reached the top of a very high and steep hill, 3670 feet above the ocean and 1026 over Camp Supply. From here you have the first view of Fort Elliott,[56] which is still about 7 miles off. At 11:30 passed a Ranch and a head of Spring Creek and at 12:15 P.M. drove into the post of Fort Elliott, Texas.[57] Here we occupy quarters, in which I sleep in the middle room. Lt. Ruffner put shortly after our arrival a theodolite up to locate the place for the monument which we brought with us all the way from Fort Leavenworth. This was set during the afternoon and the Observing tent put over it. in this tent Sergt. Lichtenberg will

sleep. nearby the Teamsters and Escort camp. Met Engineer Sergt. Moier, Corporal Wm. Holland, Batt. Engrs, Co. D. He looking very sick, in fact as I learned from him[,] he being since 24 days in the hospital. from him I learned that the promised Indian Cradle is broken and lost. Had my heavy boots resoled. paid $1.50. and a fine comb 35 cts. During Evening it blowed in a heavy gale. one could hardly stand on his legs. (West wind.) Spent evening with Engr. Sergt. Moier, who gave me a splendid specimen of mos[s] agate. about 10 o'clock Lt. Ruffner came from observatory tent and told me that he could not stand the storm any longer. found the Latitude to be 35° 28.' Went to bed at 11 P.M. The storm was awful.

traveled 18 miles

Dugouts on Sweetwater Creek near Fort Elliott, Texas, 8 May 1876.

Sunday May 7th 1876.

Had a very bad night. the wind came through the floor. it was very chilly and a rather hard bed only India rubber and one blanket, another one as cover, but I get already accustomed to it. The observatory tent was blown down during the night and buried Sergt. Lichtenberg sometime during the night. As luck would [have it,] the telescope was taken to the box and therefore no great damage done. coming from breakfast, we had fresh meat (beefsteak) [, I] found one of Lt. Ruffners correction papers driving on the prairie. In Sergt. Moiers quarters I made up my official Record. During afternoon I purchased from a Sergt. of B. Comp. Cav. one Indian War bonnet, (Cheyenne work[ )] and paid $18.00 for it. It took nearly 3 hours of talking to get it. The Observatory tent was put up again and Sergt. Lichtenberg sewed straps and buckles to it. Lt. McCauley took me to Lt. Callahan's quarters and showed me an Indian Cradle all covered with beads. The evening spent with Sergt. Moier. Lt. Ruffner had a splendid night for Astronomical work. The wind had gone down. Went to bed about 11 P.M. Lt. McCauley showed me a plant which is poison to animals and is seldom found.

Monday, May 8th 1876.

Rolled up my bedding about 5 A.M. Slept very good last night. had a wall tent fly to lay on and used the other blanket as a cover. The nights are rather chilly. At 7 A.M. the Escort, one Corp. (Carr) and 6 men, went back to Camp Supply. For breakfast we had Ham and Eggs. Lt. Ruffner asked me to see whether I could not find any Fossils in the stones used for the new hospital now in course of construction. There were none. after that I helped Lts. Woodruff and McCauley chaining the base line north and south. for dinner we had plum pudding. In afternoon the base re-chained. during evening I changed the base of the astronomical Transit to East and West, and the Azimuth screw 216 points. It read 58.8 points. It was a splendid day, windy and warm. Lts. Woodruff and McCauley had to re-chain the Northern parts of the base line. Mr. Sullivan bought a coffee mill and some crockery for our Mess. It is a nice country here. Saw the colored serving girls take during the pleasant hours of the evening rides on their ponies. The evening I spent with Engr. Sergt. Moier and after the 9:27 P.M. Reading of Instruments I walked home, such as it is. Lt. Woodruff told me that to-morrow morning a special Mail Courier will go to [Camp] Supply, so I sat down and wrote a letter. went to bed after midnight. Lt. Baldwin made nightcaps for all the hands around. Lt. Ruffner in the Observatory.

Tuesday, May 9th 1876. [Refer to Map No. 1]

As a rule got out of bed at 5 A.M. Had breakfast very late[,] Ham and Eggs. fed my Horned Toads with fresh grass. Lts. McCauley and Woodruff re-chained the southern part of base line. Lt. Baldwin, Dr. Mendenhall and two Cavalry men, all mounted went out about 10 A.M. to pick up a base monument for triangulation. It is warm this morning and no wind. Sent the letter I wrote off. The mounted party mentioned went West, and put up a heap of bones for a mark. could see it from southern Post of base line. Lts. Woodruff and McCauley measured i 3 feet on base line and worked to find Stadia readings therefore. About 2 o'clock after I refigured some calculations of Lt. Ruffner, I and Sergt. Moier rode a North Westerly direction out to the quarry about 6 or 7 miles. There was a lime kiln, some dug outs from one of which I took a pair of Antelope horns with scalp. climbed up the Chalk bluffs to look for Fossils. found none. collected some specimens of rocks and rode back. Stopped at the so-called upper town, see sketch on other page. it is the last house of a town which had here been once.[58] a very large log building with one part fixed with board flooring for a dancing hall, I hear. there were 3 women and 4 men there. all treated us coarse, but still civil. Had some beer and after my taking a sketch left the then most western civilized place in this part of the country. At this place you can still see the cellars of at least 40 or 50 houses, and there are an enormous amount of broken Whiskey bottles. On our way back from that place we saw a great many Quails which were quite tame just running a few feet from our horses. paid a visit to another Ranch near by the road but across the Sweetwater Creek, which was nearly dry. it was the scarcity of water which broke up the socalled upper town. The new town is about 5 miles down the creek below the Fort. About 7 o'clock we arrived at the Post pretty well tired. it was a warm day, not windy. The evening was splendid. Lt. Ruffner in Observatory. Lt. Woodruff and Lt. McCauley's Stadia trials close very near as I saw from calculations that Lt. Woodruff showed to me. Worked up official Report for the last three days.

The Upper Town, end of civilization three miles northwest of Fort Elliott, Texas, 9 May 1876

Wednesday May 10, 1876.

Copied this A.M. some Astronomical Computations. Lt. Baldwin and Dr. Mendenhall went out for a hunt. took ambulance. In afternoon I climbed around Sand Hills to find a place to sketch the Post but Hay Stacks were always between. Mr. P. Bauers (blacksmith) gave me for the Museum a spear point, flint. Platted the Trip of Sergt. W. M. Meyer from mouth of McClellan Creek to its head and from mouth of McClellan Creek to Fort Elliott. made a tracing on our travelling and guide maps. Sergt. Meyer being ordered to proceed to-morrow morning to Fort Sill, I[ndian] Terr., I gave him $10.00 to see whether he could find some small moccasins for the children, C[arl] and H[erman], and some articles for the Museum. He goes along with a transport of prisoners[,] horse thieves. Went to sleep after 10 P.M.

Thursday May 11th 1876.

Got up before 5 this morning. Lts. Ruffner, Woodruff & McCauley out on Stadia readings by this time. The number of the Carbine which I received is 385. it is a very old one, (Cal 45). received also a canteen. Received from Lt. Baldwin 10 cartridges. Paid for wash (50 cts.). At 9 o'clock the teams reported. Lt. Ruffner and I took angle readings from North and South point of Base line to the Monuments. The train started shortly after noon in charge of 1st Lt. Baldwin.[59] train consists of 1 Wagon master, Rich. Cavanaugh, and 7 six Mule teams. the Escort of Sergt. James Landon, 2 Corpls., 15 men Cavalry. the Infantry Sergt. Francis Hensman, 2 Corpls., 1 Trumpeter, 10 privates. And last but not least the most prominent guides, [William] Dixon[60] and the Half Mexican and Half Indian Teodoso; 52 men, 84 animals, 2 dogs.

Party Officers	4	Teams	7	Mules	42
Citizens	3	Ambulance	1	"	4
Sergt. Cook	2				
Teamsters	8	W. Master's Horses	25		[46]
Ambulance	1	Guides Horses	4	47	mules [sic]
Cav.	18	Officers "	8	37	horses
Inf.	14				
Guides	2		[37]	84	[draft animals]
	52				

At 1 o'clock P.M. Headquarters in the saddle. Lt. Ruffner, Lts. Woodruff and McCauley, A[cting] A[ssistant] Surgeon [Dr. Sabine], Ado Hunnius, 2 Cavalry orderlies, 1 Corporal, and 2 men to carry the Stadia rods. 3 men were left behind[.] north end of Base line to be marked by white and South end by red Signal Flag. rode to Mesa Point, known as Station No._____, leaving Lts. Woodruff and McCauley with 2 men at Station. The wind was very high. could see the flags at a distance of 3½ miles with naked eye on our stations on Mesa point. The wind very bad, the limestone dust driving into our eyes. Lt. Ruffner ordered our escort and ambulance in which Dr. Mendenhall rode around the instrument to brake [*sic*] the wind. It was very hot and I looked very dirty. My horse made me great trouble all the way dancing and frothing[, in] short, no walking to be gotten out of him. I had the carbine in a bad place too, what made the horse very restless. About 5½ o'clock we arrived near the place of the old cantonment[61] and found after crossing the North Fork of the Red River the camp near by. Supper being ready, I sat down but being so dirty I could not do it justice. there is a very good clear spring near by, water [which contains] much sulpher. Our tent is near a small Cottonwood tree, and we put one of our Flags in front to mark it. Before we left Fort Elliott the mail came in and I had a letter from Mrs. Hunnius. We passed through an interesting and in some places very broken country. the hills rise very steep up from long gentle slopes, [and] on the top of those hills is bare limestone. after crossing the last rise or ridge there was a magnificent view to see all the sand and limestone hills in their different colors south and south west of us. I turned the Aneroid Barometers over to Sergt. Lichtenberg to-day. Went to sleep about 9 P.M.

travelled 12 miles

Friday, May 12th 1876. [Refer to Map No. 2]

At sunrise we were called by the Trumpet, which gives the whole outfit a very soldierly appearance. after breakfast took a sketch from a bluff near Camp. Mr. Sullivan brought a turkey gobbler in he killed, a splendid shot, hit the head. Helped him in dressing the bird. he gave me a so called turkey caller[,] a bone out of the wing[,] and the beard. about 10 Lt. Ruffner told me to be ready to go with him. got my horse, but as he wanted me to ride in [the] ambulance, I turned my horse loose again, but hoppled [*sic*]. Started for Stations 6 and 7, returned about 3 o'clock. Broke down with a lot of limestone rock by catching Lt. Ruffners hat which was blown off in the wind. Station 6 was not to be seen and Lt. R had to make trial stations. made a sketch of the Ranch near Camp, the last place of civilization to the South of Fort Elliott. I wrote a letter. Lt. R. told me it might be that he had a chance to send off some mail. Lt. Baldwin and I swapped horses, got a dark brown one now, a little slow but good. my horse will do him better service. We will start early tomorrow morning. so it is ordered. Wrote another letter addressed to Edw. F. Haberlein. Went to sleep about 9 o'clock.

Saturday, May 13th 1876. [Refer to Map No. 2]

At 4 o'clock this morning we were called by the Trumpeter. had an early breakfast. the train left about 5:30 A.M. much trouble with the triangulation at the place I stood. I could not be seen by Lt. Woodruff and Party. moved farther in. from this place the Stadia readings commenced. It is very slow work. we had very sandy and sometimes steep hills to cross. about 4:30 P.M. arrived at the camp on North Fork of Red River.[62] as I was informed[,] the train arrived at 10½ A.M., but we had so many delays. I had to change the case of rod twice. standard reading was 0.730. Thence changed to 2.991 and afterward 2.000. Was very hungry and dirty arriving in camp. had a good wash and some raisin souff. Sergt. Lichtenberg, who measured the road by odometer makes the distance only. We saw some splendid scenery on the South side of North Fork on which there is much cottonwood timber. we passed a splendid grove of this kind of trees. After supper made a sketch of the camp from a hill near by. fed my horse and about 8 o'clock we went into the tent. It looks like a thunder storm. The guide, Mr. Dixon came in who took the mail this morning to Fort Elliott. He lost the book he was to bring for Dr. Mendenhall on the road. Had a big chase after a frog which I caught 200 feet from Camp, upstream near a splendid spring. This Place is called "The Big Springs." My new horse worked very well. He is a quick gentle one, and the best is [that] where you put him he will stand. Had during the morning a very bad headache, and several times I thought I would get sunstruck. Lt. Ruffner told me to-night that he will organize tomorrow two Stadia parties and I shall take independent sketches (topographical) of the country. The North Fork of Red River is about from 4 to 25 feet wide and from 2 to 8 inches deep, very clear water, plenty timber on its banks, but sand and gravel. Water alkali, like all the Creeks in this country.

travelled 11 miles

Sunday, May 14, 1876. [Refer to Map No. 3]

Had some rain about 3 o'clock, but not much, but very heavy lightning and thunder. At 4 o'clock Revellie [and] an early and hasty breakfast, and at 5¾ I and the guide, Wilson,[63] started on our mission, He to show and point out to me the country [and] I to make topographical sketches thereof. About 8:45 [A.]M. we were on the Staked Plains, the Llano Estacado. it is a level or just as good as level country. not much grass and this is very short. from time to time you will come to a depression in the ground which will be a large lake during the wet season. These are not deep and as they are more or less swampy. The last view of the Cañon of North Fork of Red River, was exceedingly beautiful and picturesque. one hill after the other was seen with a rocky top and the rocks in its different colors and shades. the river was well marked by the trees on the banks of it. after going 4 miles we came to North Fork of McClellan Creek which is a dry cañon in some places very steep. the road was here very winding as it had to be picked. Saw some cedar trees on the rocky slopes. At 12:30 A.M. [*sic*] we were on an eminent point where we could look very far up and down McClellan Creek, which lies in a magnificent cañon[;] rocky slope upon rocky slope are piled well dotted with Cottonwood, Elm and on the most rocky places with Cedar trees. It was a grand sight. We did not follow the wagon trail but Mr. Wilson proposed to bring me into the Cañon by a side Cañon and so we went, and were pretty soon between the rocks and after some down hill climbing by our horses, we arrived at the bottom. The Camp lays in a Valley about ¼ mile wide, rocks on both sides. McClellan Creek is a rather dirty looking water, but a great many cat fish are in [it] and Mr. Sullivan caught many, some very big ones. The wagon master, Mr. Cavanaugh, killed a very large Rattlesnake, a female. she had 5 large eggs in her belly. Mr. Wilson killed a Kingsnake; I carried her in my handkerchief and arriving in camp, I was just to put her in the bottle as she got rather lively again. The cook, Long, managed her, and after some fighting, we succeeded to put her in. made a sketch of part of the camp. At 4:30 P.M. the Surveying party came in. [In] The evening Lt. Ruffner asked me to platt [*sic*] Sergt. Lichtenbergs notes of the trip to-day to compare with the Stadia line run. Went to sleep about 11 o'clock.

travelled 21 miles 1281 yards

Monday 15th [May] 1876. [Refer to Map No. 3]

Revellie at 5 A.M. About 6 we had breakfast, the fishes (catfish) Mr. Sullivan caught last evening. we boiled and skinned them last night and had it fried this morning. at 7:40 the Guide, Dixon, Lt. Baldwin, Lts. Woodruff and McCauley, myself, and 2 Cavalry men went after Lt. Baldwins battlefield of Nov. 8, 1874, where he fought the Cheyennes and re took 2 of the Germaine girls,[64] which had been taken with 2 other but older sisters in June of the same year near Castle Rock on the Smoky Hill route, Kansas. The father, and mother with baby and one brother were killed at the spot. the baby was not yet born, but the mother cut open alive and the unborn baby taken from her and eaten. We did much riding and scouting up and down a creek, in which we found two water holes. the lower one has a quicksand bottom. the upper one good, and so the water. Lt. Baldwin came to the conclusion that this was not the place and we galloped on, until we came to the North Fork of McClellan creek. I pointed out to him two buttes which were shown to me yesterday by the guide, Mr. Wilson, and told him that North West of those Buttes I was informed by him the battlefield was. We rode on and soon found a Wagon wheel[,] thence some lodge poles and after a while, it was just noon[,] we arrived at the place Lt. Baldwin had his field piece[,] a mountain howitzer[,] in position. I made a topographical sketch of the country around and Lt. Woodruff made a Water color sketch of the place the Indians had their camp at that time. I picked up some Carbine cartridge shells and one good cartridge. Mr. Dixon brought 2 howitzer shells which he picked up. they were still good. they had been used as solid shot. At 1 o'clock we left the place and rode back to camp, South West in as straight a line as the country permitted. it was a neckbreaking return trip. twice we had to dismount as it was impossible to go into the cañons in another way. At 3:20 P.M. we arrived in Camp. I hope I never have to do such awful riding to do again. I think that if the Indians had chased us we could not have done better. As a matter of course I was very tired. My right leg is rather sore from the carbine rocking against it. About 6 o'clock Lt. Ruffner, Dr. Mendenhall and myself went back into the Cañon near Camp to go and see a fine Spring. Lt. Ruffner made the suggestion to follow the Cañon up. Had some climbing to do over the rocks and at last arrived at a Cave, big enough to shelter about 8-10 Persons. There was a hole in the roof of this cave and I was the first to climb through it[,] after me, Dr. Mendenhall. Lt. Ruffner would not. he took an outside road. Our Guides stated that they did not know anything about that cave and Lt. Ruffner called it Hunnius cave. For supper we had coffee and Jelly cake which Mr. Sullivan had made to the great astonishment of all who saw it. It tasted very fine and was surely a surprize. Lts. Ruffner, Woodruff and Dr. Mendenhall went out during the evening and started the points to be measured to-morrow morning. An officer _____ from _____ arrived during the afternoon in our Camp. During our trip to-day I found the botanical specimen and book of Lt. Woodruff [which] he lost in one of the cañons. Mr. Dixon shot at a deer but missed. Lt. Ruffner made Astronomical Observations. This morning there was a snake about 6 feet long coiled up under the ambulance but she managed to get away. During the evening I saw her near the Camp but had no revolver with me; it is a nice neighbor to have around the tents. Everybody got warned.

travelled about 25 miles

Tuesday, May 16th 1876. [Refer to Map No. 4]

Revellie at 4 this morning. had fish for breakfast. at 5:30 all was moving to-day. I had the Guide Teodoso with me. He speaks pretty well english and is like all true scouts a quiet fellow[;] rather dark complection [sic], a light, black, mustache[;] he wears an old hat, a ditto coat[;] a pair [of] old Cavalry pants, woolen stockings and moccasins. On his saddle he has his ever ready carbine. the cartridges he has in his pants pockets, but he rides a very good horse. We traveled in a Southwestern direction following an old and hardly visible trail. At 6:30, about 3 - 4 miles from our last camping place, we came out of the "breaks" and cañons up on the level prairie or staked plains. At 7:20 we came to the bed of a large lake, which is about this time of year full of water, but as the winter had been entirely without snow and the spring without rain[;] it is dry. We saw 6 Buffalos [sic] and after a while I proposed to Teodoso to make a chase. He said he did not care. A little after [that] the Corporal of Cavalry, who has charge of the flagging party of the Stadia line came up to us and asked us to go, and we went. [We] singled a young looking bull out and after a sharp chase we succeeded in turning him off. Teodoso brought him down. My horse was not to bring near. The Corporal gave him two shots, and I had no show at all. We took all good [meat] as hind quarters and fore quarters, liver, tenderloins, heart, liver, and tongue. Out a wagon came over from the train. We washed our hands with water out of the canteens and at 8:30 were moving on again. At 8:45 A.M. passed another large dry lake. there I caught a young bird which I tied up in the handkerchief and took him along for Dr. Mendenhall. At 9:25 came to a large break and had the first sight of the Quita Que Mountains [sic] in a S. Eastern direction about 20 to 25 miles or more off. At 10:35 A.M. I was on a "knoll" in a range of hills from which I made a drawing as I could overlook a large space of ground for miles in all directions. from here I could see our to-day's camping place. Teodoso had two shots on an antelope but no hit. He felt bad of his missing the mark. At 11:10 left the knoll on which there is a landmark used by Mexicans trading with Indians usually nearby. before we came to this knoll we crossed the Adobe Wall and Palo Grande trail. about Noon we arrived at the camping place, where the escort was busy erecting the tents. For dinner buffalo steak and liver. The water in the creek nearby is in holes and muddy. More is [in] a large Spring North of Camp about 100 yds. which is very clear but warm. The trees behind our tents are very heavy some over 3 feet [in] diameter. It was hot all day, 100° in our tent. about 6 P.M. I made a sketch of our Camp but could not bring all the tents in, they covering to[o] much ground; about dark Lt. Baldwin shot two so-called Scissor birds, which have their name of the scissor-like tail. it is a very pretty looking bird and a pity to shoot them. we are today 11¾ miles west and 8¼ miles south of our last camp. The orders are to start about 5 to-morrow morning. At 8:30 P.M. it started to rain, but not much.

travelled 17 miles 2321 yds.

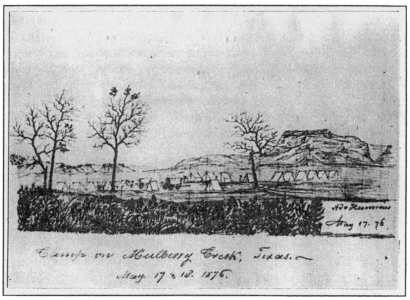

Camp on Mulberry Creek, Texas, 17 and 18 May 1876.

Wednesday, May 17th 1876. [Refer to Map No. 5]

Revellie at 4 o'clock. fed my horse about 5. had Breakfast and at 5:30 were on the road again. We expected to have such a nice breakfast of stewed Buffalo meat. Mr. Sullivan had put it last night in a covered pan and put it in a hole surrounded by hot coals, and covered it with ground. during the night someone must have stepped on the handle because it was half upset and pretty well spoiled by sand and ashes having fallen in. at 10 A.M. we came on the breaks and cañons of Mulberry Creek. Teodoso and I went up about 1½ miles the creek. from a point I made topographical sketches of the creek and country. it started to rain[,] a thunderstorm coming up. Lt. Ruffner told me on the road this morning to go down stream on a reconnaissance. must wait until the storm is over. At 11 A.M. had dinner, i.e. Buffalo meat, Biscuits, and Coffee. At Noon Lt. Ruffner told me better to start on my trip down Mulberry Creek as soon as possible as it looked much like [more] rain. Got a horse which looked like mine and at 12:30 went out with Mr. Wilson, the Guide. Passing the Mules out herding, I saw my horse between them and came to the conclusion that I rode Lt. Woodruff's horse. could not cross the Creek to saddle my horse, and it looked like rain any minute so we started on [and] rode 6 or 7 miles until we arrived on a high butte on top of the cañons. On North side we climbed the point and I had a fine opportunity for a sketch. at 2:30 we rode back. the thunderstorm came up very fast. About 3½ miles from Camp made a sketch of some sliding rock, and after this we rode as fast as the ground permitted, the rain pouring down in streams. arrived in Camp dripping wet. Lt. Woodruff made a big hallo about my riding his horse. he would not have known it if I had not told him about my mistake. the country we had passed over was really beautiful. the Walls of the Cañon about 200 feet high and often perpendicular. crossed the Creek 10 or 12 times. banks very steep. Brush sometimes so thick that we had to dismount. much Cedar trees on the cliffs. in the bottom Cottonwoods which look at a distance like oak trees. Wild Cherry, Plum, China trees, Mesquite and Chinook brush. Mesquite is very thorny as I had to find out. and [on] the rocks much Chinook or Desert oak, some beautiful cactus, red and yellow flowers. in the bottom much wild Turkeys and [I] saw a bird resembling a small Peacock. During the evening after the storm was over[,] the officers caught frogs to have fried. borrowed a candle, and washed the dishes for our mess. Before the mules were brought in[,] between [which] my horse always keeps[,] made a hasty sketch of our to-days camp. did at least the figuring of to-days march, all being ready to draw. It is getting chilly.

marched 10 miles 37 yds.

View south from the cliff behind the camping place on Mulberry Creek, with Palo Duro Canyon shown in the distance, 17 May 1876.

Thursday, May 18th 1876. [Refer to Map No. 6]

Revellie at 4 o'clock. at 5:30 I and Teodoso left and rode up the
Mulberry Creek about 6 miles to a high point from which I can see
far up the country. the heads of this creek are about 6-7 miles farther.
From this place we took a South Eastern course to strike the train,
which was effected about 9 A.M. Had a lively chase after 6 buffalos
but the men with the train did not go for them. we gave it up. we
learned afterwards that they shot two early during the morning. we
went on in a S. Easterly direction. had a shot at some Antelopes but
the distance was too great and they moving rather sharply. about 11
A.M. all at once we, that is Teodoso and myself, stood at the brink
of the cañon of the Red River, and it was the grandest sight I [have]
had in this great United States. The Sandstone Cliffs nearly 500 feet
nearly perpendicular in red and white layers, and very, very much
broken and cut up. we stood at a point [where] we could see about
15 miles down in the Grand Cañon. Made a hasty sketch, but one can
not do justice to this magnificent scenery. The Cedar and Mesquit,
the latter light the former so dark in color, and back of us the prairie
was entirely level, so also the other side of the cañon which may be
1½ miles wide. But I could not see any water. Teodoso said that it is
very deep and steep bed and terribly salty. From this place we took
a Western course to strike the trail of the Command for several miles
near the breaks of the Cañon. About noon we were on the broad plain
again. it was awful hot and oppressing. ahead of us it always looked
like water–fata morgana. it looks curious to see a train on so hot a day
like this[,] far in the distance. the animals look like Camels. they get
awfull long legs. Saw one butterfly just like our *Landhase*. At 2:35
arrived at the Camping place. it is about 180 to 200 feet above the
bottom of the Cañon. I was very tired of riding horseback. Teodoso
and myself made at least 32 miles. he proposed to walk and so we did
for about 2 miles. I, myself, was certainly quite stiff. Had no dinner.
Mallahan, the Ambulance driver, being sick and Sullivan driving, the
Ambulance came not into Camp than about 4½ P.M. it is regular
hard labor to carry water up these steep hills. Had a miserable supper.
A storm coming up, all tents were very shaky and we thought ours
would go over any time. I tied all my traps together so that they
might not be blown too far. The storm blowing awful but no rain.
It was hot in the tent. Sergt. Lichtenberg helped me figuring the last
two trips and I platted them. Traveled 22 miles, 1585 yds. Extra riding
& scouting 9 miles + about 32 miles.

Friday, May 19th 1876. [Refer to Map No. 6]

Revellie at 5 this morning. there will be a lay over today. I went
twice for water [and] could not find the Spring, but succeeded the

third time. it is under a large table or slab of rocks but you have to go right down to the Cañon. No walk up to the place. It is impossible to go straight to the Spring. The water is clear but has a flat taste. at 8:00 I went on a sketching tour down the Cañon. climbed over huge rocks in head of Dry Creek. some stoops are from 10 to 20 feet. I arrived in a place [where] I could not go farther. there was a small opening between the rocks. I could not pass through, so I made a halt and the drawing on the next page. by the way, this must have been at least 100 feet lower than the foot of the cañon near Camp. This evening Dr. Mendenhall found an old War axe in the shape as drawn. It was a lovely day after so hot and close a day. Observation this night. Dixon the Guide expects to bring us tomorrow to the place where the permanent Camp shall be established. I hope that water will be handier as in this lovely place. Somebody of the infantry escort shot a deer to-day. I used much strategy to catch a bull frog for my alcohol bottle. the salamander I caught in our last camp near our tent.

Rocks at the head of a dry creek near camp on Mulberry Creek, Texas, 19 May 1876.

Saturday, May 20th 1876. [Refer to Map No. 7]

Revellie at 4 A.M. at 5:30 all was moving. Caught a little frog. Teodoso said it means soon rain if these crawl on the prairie. We had during our to-days trip the cañon of Palo Duro was on our left within one mile, or more or less, the side cañons of which extend far. These

Cañons are first very small ravines, but all at once they go down 50 to 100 feet nearly straight. they are well grown with Cedar. some have an enormous size, some pointed but mostly flat or rounded at the top. The mesquite bushes are pretty tall. they are blooming now in long grape form. at about 10 A.M. arrived at the place picked as our permanent Camp. It is again on the bluff about 125-150 feet above the little Creek running in the Valley. The water seems to be very good, so far, anyhow clear and not such a salty taste. The valley which we overlook is about 400 yds wide with not much timber around, though plenty, but against other places. The ground being very rocky and as expected our tent was blown down. After the figuring of the to-days trip [I] went to the Creek and washed my clothing. it did better than I expected. surely it is not snow white, but clean. Went to bed at 10 o'clock.

11 miles 421 yds.

Sunday May 21st 1876.

Got up before Revellie about 4 o'clock and after finding my horse wrote a letter the larger part of it so as to be used by Haberlein if he should see fit. Heard that the mail Curier shall go after the train, which train, it goes for more forage and other necessities. Sergt. Lichtenberg and I compared the Stadia and Theodolite readings from the 13th up to the 20th day of May. All correct. Thence Lt. Ruffner set me to work on the Stadia papers, he going about 1 o'clock with Teodoso and one Cavalry man out on an exploring tour. it was very windy[,] the dust flying like anything and covering everything. I worked until 5 P.M. and finished two days. [In] the evening I asked Lt. Ruffner to get for our mess 12 cans of green Corn[,] 10 Cans of Milk[,] 1 btl. of flavoring Extract[,] 2 lbs. of Candles. 6 teams under Mr. Cavanoughs charge and [an] Infantry [escort], left about noon. Handed my letter to Mrs. Hunnius to Lt. Baldwin to see it off. there was talk of moving the [permanent] camp to the falls of the Red River, but Lt. Baldwin objected and so there will be no move. To-day we had Deer for breakfast and the other meals.

Monday May 22nd 1876. [Refer to Map No. 7]

It was rather chilly this morning. my horse broke the halter and I had a lively time to catch him. Patched the halter with a piece of rope. after breakfast I worked on the Stadia papers, from Fort Elliott to here. there are 217 full and 2 bisect readings. Messrs. Sullivan and Mallahan moved their Wall tent up to us on the hill. the horses made it too bad for them on the old place. for dinner we had rasin duff. at 1 P.M. the west wind set in and the dust and flying sand was awfull. Lt. Ruffner retreated into the ambulance and I to the teamsters['] Wall tent, and I worked Stadia distances until 5 o'clock.

Mr. Sullivan killed a young deer, another party 2 antelopes, one of which ran about 4 miles with 3 legs until Teodoso caught it, he having the best horse. Lts. McCauley and Woodruff tested the Stadia rods. There will be no moving of our Camp. I had after dinner a good wash in the Red River Creek. Mr. Sullivan went with me. Observations to-night. Sergt. Smith of 4th Cavalry went off early during morning and took our letters with him. During the evening shortly after sunset the bullbat birds [night hawks] were around the rocks very thick. they will go and fly quite near a person. they scared me with their sharp cry several times. Dr. Mendenhalls red shirt shrunk awfull. I found him washing it in the creek. he thinks it is a horrible place we are staying but has the consolitation that every day we come nearer to going home again. surely I did not like and do not now [like] this place but since I have plenty [of] work on hand, do not feel it any more so bad. But such a dirty Camp will make the cleanest man careless and slop[p]y. It was very hot during [the] afternoon. Made during the evening a sketch of the camp, looking east.

Tuesday May 23rd 1876.

North West wind this morning at 5 o'clock. Thermometer showed 56° Farenheit or 11° Reaumour, and yesterday about 2 o'clock P.M. it showed 100° Farenheit or 30° Reaumour. The changes are so great because the Rocky Mountains are not so far from us. It wanted to rain very bad but could not afford it. Lt. Ruffner took the Magnetic Variation this morning. It is _____ after which I worked on the Azimuth of the Stadia readings[,] which I finished about 5 o'clock in [the] afternoon. got a little black and yellow snake by one of the Cavalry men. To-morrow Lt. Ruffner, myself[,] Teodoso and some Cavalry men will go up the creek. also one team [and] 10 day's rations is the order. Lt. Woodruff; Lt. McCauley, Sergt. Lichtenberg, Mr. Dixon as guide will strike with some Cavalry as an escort and a team and 5 day's rations, North for the Canadian River. it was very warm; about 2 o'clock 102[° Farenheit] in tent.

Wednesday May 24th 1876. [Refer to Map No. 7]

It was raining a little at 5:10 A.M. Lt. Woodruff, Mr. Dixon as Guide, Sergt. Lichtenberg, 16 mule team, 1 Corpl., 6 men Cavalry [and] 1 Infantry started to run a Stadia line North to the Canadian River. [Refer to Maps 14-15] Sergt. Lichtenberg [in] charge of Odometer, Barometer C, and Thermometer. Got from Sergt. Lichtenberg a pair of suspenders, of which he has no need, and mine are nearly worthless. turned over to Cavalry Sergt of Detachment, my horse, saddle, blanket, bridle, picket rope and pin. Lt. Ruffner and I tested the Stadia instrument and rod. At 8:15 Teodoso, myself and the teamster, Hunter with [by] name, left the permanent Camp. caught a little rattle snake, several insects and a variety of bugs and beetles. Teodoso shot an Antelope. about noon we passed the place where General Getty was jumped by the Indians in 1872. The place looks very dangerous to camp in. At 2 we arrived at a place Teodoso had selected to camp, but it is not 8 but 11 miles 209 yards we had traveled. there is plenty wood, grass, and very good water in [the] creek here. by very good, I mean considering the country we are in. For dinner we had Antelope and Tomatoes, which latter I can eat now like a good fellow. I waded the Creek to get some dry driftwood; by my return I had only three leeches on one foot. About 5½ o'clock, Lt. Ruffner came in and by and by one after the other of the party. Lt. McCauley went back[,] he having lost his notebook by riding over very rough ground. I found here a great many wild roses but not in bloom yet. Got a good pile of wood from the other side of Creek. Lt. Ruffner and Lt. McCauley out on a little run in the open air. I heard one of the Cavalry fell this morning with his horse from the rocks, but nobody hurt. We are not many. our party consists of 11 men, viz, Lt. Ruffner, Lt. McCauley, myself, Teodoso, 5 Cavalry men, 1 Infantry man and the teamster, Mr. Hunter. The latter and myself are tenting together. Lt. McCauley was preparing the Antelope head during the evening, and nearly set our tent on fire. He moved his shop to the other cooking place. a thunderstorm is slowly coming up from the West. about 8½ P.M. we could hear the thunder. right back of our little Camp on the Bluff is a Mexican landmark as used by their Buffalo hunters. it consists of 3 large stones and is about 10 feet high. [Refer to stadia 235 on Map No. 7]. It was very hot during the noon hours. about 4 o'clock in the afternoon a North East wind set in which made it quite pleasant, but in late evening it got chilly. We are 4275 feet above the level of the sea.

travelled 11 miles 209 yards all walking

Thursday, May 25th 1876. [Refer to Map No. 8]
During the night there was a very heavy thunderstorm and plenty rain. we did not get so very wet but everything is damp. One of the Escort tents was blown down and they poor fellows got wet. At 8 o'clock we started and Lt. Ruffner gave orders to go about 5 miles farther, and then make camp and put things on the sun to dry. about 2½ miles from our last camping place I saw to our left about 3 miles distant a big Cañon and learned from Teodoso that this is Cañon Blanco. Stepped on a Rattlesnake, but a small one, which I put into the bottle. Saw a big one, but she went into her hole before we could get some sticks we have along in case of a snake. Caught 2 big bugs, one the smaller with the feathery feelers is the male, the other with single feelers and rather white body the bigger of the two is the

female. About 10½ A.M. arrived at camping place[;] plenty wood and good water, but bed of Creek rather swampy. There is a mocking bird singing all the while I wrote [this], just on a tree near the tent, but on the other side of the Creek. The Spanish bayonnets are near blooming. This plant is the Mexican Soapweed. Saw much cactus on the prairie this morning. For dinner we had green peas and antelope. As I do not know much of cooking I do the washing of our "Mess Kit" [consisting of] 2 tin plates, 2 tin cups, 2 knives and forks, one spoon. The big frying pan has to answer as [the] article to wash the dishes in. Well out here anything will do. Plenty [of] small ants are crawling all over us which is rather not very nice. It is very hot now about 1 P.M. During [the] afternoon I gathered some sweet water shells for Lt. Ruffner. I had some also for Prof. Leuckhardt. After supper what looks like a thunder storm made his appearance from the West and the Wind is pretty stiff from South East. At 9 o'clock the storm started in good earnest. it was an awfull rain, to say nothing of lightning and thunder. I was all the time afraid that our frail little tent would break down. there was much hail also.

travelled 5 miles 12 yds

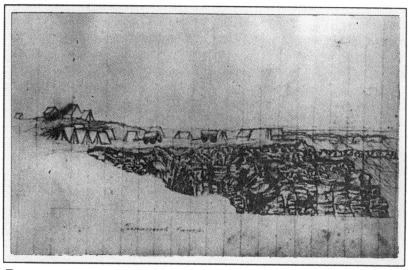

Permanent camp on the Prarie Dog Town Fork of the Red River occupied from 20 May to 1 June 1876.

Friday, May 26th 1876.

Got up about 5½ this morning, everything pretty damp. The tent leaked a little and I had during the storm my old india rubber raincoat as additional cover. It is chilly. The fire would not burn but without

much coaxing, though we took some wood last evening into our tent
to keep it dry. The Creek is very high, in fact so [high] that we have
to lay over all day probably. At 7 o'clock I erected a Water Gauge. Lt.
Ruffner, Lt. McCauley, Teodoso and two Cavalry men went up the
Cr. on an exploring expedition but without the instruments except
my Prismatic Compass, and I got commissioned to go out and catch
as many butterflies as possible for Lt. Ruffner. had been on butterfly
chase from 9 A.M. until 12:30 P.M. Had Tomatoes for dinner. on
my little excursion saw 4 Antelopes. they were very much surprized,
and as I had nothing [other] than a butterfly net and two pocket
knives, I let them go peaceable. After 3 o'clock a rattlesnake with 6
rattles was accidentally discovered a few feet from my tent. I helped
killing her. at 4 Lt. Ruffner and party returned. He, Lt. R., showed
me a splendid Hawk he [had] killed. the Creek fell since morning at
the rate of 3 inches an hour. At noon the velocity of the water was
about 3 miles per hour. It looks very much like rain again. During
forenoon I washed two undershirts, 1 pr. drawers, one pr stockings.
Got part of [a] root of Spanish Bayonnet, also one leaf for Museum.

Saturday, May 27th 1876. [Refer to Map No. 8]

Got up at 4 o'clock this morning for breakfast [of] Beans and bread
and Coffee. At 6 we started for T[i]erra Blanco Cañon in a South
Western direction. I had odometer, Prismatic Compass and Stadia
rod readings to do. Lt. Ruffner thought he could move more rapidly
this way. But he soon found out that he was very much mistaken,
because I had to walk every step. at 1:00 P.M. we struck at last the
Cañon, bad muddy looking water, no wood. Teodoso went and brought
some [wood] lashed to his horse. We had Lima beans for dinner. It
was very hot. The country we traveled over to-day was a splendid
sandy soil, the best a gardner would wish [for]. any amount of young
grasshoppers. Lt. McCauley, who rode ahead and acted as fore
flagman[,] killed an enormous rattlesnake. The Cañon we are [in] is
red sandstone rocks about 50 to 75 feet high. very steep and much
sliding rocks. The valley is about 100 yds wide. we passed some large
lakes on the prairie during our day's trip with water [in them] from
the last rains. Platted the trip, also one Reconnaissance of Lt. Ruffner
of yesterday up to the Spring and head of Palo Duro Cañon. About 1
mile South or up the Cañon from the place we are encamped is a
Spring called Ojo Frio. Made a sketch of the mess tent of the Escort,
made out of Extra Wagon cover, shelter tent, Jacobs staff and Signal
Flag props. The table consists of 4 pieces of wood driven into the
ground and the tail board of the wagon as top of table. Mr. Hunter
the teamster burst my folding stool and I had to sew it together again.
it is not more so comfortable as it used to be but answers the purpose
still very well. Scrambled up on top of bluff and made a topographical

sketch. The rocks are very loose coarse red and white sandstone, and the tops of the layers form most grotesque contour lines. For supper Coffee and Hard bread. Teodoso and one Cavalry man was out hunting antelopes but came back home empty handed. The Hard bread or Crackers, branded and marked Purchased by C. B. P. October 12/74 A. C. U. S. A. have a taste like rancid oil, and are after my opinion bad for food. As usual a thunderstorm is coming up from the South East and at 8 o'clock it was blowing at a fearful rate. On the hills between the rocks are plenty wild Gooseberries. Here I saw a morning glory, white with red inside. I picked up from the prairie some very nice red and white agat[e]s. Caught a bug half red and half black.

walked 10 miles 1628 yards.

Wednesday, May 28th 1876. [Refer to Map No. 8]

Got up at 4 A.M. as there should be an early move. Part of our tents, which consists of 1 Wall tent, 2 escort and one A tent, the two escort tents were already taken down. As Lt. Ruffner said we should stay here and he, Lt. McCauley, Teodoso and 2 Cavalry men would go up the Cañon and Creek on Horseback reconnaissance. I was very glad to have a rest day as last night I had a bad cramp in my left leg from over exercise during our yesterdays march. That Thunderstorm last night passed over us with a drop of rain. It was pretty cool this morning, as have all been[,] and in the hours from 9 A.M. until 5 P.M. it is very, very hot. Notice that a heavy dew falls every night, just as much as a light rain would wet the ground. For dinner, Tomatoes and as an extra I put the box of Salmon, I bought at Bluff Creek Ranche, Kansas, on our table. This was anyhow something like Sunday. Worked up the official Record book, which I had not done since May 10th. About 6 P.M. Lt. Ruffner and party returned from their trip to Agua Punta. I heard they saw a herd of Mustangs. They had a great many shots at Antelopes but no hits, but they succeeded in catching a young Antelope which was brought in, and is fed on condensed Milk. The poor little thing, with its so beautiful black eyes cries after its mother like a child. There was a beautiful evening and not much wind.

Monday, May 29th 1876. [Refer to Map No. 8]

Got up and broke camp at 4½ this morning, but did not leave the place until 6:30 A.M. Only Odometer measurements taken. Travelled through a small cañon about 100 to 150 yds. wide. the height of the rocky bluffs ranges from 30 to 75 feet but they are very steep and all in all look very pleasing to the eye. The Small Creek we travelled down was very winding with no other water than from time to time in a pool, one of which was quite large. passed a number of side streams, all dry but with considerable timber on their banks. Saw a few Cedar trees on some of the bluffs of the main Cañon. On the banks of the Creek is some small willow brush, and very good grass near its banks. About 10 o'clock near the end of the Cañon on the West side of it, there are 2 Monuments on one rocky bluff. Landmarks very likely put up by Mexican buffalo Hunters. After passing this point we came to quite a basin in which there is a rocky point, a kind of a mound with a horse's head on a pole as a landmark. thence we came on the level Prairie and shortly afterwards into our old camping place of May 24th & 25th [which was] the first Camp we made out of the Permanent Camp. Most of the rocky bluffs we saw to-day have the following profiles: [two small sketches]. They are very sharply cut and very few regular side Cañons. There was an Antelope hunt but without success, but Teodoso went out from Camp and brought one in after a short absence. The guide Mr. Wilson came to our Camp[,] he being out on a private Scout[,] and told us that the other exploring party under command of Lt. Woodruff is back in Permanent Camp. Theodoso and one Cavalry man went back to see whether they could not find the other antelope which was supposed to be shot about 5 P.M. they came back without [it]. They found the animal but the Coyote wolves had been already at it. Teodoso rode to another place where he [is] supposed to let have dropped his hunting Knife and sure he found it. I was told that it has been on the level Prairie. He has a splendid memory for ground, and an Eagle's eye. As the flies were horrible on the antelope meat, Lt. McCauley constructed out of a mosquito bar a safety place to put the meat out of their reach. It proved a success.

travelled 11 miles 442 yds

Tuesday, May 30th 1876. [Refer to Map No. 7]

We got up at 4 A.M. and after a breakfast of Antelope meat and Coffee all was packed up and at 5:30 were on the move again. Lt. Ruffner and Party went down the Palo Duro Cañon. Teodoso went with us. Not far from the Permanent Camp Teodoso shot 2 Antelopes, which were, of course, taken along. Met Lt. Woodruff and the Surgeon who were on a hunt. At 10:30 we arrived in the Permanent Camp, where everyone seemed to be very glad to see us return in such good health. We saw and were informed that this morning the men had a successful Buffalo hunt. Mr. Mallahan got pretty near Killed by one he wounded only, and he had to run for his life. It is the same dusty, windy place as ever and looks very desolate. every thing is full of sand and dirty. During afternoon had a good swim in the Creek which is very high and deep. It rained a few drops. Teodoso burned his hand pretty bad from [the] explosion of a metallic cartridge in his hand. The Barometer fell to 25.82 [*sic*].

travelled 11 miles 232 yds

Wednesday, May 31st 1876. [Refer to Map No. 7]

Sergt. Lichtenberg showed me the rattle of a rattlesnake which was killed by Mr. Sullivan some days ago. 13 rattles, she has been about 7 feet long. She was near the Creek. Last night the wind was very bad and this morning everything is covered with a thick layer of fine reddish sand. During forenoon [I] platted our yesterdays trip and Lt. Woodruffs North from this place to the Canadian [River]. the distance of Sergt. Lichtenbergs notes give only 28 miles and some yards. For dinner Mr. Sullivan had buffalo meat chopped and some bacon fried with it. it was a splendid meal. Lt. Ruffner and Dr. Mendenhall with Mr. Wilson as Guide have been out and returned about 4 P.M. I found Lt. R., as I brought him the plattings[,] very much used up and with two crackers. The wind and dust was horrible to-day. after Supper Lt. Ruffner gave orders that I and Sergt. Lichtenberg should be ready to run a Stadia line by 4 o'clock to-morrow morning and should the Currier with the mail come in to-night or early to-morrow morning the whole Camp will be moved. Will be more than glad to leave this dirty place. The Barometer has been down to 25.72 [*sic*] at 3:00 P.M. and to-night the moon has a court. Will be more than glad to leave this dirty place. the wind was so bad that the men could hardly make coffee. some baked bread down on the Creek behind the rocky bank. [I] did some washing during the afternoon. Begged some bread at the Infantry as our Mess has none for tomorrow a lunch and dinner. This and water and some of the Sausages (Volz's) will do very well.

Thursday, June 1st 1876. [Refer to Map No. 9]

Revellie at 3 o'clock this morning; it was quite dark. warmed myself some coffee and after packing everything. by this time it was about 5 o'clock. Private Replog[l]e and I started for the other, the South Side of the Palo Duro Cañon, as Station No. 2. [With] Mr. Dixon as Guide, we went in a due south course and after passing several dry Lakes, over the level prairie we struck Gen'l. [Nelson A.] Miles Trail at about 11 o'clock. about 9 miles. Lt. Ruffner sent several messages up to me complaining about stations to[o] big, or Prairie Dog holes and ants' nests, and at least twice about my stooping down to watch his signals. I forwarded a rather uncivil note to him which he answered in a rather cutting and sharp way. I had stepped into a prairie dog hole and hurt my leg. Was in much pain. leg was swelling badly. Of all of which Lt. Ruffner did not know. Anyway, he wrote that he would discharge me on the spot, then and there, but he would allow me to follow the column. But nothing was said by him afterwards. He demanded his note back and tore the same up. After the Signal Flags were planted we went back to the New Camp which we struck about 1:00 P.M. The New Camp is about 3 miles up the Cañon near Gen'l. Miles crossing. This Camp everybody was surprised to find down in the bottom and not on the crest. Had some coffee at Mr. Dixon's mess. at 2:30 P.M. Corporal Smith came in with messages and mail. Had two letters from Mrs. Hunnius one dated May 7th [and] the other 16th of May. it was windy to-day, but there is no dust at least. There was a splendid evening, no wind and strange[ly] no mosquitos. Since this evening everything goes by the bugle call. as I was pretty well tired and as the orders are [that] the surveying party will start at 4 A.M. tomorrow I went to sleep about 9 o'clock.

   travelled 19 miles

Friday, June 2nd 1876.
   Revellie at 3 o'clock this morning, breakfast at 3½ A.M. and at 4 A.M. the surveying party was moving up in sharp gait to 9 miles signal Flag, where work was stopped yesterday. arrived there about 6 o'clock. I had with [me] Moore, the uneven, and Lt. Woodruff with Repogle, the even numbered stations. Everything went on smoothly and quick. had a shot at an Antelope but too short; the air was perfectly moving by heat. Mr. Dixon, the Guide, lost the trail and found it again, which he marked by burning some buffalo chips. we thought something was wrong, Indians or so. at 11 we came to camping place. Lt. Woodruff in ambulance, being very sick. the heat had been to[o] much for his constitution. I rode his horse. mine came up with the ambulance. After unsaddling, went into the Cañon for a canteen of water. The Cañon is deep and pretty steep, on places perpendicular Sandstone Rocks, Plenty wood, but the water is rather muddy in oblong pools. Dr. Mendenhall found some running water about ½ mile down the Cañon, which was very clear, cool and good. The coolest and best tasting water I had since leaving Fort Elliott. For dinner we had Buffalo. Teodoso shot one. On the little Creek in [the] Cañon we found what looked and smelled like wild Celery. There is an order issued to-day that nobody will leave camp unarmed. The Cavalry which have their ententment down near the foot of [the] Cañon go with their carbines to their meals. During afternoon it appears that they travelled on a much shorter trail than we. Sergt. Lichtenberg brought me two Daysies. From the doctor [I] got 6 Quinine Pills. The Observatory tent was put up and observations taken.

   17 miles 590 yds.

Saturday, June 3rd 1876. [Refer to Map No. 9]
   During last night a thunderstorm came up. it was very windy and much lightning. I regretted of not having made a ditch to carry the

water away from our tent, which stands on a gentle slope. Put everything up as high and dry [as possible], and dressed myself in case the tent should be blown down. As the wind was [from the] N[orth] West it was a great change [in temperature] since last afternoon. it was getting very chilly. This morning it was actually cold. There was not much rain after all during the night, but we had some in the morning. Went on the crest of the Cañon and made some sketches of the Rock Wall. This wall is some 60 to 70 feet high and quite smooth. The sandstone is poreous, and full of holes. by going down into the Cañon I came near a place where a hawk had his nest and the old ones went for me, with shrill cries and angry flapping of wings. During early afternoon the wagons (4) and Escort (5) came up from Fort Elliott, so the Sergt. and 3 men which were left in the Palo Duro Cañon to show the train the road and help them across. Copied Astronomical computations of culminating stars. Received the Commissary articles ordered and paid to Lt. Woodruff 5 Inf. for[:]

12 Cans green Corn	1.96	
10 ” Milk	2.18	
1 bottle flavoring Extract	.19	
2 lbs. Candles	.30 ⁓	$4.63

Collaborated with Sergt. Lichtenberg [on] the Stadia rod readings and Theodolite No. 2 (Aloe) up to our last station here near the West bank of Cañoncito Blanco (The Little White Cañon). this evening I had a very pleasant walk with Dr. Mendenhall. we spoke about the opening ceremonies of the Centennial Exhibition and our ignorance of it here in the wilderness. Also about the outbreak of some 160 Northern Cheyenne warriors and of some unpleasantness at Fort Sill, Indians. as we are going some 28 miles more south we may have a chance of striking the latter. It was very chilly near evening, and I tried to make our tent as close and warm as possible. most of us go around in their overcoats, which is not to[o] warm to-night. At 9 o'clock this evening it was 53° F and no wind. After reading in some old Newspapers, but all news to me, I went to sleep.

Sunday, June 4th 1876.

Got up at 5 o'clock this morning, actually cold, 48°, quite wet with dew. The warm coffee was quite the thing. This morning after breakfast, Teodoso and some men went out to find a buffalo, as fresh meat is gone since yesterday noon. Copied Lt. Ruffner's Reductions on apparent places of Lunar Culminating Star. Lt. Ruffner, Dr.

Mendenhall and guide Wilson went out on a ride. they returned about 3½ P.M. The hunting party came in without any success. It was very warm at 3 P.M. 90°. Teodoso found some [of] what are called "Rolling Stones" in the Cañon. They are sandstone and I believe they are formed by bear pups playing with them. Sergt. Lichtenberg has a very inflamed eye. Dr. Mendenhall fill[ed] Mercurial Barometer tube some weeks ago and Lt. Woodruff filled the Cistern to-day. two posts were erected in front of Lt. R tent, the middle one. Climbed up the other side of the Cañon and went over to the Rocky Wall, which is only about 5 feet wide and runs out to a knife edge. made a sketch of the Camp. At the foot of the picture is the Cavalry and Infantry kitchen tents. The evening I spent in reading in a newspaper of the date May 6th, quite news to me. Observations to-night.

Monday, June 5th 1876. [Refer to Map No. 9]

Got up at 5 this morning. it was not so chilly as the two previous ones. And as there were two Surveying parties to go out I apprehended that I was surely to go also. After breakfast Lt. Ruffner asked where my horse was, so I saddled up and went out with his party to read one of the Stadia Rods. There were two. Lt. McCauley doing the topographical sketching. This party went down the Cañon and Lt. Woodruff and party (P[r]is[matic] Compass) up [the] Cañon. Saw a buffalo on South bank of Cañoncito Blanco and sent word back to camp to hunt him, as there is no fresh meat. At 9:30 we came to what is considered the Mouth of Cañoncito Blanco, but I think it is not. There are so many Cañons and bluffs and Rocky walls seen from Station 343 where the last Readings and Angles were taken that it is very difficult to say which is which. The Cañons are all very deep and rocky but it is not so great a sight as I had expected to see. it is all so ruggy [rugged] and wild, rock cropping out everywhere, but I think our point must have been from 3 to 400 feet high. Plenty cedars in the Cañons. Lt. McCauley, Dr. Mendenhall, myself and two Cavalry men went farther on an exploration. Lt. Ruffner with Mr. Dixon the guide and Escort returned to camp. We found a place where the Indians in their flight for Gen McKenzy dropped the lodge poles.[65] There were always 4 together some sets with leather fastenings at the top ends, others tied up in bundles of four. The Indians must have been in an awfull hurry or else they would not have dropped these for them so valuable articles. We stopped at a point where I had the best view of our to-days little trip. There was quite a detached mountain in the Palo Duro Cañon, which we voluntarily went up, [and] down we saw the dry bed of a Creek. the colors of the different layers of sandstone, white, yellowish, red and chocolate color, looked by the sunshine very well and pleasing to the eye, but it is after all a failure to make a great impression to a persons eye only. there is no life. all so dry, and the heat is the only wonderful thing out. Lt. McCauley caught a young antelope which was asleep near this point. They, that is Lt. McCauley and Dr. Mendenhall[,] were going to shoot the mother, but had no success. I got tired of waiting for them to return so rode home, that is, back to Camp alone. It is rather a curious feeling to be on the Prairie a lone person. In one of the Side Cañons of the Cañoncito Blanco I saw a great many tall Cedar trees. Arrived in Camp 2½ P.M. Barometer (Mercurial) readings were started to-day at 7 A.M. this morning by Sergt. Lichtenberg. About 7 o'clock this evening Lt. R. changed the tent to South for observations. There will be work pretty near all night in [the] observatory. Lt. Baldwin and party came in late and brought quite a number of fossil shells in. 3 young hawks are alive taken from a nest in a hole on the big rocky wall near camp. One of the fine things on these Staked Plains is a bug about ½ inch long[,] head and end part of body dark grey [but] in the middle nearly white. they are here in great numbers and running over ones face and body. The places we visited on our trip to-day were covered with grasshoppers.

travelled about 12 miles. N. B. used chronometer (pocket) as compass.

Tuesday, June 6th 1876.

As I heard from Lt. Ruffner yesterday that there would be no surveying or more to-day anyway not this morning, I took the opportunity and after breakfast over I went down into the Cañon and wash a set of clothing. It went off all well because I took our dishpan to wash in with me. but should I ever go out on a trip again I [shall] take some cloth[es] pins along as they will and would come in very handy. the water must have been, lately too, pretty high in this Cañon as I saw many a tree where the deposits of grass and other matter was at least 15 feet high. I saw in a newspaper to-day that one of the standard industries of Texas is likely to be interfered with, if not wholly discouraged, by Legislative enactment. A bill is pending in the State Legislature to punish Horse-Thieves for the first offense by the whipping-post; for the second offense by whipping and branding; for the third offense by hanging. During afternoon copied for Lt. R. Reductions on the Prime Vertical for Latitude. Had a pretty good sleep as it was very hot and awfully windy. about 7 o'clock a rainstorm came up, in fact [it] was around us since about 4 o'clock. Wind sprung from South to East, [and] it started to rain and we was not long in tent when we heard a couple of heavy knocks against it. Thought that Lt. Ruffner wanted something, so I put my head out and saw hail. Hailstones as big as pigeons eggs. We gathered them and made ice water. in each of these ice pieces which were all in egg form pointed at one end there was another one as big as a good-sized pea. There was a buffalo hunt. it looked fine to see Teodoso chasing the animal. 2 shots brought him down. His horse goes right along side any buffalo and there he has the advantage of all of us. there will be Revellie very early to-morrow. everyone went in good time to sleep. Late in [the] evening heard that there will be no buffalo meat in Camp because the mule they took along, to pack on, would not allow it. there are mules that do not like the smell of Buffalo. The worst is [that] there is no oil any ore to fill the dark lanterns for illuminating the Astronomical Transit. Lt. Ruffner thought of making some out of the tallow of this Buffalo.

Wednesday, June 7th 1876. [Refer to Map No. 10]

Revellie at 2 o'clock this morning. it was a very busy scene by [the light of the] full moon. the wind was still high. We had a very short breakfast about 2:30 A.M., some of the buffalo meat but you could hardly like it, so hard and tough, must have been an old one. At 3:30 A.M. the train pulled out. it was a nice scene by moonshine. Lt. Woodruff and party had the uneven, I and Moore the even numbers of Stadia Stations. We saw after we crossed the Cañoncito Blanco, something coming up towards our camping place. It was still [too] dark to say whether buffalo, indians or mexicans. It turned out to be the latter, 4 men on horseback, 2 wagons drawn by bulls, and a lot of cattle. Got very damp from the dew falling. it was pretty chilly. Sun rise and moon set at [the] same time. Travelled all day over level prairie with any amount of dry Lakes[,] some of very large size. Made several "cut-offs" on the trail and at 1:45 P.M. arrived in Camp. Our line gave 20 miles some feet. Passed some places full of grasshoppers, yellow underwings and blue legs, some with red wings. The place we camp is near a Cañon, which is a great place for indians hunting bears. It is a hardship to get a drop of water, which is in great abundance about 600 or 800 feet below us, running very swift. The road leading down to it is on places very dangerous and on others so steep a person has to slide. The water is good and clear as crystal, but to fetch a bucket full into Camp is regular convict labor. Here are very imposing Cedar trees, tall, and to look down on them is a great sight. We are near the Cañon of the Red River. you can see it distinctly from Camp running in an eastern direction. It was ¼ past 8 [when] Lt. Ruffner asked me to plat the to-days trip as he liked to know where we were. finished the work about 9 o'clock. Lt. Ruffner told me he explored the Cañon down to the Red River, and that he and his party found a cave in which they went in. The camps name is Camp Cent.

travelled 22 miles ____ yds.

Thursday, June 8th 1876. [Refer to Map No. 11]

Revellie at 2 o'clock this morning. The train pulled out at 3:30 and so soon [as] it was light enough to see we followed. The first 3 miles in a southern direction, thence East until we struck the Cañon of the Red River. We descended about 1400 feet on some places awful steep. The wagons had to be held on extra guide ropes. It was very hard work on the men, but if one of the wagons had slipped it would have been surely the last of it. The scenery was sublime. On many places we had to lead our horses to go down the winding path. The Rocks in the Cañon have very much gypsum. After an hour down hill travel we came to a bottom about ½ to ¾ mile wide in which the Red River flows. its bed is about 100 feet wide and at this time there is only a very shallow narrow stream running in it sometimes on one, sometimes on the other side, and from time to time underground. Bed very sandy, red, very red sand. Saw heavy Mesquit trees, some nearly yellow leaved Chinaberry, Cedar the round to pointed kind. Another kind was pointed out to me which is called chapparellwood, very small leaves. The water in the stream is very alkali and warm. At 10 A.M. arrived in Camp. The Cavalry escorting [the] train shot a buffalo and Mr. Dixon and Dr. Mendenhall [shot] an Antelope. It is very hot[,] 100° in shade. Our Camp is near the junction of Palo Duro and Tule Cañon with Red River. Just before dinner a big Tarantula was caught and given to me. It was going to fight us, a very big animal. I omitted to mention the fact that there was two Cañons we went into. First we went down about 1,000 feet and after travelling over very hilly ground on a winding road we went down a second [time] about 400 feet and after this we came on the Red River. The place where we are at present is the Mouth of Tule Creek or of Pleasant Valley, as it is called on our map of the Indian Territory, Jan. 1875. During afternoon went, or rather climbed up the hill rear of Camp (to the North) about 200 feet and made the annexed sketch of our Camp. Our Tent is the A tent on the Officers line of Wall tents. The 7 A tents on East side of Camp are Cavalry escort. the others are Infantry and teamsters. From the station I made the sketch, looking East and North. I had a fine view of the Red River or Palo Duro Cañon, the bed of the River being dry, at least so it appeared to me. about ½ mile, from my station, was the distance to the River. Back of Red River the mountainous bluffs rose in two tiers, just in the way we came down to-day and as is shown in this sketch. Found upon the hill a black stone with a white vein through it. There was much Gypsum on these hills and any amount of bright red Clay. Mesquit and Cedar brush and stunted oak (Chinoak). Good water (rainwater) was discovered ½ mile back from Camp. Plenty tarantulas black and brown [al]so some centibedes [centipedes] were caught and killed. It was very hot all day. At 5:45 P.M. 102°. Attached Thermometer to Greens Barometer No. 392.

During the evening Mr. Dixon told us the story of a supposed tenderfoot, a man by [the] name [of] Williams, and how he rode a bronco whose name was Walking Bear. All got fooled. Williams had been a circus rider.

travelled 11 miles 1429 yds.

Friday, June 9th 1876. [Refer to Map No. 16]

This morning at 7 A.M. Lt. Ruffner, myself, Dixon the Guide, the Ambulance and 4 Cavalry men started on a 4 days surveying scout up the Tule Cañon. Orders were all as light as possible. I rode in [the] ambulance and after going back over the yesterdays trail to the point where our[s] with Gen'l. Miles trail crossed, I put the Odometer on wheel and started a regular business. Every hour, Aneroid Barometer and Thermometer readings besides. Well, we travelled and travelled, sometimes in a walk sometimes in a gallop behind the party ahead. At noon we watered. About 2 P.M. we were in a very broken Country, Breaks of the Tule Cañon which has been all the while in sight. I received an order to make a topographical sketch so I did and as this consumes much time, they left some Cavalry man from time to time to mark for me to sight and drive at. Well we drove on and on all at once we had 3 Cavalry men ahead of us, one of which was stationed on [an] old road near a smooth break leading into the Cañon. These markers went on until they and we arrived at a place where there was a Mexican encampment (2 Wagons) in the Cañon. But the three men came up again and motioned us to drive on, so we did. Nobody could see anything of Lt. Ruffner, Dixon and one Cavalry man. at last we saw something far off West of us, and we drove on until at 4 P.M. we struck water in Tule Cr. in the Cañon which is dying out mighty quickly now. there are very low hills here on both its sides. We watered Mules (one took 4½ buckets of water), and had a big consultation [on] what to do. all at once we discerned far in the distance 3 Men on horseback seemingly coming toward us. It proved to be so our missing Chief and party. He was red hot and accused everybody, me and Manahan the most[,] of driving past his camp, and it was nothing than his, Lt. Ruffners, fault. We had not the slightest idea where about he could be. But he came pretty soon to himself again, as he found out the ground had been measured from [the] crossing this morning 21 miles, 3609 feet and about 7 miles from our Camp. There were several hunts but no success. Mr. Dixon made a nice spring by digging out the ground a little only. In creek [the] water tastes bad, brackish. As there are no tents along, we all will sleep in the open air. The grass is very high and one will sleep very soft. From 9 to 3 to-morrow morning, there will be 6 guard hours. Mr. Manahan and Mr. Dixon have to stay an hour guard each too. I told Lieut. Ruffner [that] I liked to do my share in the watching just as well as anybody, which of course all are like to hear as it will give somebody an extra few hours sleep. it was very windy, and nearly an impossibility to smoke a pipe.

28½ miles

Saturday, June 10th 1876. [Refer to Map No. 16]

At 3 this morning we were all awake and getting breakfast ready. People do not like to sleep long into the morning in this part of the country, as the early morning hours are very favorable for Indian attacks. They woke me every hour to ask the time for relief. there was not much trouble as everyone slept in his clothing and [had] the carbine ready by his side. At 4 we pulled out and in a western direction until we came to a place about 13 miles from our last Camp. it was by this time 10 A.M. on our trip here one buffalo and two Antelopes got shot, and we have plenty, fresh meat. the Tule Creek is very, very winding, and the valley is only [at] the widest ¼ mile. There is no water except about 10 miles up from last night's camp[,] a waterhole on a rocky bank. the last point we reached at 10 o'clock. There was a rocky bank, a Hackberry tree with several nests in [it]. took some sight measurements to another tree about 1½ miles from this place[,] which is really the head of the Tule. We retraced our trail. as we came to the place, the 1st Antelope was shot. we saw a great many little blue butterflies sitting and sipping the blood. caught some of them. At 2 P.M. we camped on the same place we left this morning, as [it is] the only place with drinkable water. The pool or pond here is very deep and one may find water here at all time[s]. it is not running and tastes very brackish but it is water and wet. Had a good dinner, Buffalo meat, coffee, bread and some liver. We travelled a part of the day on an old, and very indistinct trail. Right near our camping place two trails go north. Lt. Ruffner told me that very likely we will be in Leavenworth by July 4th or 5th, and he being afraid of having by this time no jurisdiction over me any longer, as there was no money up to his knowledge appropriated for any Office. Well, one must not say anything until he is actually hit, [so] told Lt. Ruffner that I would under all circumstances work until our coming back to Leavenworth. The Buffalo hunt was funny to-day. There were 8 of them and as all [hunters] dismounted from their horses, they [the buffalo] likely thought another herd we were, and as one was shot down the others would not run, but wondered what had happened to their fellow buffalo. The same with the second Antelope, (Mr. Manahan shot it.) she did not move and looked all the while on us and wondered. We saw a great many herds of antelope to-day. After dinner Mr. Dixon built himself a sun shelter out of willow branches and a blanket. It worked very well. Lt. Ruffner sits under the Ambulance and watercolor sketches. It is very hot. I am laying in the deep grass near a young cottonwood for shade. Camp on Scare Spring in Tule Cañon. The mosquitoes was very bad near evening. Some ducks and mud hens came to the Creek. Had to move my blankets higher up the hill to have more air and be out of the mosquitoes. Went to sleep about 9 o'clock. from midnight to 1 A.M. I have been on guard. Very chilly but bright moonshine.

    travelled 26½ miles

Manahan flagging antelopes on a hunt near Scare Spring, 10 June 1876.

Sunday, June 11th 1876. [Refer to Map No. 17]

    Got up at 4 o'clock this morning, it being very cool, 60°. Mr. Dixon shot an antelope, which ran right into Camp. at 6 o'clock we started and ran nearly over our trail of the 9th inst. Saw a great many buffalos. Made a very close survey over the broken ground which will give with my first measurement a very good idea of the country. at 9 A.M. we stopped at a Spring named by Lt. Ruffner after to-day, as Sunday Spring. pretty good water, some cottonwood trees along the Creek, which latter is dry, only water near Spring. Lt. Ruffner, with Mr. Dixon and 2 men went over to the main Cañon for exploring and watercolor sketching. he took the Aneroid Barometer along with him. Saw some white wild roses but at a place where I could not reach them, the rock too steep and I not having too much time to loose. Lt. Ruffner named the Spring we left this morning "Scare Spring" after a certain scaring Mr. Wm. Dixon gave to Mexicans, at the very same place on the morning of July 7, 1875. He being out on a scout with 2 others after Indians and surprised the camp of some Mexicans, pretty near shooting some of them. He scared them awful. Had a good antelope steak for dinner, bread and coffee. as there was no dry wood except a very few dry bushes I found about ½ mile below our Camp all was cooked on and by buffalo chips, which make plenty heat but smell very sickening. About 4 o'clock Lt. Ruffner and party came back from the exploring trip. Lt. R. told me that after a ride of about 4 miles in Southeast direction he struck the main Tule Cañon which is about 500 feet deep and about the same width. He showed me a pencil sketch made by him and after the description and the picture it must have been quite a picturesque place. the rocks are at that place very red and perpendicular. During [the] latter part of afternoon I caught several species of grasshoppers, two of which are of a striped kind. saw only the two of the kind or else I would have tried to secure more. About 7 we had supper, viz. Coffee and Crackers and at 8 I laid down to sleep. it was rather chilly looking weather. It looked like rain. Was on guard from 11 to 12 P.M.

travelled 10½ miles.

Monday, June 12th 1876. [Refer to Map No. 16.]

Woke from a sensation like being in rain about 2½ A.M. this morning and so it was. Raining and strong wind from the North very chilly, 52° Farenheit. we made coffee as quick [as] we could by the storm, packed up and started at 3:30 A.M. it was a very cold ride. We put a buffalo robe around us to protect ourselves. travelled on a Wagon trail and at 7:30 we struck our trail of [the] 8th inst. from Camp Cent to Camp on Mouth of Tule Cañon. arrived in Camp at 9:30 A.M. from foot of bluffs to Camp the whole road, I made a careful survey of [the] road and bed of Tule Creek. After arrival in Camp, heard that our Mess is in a most poor condition, in fact nothing left to eat[,] so I laid down and slept dinner away. During [the] afternoon I arranged my meal and Board matter with the Infantry Sergeant and had first meal this evening, supper. Mr. Dixon gave me ? plug of Tobacco as I am entirely out of it. Received from Sergt. Lichtenberg, Engr. an Indian relic which he found near Camp, for the Museum. it seemed to have been worn either on a horses bridle or as a breast ornament. The Monument was sunk during [the] afternoon and observations taken. As an experiment for lard oil, Buffalo tallow was used. Caught some fishes in butterfly net for bottle.

travelled 16½ miles.

Tuesday, June 13th 1876. [Refer to Map No. 11]

Revellie at 2½ o'clock this morning. about 3 o'clock we had breakfast and at 4 the Train started. The Red River which we soon reached; its bed being only ¾ of a mile from the camping place just left, is dry and at least ½ mile wide. The bed is fine red sand with much alkali and other bitter matter. some places looked quite white of salt; the banks proper of River are not high, about 4 to 5 feet which is all told. on both sides rise bluffs and hills upon hills and hills. It is a very rough country, much water-worn. Travelled about 2 miles up the and in the River bed. Thence we ascended the first rise of Cañon about 200 feet very steep. I did not see it, as the Surveying party was far behind, but was told that it has been much labor to get the teams up. had to double, that is each wagon, 12 mules. Then we came on a large wide rolling and hilly stretch for about 3 miles and thence we had to ascend the second big and high [bluffs], but where the road was not so steep rise of country. About midway in first bottom I made the annexed sketch of part of the second rise. This rise is for several miles a continuous line of hills and rocks, one ridge behind the other and all more or less cut and pointed. Thence we had a descent for some time until it got more and more level to Battle Creek. Saw some very fine colored sandstone; one layer yellow, shaded to nearly white, darkest ochre, and next layer purple. It was a very fine sight to look at. many rocks standing 38° dip. Saw many fine specimens of petrified Cedar and Cottonwood and also finely colored and shaped pebbles of all kind and color. Arrived at Camp at 11:30 A.M. very tired, it being pretty hot, and as we had had nothing to eat since 3 o'clock this morning pretty hungry. But as soon as I had unsaddled I was called to dinner of Buffalo meat, potatoes and bread & Coffee. The first potatoes I tasted since leaving Camp Supply. Surely very bad they were under ordinary circumstances, but a real delicacy under existing extraordinary circumstances. The place we camp is a large level flat for several miles surrounded by hills, with pretty short thick grass. There is no dust, of which latter we had any amount in former Camps, which the whole command occupied. The Creek nearby has its name of a battle fought under Gen'l. Miles, Col. 5th Infty. in 1874 (Aug. 30) against hostile Indians. The Creek is not very wide but has running water, [the] color of which is pretty red, and tastes alkali, but not so bad as Tule Creek. Counted 9 herds of buffalo near Camp. On trip caught big animal known here under name of "Sawbook." Had through kindness of Lt. Baldwin a good drink of whiskey. During survey had the even stations and as Moore, my rod carrier, is sick (diaorrhea), Hazen, a very green hand[,] carried it. I had to do everything. About 5 this afternoon there was a buffalo hunt to all directions as the animals came nearly into Camp, but plenty shooting though no kill. Right after dark about 8 o'clock big excitement. Lt. Thomas M. Woodruff, 5th Infty., had not returned from his watercolor sketching excursion. Fires were kindled on prominent places and all the Cavalry mounted to look for him. Lt. Baldwin blowed the bugle. It was very effectful, I mean the tunes he brought out of the instrument, serious as the matter was, we all had to laugh. All at once Lt. Woodruff made his appearance. During [the] afternoon [I] made a sketch of our tent with Sergt. Lichtenberg and Sergt. Hensman of Infty. Escort. The picture shows, also, the Mercurial Barometer, attended by Lichtenberg. Wrote a postal card to Mrs. Hunnius and a few lines to Corpl. Wm. Holland Engrs. in Ft. Elliott asking him to send me by Mr. Wilson, the guide, 2 packages of smoking tobacco as I am out of it; and that I was going to refund on our return to his post on or about the 24th inst.

    travelled 12¼ miles

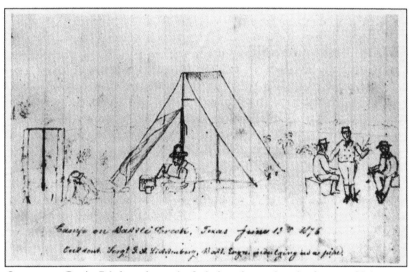

Sergeant G. A. Lichtenberg indulging in a pipe in front of his tent in camp at Battle Creek, Texas, 13 June 1876.

Wednesday, June 14th 1876. [Refer to Map No. 12]

    Revellie at 2½ A.M. rather early. had breakfast at 3:00 and started at 4:00. the train and an Escort of same went on [the] road and our surveying party with Mr. Dixon as Guide took a North West course. First over a large open space and that is broken twice with a range of hills which are very sharply cut and rather steep. bad ascent as they are covered with large round pebbles which give way as you step on them. after 8 A.M. we were in the foothills of a very high range

of hills, very rocky and steep. at 10 we were at the summit, and now
it went down and up and up and down in the Cañons. it was a dazzling
and dizzy ride. plenty buffalo, large herds. Saw some long billed
snipe. crossed several dry streams with very steep banks. We followed
always buffalo trails as they will surely lead to some accessible point.
At 2 o'clock arrived at Mulberry Creek where we found the Camp.
We all was very tired and certainly our poor horses the most. they
had to work very hard all day. The train which came by the direct
and generally travelled road had a very rough days work so I heard.
They brought an Antelope, one buffalo and a bear in. the latter was
shot by Lt. Baldwin. It must have been a large animal. I did only see
the meat and skin, as he was already cut up. There were several bears
seen during the day. The water here in [the] Creek is very good,
considering our so bad water we had in the 2 last Camps. There is
some alkali in it and if a person would come to it the other way [than]
we did, that person would say it is very bad, but he would soon change
his mind by tasting Red River. During the day, near and after noon,
the water in the Creek sinks until hardly any is left, but as soon [as]
the sun has set it comes up again and in early morning is quite a
lively little stream. for supper bear meat. it is splendid and goes well.
I did it all honor. Platted to-day's trip and stuck all our surveys
together. after this, we can only be about 15 miles from our Camp
on Mulberry Creek (May 17 & 18) below. Before we struck Mulberry
Creek passed a large place we had to go down[,] a very steep hill and
you had to lead your horse very careful or else it would have fallen
down the Cliffs. in all these Cañons one has to take the zig-zag mode
of travelling. on places the mesquit brush is very thick and as it is
most exceedingly thorny, our hands and faces look very much like
having had a fight with cats. but just as bad as these are the dry old
sunflower stalks in the level bottoms. Saw some sandstone rocks
which slided into all possible directions, besides being on places oval.
Much yellow and very red sandstone, also some pure white and some
purple. over this then comes generally very hard white gypsum. on
some places chalkstone and limestone, the latter with very sharp
edges. Splendid Cedar trees, some Hackberry and Chin-oak. along the
mostly dry Creek beds scattered Cottonwoods, some of which are of
large size and limbs so crooked shaped that they can from a distance
be taken for an oak tree. Part of the train left us today as Guide
Wilson, 4 6-mule teams, 1 Inftry. Sergt. and 5 men, and___of the
Cavalry.

   travelled 17¼ miles

Thursday, June 15th 1876. [Refer to Map No. 13]
   Revellie at 2 o'clock this morning. I was still very tired and could
hardly get out of my blanket. We felt cold as none of us had shut the

our tent, and so we were just as good as in the open air all the night. But the rousing [of] everybody at 2 o'clock in the morning deprives anybody of sleep. About 3 o'clock it was discovered that the 2 Ambulance lead mules were gone, and at that time it was too dark to see their trail. By this time all was nearly ready to move, and the news of this loss was like water on hot iron. Teodoso went out first and right after him Mr. Dixon. So soon as daylight was breaking Teodoso came back on a trail made with a moccasin. But that lead right into camp, and may have been made yesterday by Sergt. Lichtenberg, who wears a pair and had been out walking last evening in this direction. Dixon came in and could not see anything. Myself and Hazen went out as we had the first Station this morning (No. 528). [We] went with Dixon to guide us, and now he pointed out to us the trail of the mules. one could see the tracks where they crossed the Creek and the impression made by the dragging their lariat ropes. Hazen went back to Camp to report the trail found. on the prominent Hills sentinels appeared to look out for the Mules and Indians which might be around and [who] might have taken them. After a time Dixon came back from Station 529[,] a high hill on our proposed to-days route. This latter Station being Lt. Woodruffs and he having a spy glass, [he] kept on top on [the] Hill to look out. Dixon passing near by Station, I went to meet him and asked how matters stood. And there he all at once discovered in the grass the trail of those two mules. it lead near my station up a very high and steep bluff. I sent Smith, Lt. McCauleys orderly, to Camp to report the fact. Lt. Baldwin came out very soon and I put him on that trail. between that time Hazen had returned and Lt. B. gave him orders to send out the Cavalry Sergt. with all the mounted men available as soon and quick as possible, and sure they came soon on a regular charge over this rough rocky country. it looked very fine to see them jump and ride. I put them on the trail and off they went. I and Hazen kept our post, and after Lt. Woodruff and party came back again and we saw the tents being in course of erection we mounted and returned. I tried to take a big lodge pole along with me, but my horse got so wild that he nearly throwed me. In one way I was very glad to hear that Lt. Ruffner was going to lay over as I and [al]so everybody was very, very tired. Had a good sleep from 8 to 12 o'clock when I was called to dinner [of] bear meat, Potatoes, Bread and Coffee. Lt. Baldwin and the Cavalry came back in troops. they had trailed them mules and think they must have gone to Fort Elliott. that would not be unlikely at all. about 2 o'clock the Cavalry Corporal, Hall, Teodoso, and 4 men (Schuemaker between them) started for Fort Elliott to report and [to] ask that some parties from there should be on the lookout for those two Mules and the one that strayed from the train which brought supplies to us to Permanent Camp on Palo Duro Cañon. Gave Corporal Hall a section of Indian Territory map along

which I had, to guide the party in case of their loosing or changing
trail. During evening I heard that Lt. Ruffner discharged Mr. Manahan
from driving Ambulance, and with this he lays the fault of losing the
mules to him.

Friday, June 16th 1876. [Refer to Map No. 13]

Revellie at 2:30 this morning. It was raining. there was not much
of it as the thunderstorm moved more to the East. At 4 we started
in a North western direction[,] some short distance up the Creek
we had camped on, and thence ascended the hills, up on top of which
there was a fine view down stream. It rained pretty lively just at
reaching this point. from here we had one hill after another, some
very sharply pointed. These hills are all more or less overgrown with
grass and as tops are covered with smooth pebbles of all sizes, we
travelled on a ridge, about half way between Mulberry Creek and the
Creek we had camped on. From one of those little peaks I made a
sketch of a continuous set of them which is really very pretty,
especially as the rain clouds just broke and the sun was shining
through on them. The rocks are hard red clay and limestone. We saw
a great many buffalo. At 7 o'clock we came to the last high rise, and
this is the one shown in the sketch, which projects far into the valley
of the two streams and forms this point [and then] falls back very
much to both sides. passed a very narrow passage about 6 feet wide
and on both sides steep, deep Cañons. Thence a few hills more and
we came to the level Prairie again on which we saw great numbers
of buffalo grazing. Travelled up the North side of Mulberry Cañon
and at 11:30 arrived at the very same place we [had] camped on May
17th & 18th. Stadia Station No. 560 was at a Monument placed at
that time and here we had at least reached one closing point on the
Survey. Had several opportunities to shoot at buffalo, but as the train
was far away from us and there would have been no chance to
transport the meat and otherwise could not see why [to] waste
ammunition. Lt. Ruffner spoke to me about my being with the
Infantry detachment and he said he wanted me to pay the men. [I]
Told him that that has been my intention from the very beginning.
He said he did not like it at all, it looked so small [for me to have to
pay for my rations]. But he remarked, that he is afraid, that his Mess
will run rather short too. During the afternoon Lt. Ruffner told me
that he had to leave me here, as the trip he is going to make over to
the Cañon of the Red River, would be too much for my horse. He
left everyone here whose horse has a sore back. Lt. Ruffner told me
to go with Lt. Woodruff down Mulberry Cañon. Went to sleep at 9
o'clock, but before [that] we drove all the tent pins [in] once more
as it looks much like rain.
     travelled 15 m. 1278 yds.

Saturday, June 17th 1876. [Refer to Map No. 13]

Got up at 4 o'clock and had breakfast at 5 A.M. Lt. Ruffner, Dixon as Guide and 3 Cavalry men and one Pack mule left about 5 for the Cañon of the Red River. At 5:30 Lt. Woodruff, 4th Infty, with Theodolite No. 2 and Lt. McCauley[,] 3rd Arty. and myself on Stadia rods. Lt. McC with Freimer, and I with Hazen, left to meander down the Creek. at about 9 o'clock after having crossed and recrossed the Mulberry some 10 or 12 times, I came to a crossing that looked pretty fair. went down the bank and my horse fell in the Quicksand up to the breast and right after with its hind legs too. I just managed to jump off, partly drowning myself. I looked very dirty and the horse not much better, but as none of us two was hurt, only much scared[,] all was nothing and just the thing to happen on a trip. At 12:30 Lt. Woodruff sent me word that the station of mine would be the last so we put up a big rock monument and prepared to go home. Here I saw two wild turkeys but they were too swift to be chased. Lt. Woodruff proposed to strike for the level Prairie and we prepared to ascend the hills. after the first we came to a second, and after that to a third[, a] very steep rise[,] in all about 300 - 400 feet. found some shells[,] some lava and some red so called corral stone. At 2:50 we arrived in camp again. [I] Was pretty hungry as I had [eaten] nothing since 4:30 this morning. Think 10 hours riding ought to make a person ready for a meal. The trip to-day was very interesting; the country on places real pretty, and some places very rough. Mulberry Creek being on most crossings dry[,] on some places there is water standing in deep pools. water where it is running [is] clear and of good taste. Creek very well timbered, about 6 miles below our camp, Cottonwood predominates. The Creek has a wide, about 35-40 feet, sandy and gravelly bed, with steep banks on which is much brush. On a great many places the hills close so near the Creek that there are perpendicular walls of at least 100 feet in height. (red sandstone and very hard red clay.) Think Lt. Ruffner might have taken me along because I think there could not be any harder service required of my horse as it had to undergo to-day by a ration of two quarts of corn for 24 hours. Near evening went up part of the hill facing the Camp and made the sketch, to be found on the next page. Dr. Mendenhall and Mr. Sullivan had been out in the breaks of the Cañon and found in a tree the nest of an Eagle. They brought both young ones in. Mr. Sullivan presented his to Sergt. Lichtenberg, who put his to Dr. Mendenhalls box and takes care of those animals. They are very young, but of large size. About the same time a Bull frog of enormous size was caught. A[cting] A[ssistant] Surgeon Sabine, took measurements which will be found on next page. There were several nearly as large as the one caught seen, but the men selected this one.

1 foot	5 1/4	inches from tip of Nose to toes of hind legs
1 "	8 1/4	" " " of toe from hind leg to hind leg
— "	10 1/4	" " " " " " fore leg to fore leg
— "	8 1/2	" length of body
— "	10	" " " hind leg
— "	3	" " " fore leg
— "	11	" circumference of belly
— "	7	" " of neck
— "	5 1/2	" " of thigh
— "	3 3/4	" " of leg
— "	2 3/4	" " of foot
— "	2 1/2	" across mouth
— "	5	" around "
— "	2 1/2	" length of neck
— "	3 1/2	" spread of web of hind foot
— "	3	" " of fore foot
— "	2 1/2	" length of longest hind toe

Weight of the animal about 3 1/2 lbs. good (estimated.)

travelled about 20 miles

Sunday, June 18th 1876. [Refer to Map No. 13]

After breakfast and about 7 A.M. I went out on my survey with Teodoso as Guide. the North Fork of Mulberry Creek is only ½ mile up stream from Camp. went up the Fork to breaks in level Prairie. There is no water in [the] Creek, but some scattered trees. About 9½ o'clock we arrived in camp again. The country was, and is, very rough[,] the hills rather steep, even buffalo trails are not always what is wanted. Washed my old blue woolen shirt but the water would not clean it. Worked up the Journal of the trip, which was not done since May 28th. Lt. Woodruff is out with Sergt. Lichtenberg after the course and direction of a certain steam we saw yesterday and which Sergt. L. marked in book the day before yesterday as a Creek running N. East. At 12:15 P.M. Lt. Ruffner and party returned from the trip over to the Red River Cañon. About 2 P.M. Lt. Woodruff, Sergt. Lichtenberg and Escort came in. it was raining already all at once[;] we had a thunderstorm closed upon us, and the storm coming from [the] West upset our tent. Hail and rain finished to wet nearly everything. Only the Wall tents, the Infantry Bell tent, and one Cavalry A tent stood the storm. All others was down. The hail was laying very thick on Sergt. Lichtenbergs side, water running through our tent. about 1 inch of rain fell in ½ hour. Sergt. Lichtenberg was very hostile. We managed to save the books, though some got very wet. About 3 o'clock all was over. the dry Creek right in rear of tents is very high. Mr. Wilson, the Guide, came in with the mail. [I] got 2 small packages of tobacco and a letter from Corpl. Wm. Holland, Comp. D, Batt. of Engineers. He informs me that Sergt. Moier is in from Sill and brought a cradle with a papoose in it, also some other trinkets along for the Museum. Mr. Dixon would not take the tobacco I owe him. He said it made him pleasure to help anybody and he had still plenty of it. Now after the rain is over[,] we got some new tent pins (7). Sergt. Lichtenberg is very hostile that Lt. Ruffner asked him to copy some notes of his, he being so wet. The Portable Transit monument was sunk and Astronomical Observations taken. The two old Eagles have been pretty near all afternoon over our Camp, watching their young ones, sitting in a box in front of our tent.

travelled 10 miles

Monday, June 19th 1876. [Refer to Map No. 4]

Revellie at 3 o'clock. breakfast shortly after and at 4:50 the train and Command moved off together. but before leaving Lt. Ruffner made some final Instrumental Readings on points. Our course was as a general direction, North North East. Saw hundreds and hundreds of Buffalo sometimes in front [and] sometimes on both sides of our route. Did not travel on a trail but Mr. Wilson our Guide for to-day took us more East than the trail [by which] we came to the camp [we] left in May. About 9 A.M. we crossed the Salt Fork of Red River. it was very Clear and swift running about 20 feet wide. Rode back 3½ miles to hunt for pocket knife. found it at the last place I sketched. Had it since June 28, 1864. Folly Island, S. C. [The water] to me [tasted] not very salty, in fact, it was excellent water. There is not much timber on the Creek where we crossed. Here at the crossing, as Dr. Sabine, Acting Assistant Surgeon, and Mr. Dixon, were riding through the water, the Doctors horse laid down with him and he was wet up near his waist. He did not feel bad about it and all laughed. It was very hot all morning. After a ride of about 3 miles more we crossed the Whitefish Creek and camped 10:45. This Creek is partly dry, but water [which was] rather dirty looking was found about ½ mile from Camp, down bed of Creek. a very pretty grove of high trees are near our crossing of the Creek in which there was an encampment of buffalo hunters. Buffalo are very thick in this part of the country; it is quite a sight to see a herd of 1500 to 2000 or more in move[ment]. After the tents being up and dinner over, I platted the to-days march. There came several thunderstorms up about 2 P.M. but not much rain fell, except a few drops. Before we left Camp this morning, it being still dark, a detachment, the Cavalry Sergeant and 4 men[,] Teodoso as Guide went out to look after the lost Mules. (Ambulance)

Teodoso, one of the civilian scouts guiding the survey expedition, sitting on his Indian pony, Jim, 19 June 1876.

Heard from Mr. Wilson that the Mule lost from our supply train was caught by buffalo hunters and brought to Fort Elliott. Teodosos father, a full Mexican, travelled with us. he came to our camp yesterday, from the Quita Que Mountains,[66] where he had been with the Officer mentioned on May 15 th[,] who was on a leave for some twenty days and used these to look for Gold in those mountains. There was after all a thunderstorm with hail and much wind. Before dark Sergt. Lichtenberg and I walked to the Whitefish Creek to fill our Canteens. found two good springs. Some rain about 9 o'clock [in the] evening.

   travelled 17¼ miles.

Tuesday, June 20th 1876. [Refer to Map No. 3]
   Revellie at 3 o'clock this morning. the train started at 4:30 A.M. a mile from our camp we passed over a great many places where the buffalo hunters had made a stand and killed the animals up to 25 in a small place. The stench of the carcasses was awful. The hunters cut the heads off to turn better the bodies. Carried during to-days trip the Mercurial Barometer, which by the way is conveniently cased and strapped. Private Micue was ordered by Lt. Ruffner to go back to the Ambulance and get him some cartridges. On his return he came in full gallop, and he was near passing me [when] the horse stumbled and fell with him, he coming to lay under the animal, which tried to get up but fell a second time and this time on his chest. he looked very pale and said he had much pain in his chest, but mounted after a short time the horse again and rode slowly on. but it did not last long. he had to sit on the ground and was put in one of the teams [wagons] where a bed had been made for him. There was any amount of buffalo seen and near us, one little calf came up to my horse thinking it was his mother. I could have held him but I pitied the little thing and let him go again. Once a herd of buffaloes passed so near I might have thrown stones at them, but all old bulls. Dr. Mendenhall shot at them just for fun. I cannot see the use of killing if it is not actually needed, but I suppose he having nothing to pay for the wasted cartridges [could not resist]. Saw in the distance to our left our old camping place of May 14, 15 & 16. There is much and heavy timber on McClellan Creek, mostly Cottonwood. Plenty and clear good water at present in Creek. At 11:30 A.M. made Camp about 100 yds from junction of North Fork of McClellan Creek with the main stream. There is some good and running water in the N. Fork. After dinner platted Sergt. Lichtenbergs notes of to-days trip. at 2 this afternoon the Barometer being very unsteady we made our tent as tight and stormproof as possible. Washed a set of underclothing and put on one of the new woolen shirts on with the new red necktie. It is quite a sport at such a place like this. Very hot

to-day[,] in [the] shade 108° in [the] sun 128° at 2 P.M. Near dark
a rattlesnake with 5 rattles and a butt[on] was caught alive by Mr.
Sullivan and others and put in a bottle. She was afterwards killed by
pouring alcohol on her as she pushed the cork on the bottle out twice,
and for fear she might get away and bite somebody. There was a little
rain during [the] night but not much.
    travelled 22½ miles.

Wednesday, June 21st 1876. [Refer to Map No. 2]

    Revellie at 3 o'clock this morning. at our breakfast that we had
right after it was still dark and one had to feel what he was eating.
The train left at 4:15, but most of the things had been packed already
yesterday evening, which will account for the early leaving. At about
8 A.M. we crossed the North Fork of Red River and at 11:20 arrived
at Fort Elliott. It was very hot and oppressive during our trip. on the
N. Fork we made a short halt and I had a little lunch of dry bread,
sausage and water. saw some Buffalo but not so many as yesterday.
On North Bank of North Fork of Red River a halt was made of about
½ hour to allow the train to catch up with us [who were] on horseback.
The roads being very sandy. the bed of North Fork is 100 yds. wide,
the stream of water in it some 20 or thirty feet wide and 2 feet deep.
Miccue [*sic*], the man that fell yesterday with his horse[,] rode in
[the] Ambulance. The country and soil between our last Camp and
North Fork is very rich black soil but wood [is] scarce except on
McClellan Creek. From North Fork of Red River up to Fort Elliott
more or less sandy[,] some places very. For dinner bought a box of
canned peaches and some Crackers. Paid to 1st Sergt. of Co. H. 19
Infty. (Mr. Minty) $2.25 for my eating meals with the escort and
arranged for meals until we leave here. Paid Corpl. Wm. Holland[,]
Engrs. 60 cts. for tobacco he sent me. Sergt. Moyer [*sic*] Engrs. brought
from [Fort] Sill a little Baby Cradle with a doll in [it] and other
trinkets. had a good supper. Went with Corpl. Holland to Spring for
drinking water. As it looked like rain I slept in [the] house on [the]
floor. There was a very heavy storm last night with much hail but
no rain.
    travelled 25¼ miles

Thursday, June 22d 1876.

    Got up at 4:30 this morning, nice cool morning. I am getting
civilized, blackened my boots, which seem to be quite astonished
about this as it took quite a while before I could made the blacking
stick to the leather. Lt. Baldwin signed for me my requisition on the
Commissary. bought at Post Traders 1 plate, 1 Quart cup, 1 Knife
and Fork and Spoon, 1 Cooking pail, $1.25. Tobacco 50 cts. wrote a
letter to Mrs. Hunnius, and told her we would arrive about [the]

30th or 1st of July. At the Commissarys I bought 1 tin box of Crackers, 2 Cans Condensed Milk, ½ lbs. of black tea, 2 lbs. of sugar, 3 Cans of green Corn, 2 cans Lima beans, 2 Cans green Peas, 2 Cans of Salmon, 4 Boxes of Sardines,and paid $5.20 for it. Bought of Sergt. Moier, Batt. of Engrs. one Buffalo robe and gave $6.00 for it. Since 5 o'clock this morning I relieved Sergt. Lichtenberg of taking meterological observations. During forenoon Sergt. Moier and I measured off 1000 feet on the parade ground. Measured it 4 times over, 1st 1000 ft., 2d 1000' 2.8", 3d 1000' 3.8", 4th 1000' 3.5". about Noon Lt. Ruffner tested the Stadia Rod. 10 readings were taken, and Lt. Ruffner will take another set about 6 o'clock to-night. After these readings were taken packed my "traps" and had at Sergt. Moiers milk punch, which by the way is a very good drink. Went to sleep about 10 o'clock.

Friday, June 23rd 1876.

Got up at 4 o'clock and after breakfast the wagons came and got loaded. there were three wagons, one with all boxes and heavy things, which will not be unloaded (Sullivans team), the 2d wagon has all mess chests, bedding and packages, the 3rd carries the forage and some of the Infantry escort (Co. E 19 Infty). We have 3 ambulances, our own with the officers, driven by Sullivan, 2d Escort and some civilians (Mr. Carter (colored) Barber at [Fort] Elliott), 3d Ambulance, driver, I, Sergt. Lichtenberg, Manahan, a discharged soldier and one Civilian. These Civilians are nearly all witnesses in a trial now pending at Camp Supply, "the United States against Lt. Col. Bankhead, U. S. A." The teams left about 6 this morning and at 7 o'clock after a general "Good Bye" to all the hands that had been with us on the Expedition, we drove off.[67] Mr. Wm. Dixon, Chief of Guides at Fort Elliott, presented me with his likeness; which he had taken for me, by the Hospital Steward at the Post.[68] We drove very fast. at 9:30 arrived at the Washita River, where we had been in Camp May 5th and 6th. The Ranch (Whelans) is improving. they erected a corral just now. saw a small herd of Buffalo about 5 miles off to the West. The Mercurial Barometer, which was carried by the officers, got broken, but the Mercury [was] saved. Started at 10:30 again and arrived at Springers Ranch, on North Side of Canadian River at 12:30. The wagons arrived two hours later. Had supper at the Ranch, 50 cts. a good meal. For dinner [and] lunch bought a can of peaches and Crackers 50 cts. Near evening made a sketch of Ranch. It is very hot.

travelled 34 miles.

Tintype photograph of William "Billy" Dixon, one of the civilian guides for the expedition, made at his request by a hospital steward at Fort Elliott and given by him to Adolph Hunnius on 23 June 1876.

Saturday, June 24th 1876.

Very shortly after midnight, the Corporal of the Escort woke me to ask what time it was, and from that time it was impossible for me to get any more sleep. The heat and the mosquitoes was rather too much for anyone. We started big smokes to keep the beasts away from us but it was not much gained. The poor mules had no rest at all on account of the mosquitoes. About 2 o'clock I made my breakfast, Tea, Lima beans and crackers. It was still very dark as the sky was very cloudy. At 4:15 we started. between our last Camp and Commission Creek there were immense herds of buffalos, thousands and thousands. Mr. Springer told us last night that the herd which passed his Ranche two days ago was about 4 miles wide and it took them nearly 48 hours to pass. Those immense herds we saw this morning are parts of which the whole consisted. On South Commission Creek we made a halt for lunch ¾ hour, and also to give the teams a chance to gain road on us. very heavy sand, very hard work on the mules. had some fine views of the "Antelope Hills." at 1 o'clock arrived at "Willow Springs Mail Ranche." It was very hot. had a little rain to-day but not much. At 4:15 P.M. the teams arrived. For Supper I had Tea, Salmon & Crackers, which was quite a good meal as I was very hungry. Near dark made a sketch of Willow Springs Mail Ranch. This Ranch is under Military control and there are mules kept for relays. Right under the Kitchen they have a good spring with clear cool water. Wood is rather scarce on the Willow Creek. there are only a very few trees in sight. some large water holes near Ranche. Buffalo also came very near camp for water. It looks much like rain.

travelled 34 miles

Sunday, June 25th 1876.

Got up at 3 o'clock this morning. At 4:30 we started. at 6 o'clock we crossed Wolf Creek, near the place we camped on May 3rd and 4th, and after a brisk drive arrived at Camp Supply at 9:45. Passed several Wood wagons of Lee & Reynolds,[69] 12 oxen spanned. The butcher Schlick of Camp Supply passed us, and told Mr. Manahan that the Mules lost by him [the ambulance lead mules] were caught yesterday near Buffalo Creek. Mr. & Mrs. Moller received me very well and after a shake-hands and a wash, had another, the 2d breakfast. It was hot and dusty. At noon had dinner at [the] Mechanics Mess house. Got 2 pairs of moccasins presented to me. At 4 P.M. another dinner at Mr. Carl Mollers (Soup, Roast (filled), green Peas, Macaroni, Tomatoes (sweet) and 2 Pudding[s].) The Chief Clerk, Mr. Dahn of the Quartermasters Office at Fort Elliott, I met at the table. [I] could not get small moccasins for Carl and Herman [as] there have been no Indians near this Post. About 9 o'clock went to sleep on the floor. it was very warm but at least some air stirring though only from time to time.

Monday, June 26th 1876.

Got up at 4 o'clock. made some tea and green peas. Said good bye to all and at 7:14 we started. the two teams left about 6:30. We had an Ambulance and a so called Spring Escort Wagon, which vehicle has its name from two springs under the drivers seat. Otherwise it is not springy at all. Mr. Crayton, 2nd Clerk at Quartermaster Office at Camp Supply, went off in the Mail Coach. [I] gave him one of my visiting cards and address. he will be 24 hours earlier than me in Leavenworth and I requested him to see Mrs. Hunnius. between the Post just left and the high hill [we] met a large Emigrant train. a great many women and children all going to Arizona up the Canadian to Fort Bascom, to Anton Chico, to Albuquerque and thence via Fort Wingate to Prescott, Arizona. At the Devils Gap made a drawing and after that I collected fossil specimens. Dr. Mendenhall had a whole Water bucket full. at Buffalo Spring we made a halt, had some lunch. it was very hot. a second halt was made at Snake Creek to water the horses and at 3:30 P.M. arrived at Redoubt Creek Ranch. spoke [to] Mr. Crayton once more. the Stage had just changed horses. Had a good supper at Ranch, 50 cts. One of the big dogs bit me but only into the heel, she having young ones. The Mr. Ranchman treated me to a cigar, a pretty queer one by looks, but by the smoke very good. The road was very sandy and dusty and it was very hot. we could hardly quench the thirst. All water we passed was so muddy and warm and of a very bad taste. Train arrived at 7:15 P.M. Plenty Mosquitos. went to sleep at 9 P.M.

travelled 37 miles.

Tuesday, June 27th 1876.

Got up about 2 o'clock this morning, the mosquitos being too bad and the air very thick and oppressive. After an early breakfast such as it was, we started at 4:20. it looked very much like rain. at the old Redoubt made a halt for watering mules, lunching and running around to find fossils. There was another long halt made at the head of Bear Creek. Everybody interested in Geology was fossiling, while all not interested grumbled more or less about it. saw a large herd of Texas Cattle, one young bull going for the ambulance. Got several times a little wet but as the sun came out from time to time we got dry again. Arrived at Bluff Creek Mail Station 12:20 noon. wood very scarce, but good water near camp. [I] made dinner on a box of peaches, crackers and Tea. About 2 P.M. the train arrived. I was so tired I slept on the hard prairie for some time. As I awoke all the tents were up.

slept until 5 P.M. It got pretty cool near dark. Went to sleep for the last time on this trip on the ground. [I] had to bank up the extra linen on [the] tent with pieces of ground to keep the wind out. About 10 feet on [the] N. end of Oaks Ranch is a new building.

travelled 34 miles.

Wednesday June 28th 1876.

Mr. Leny the Cook woke me at 3 o'clock this morning. it was raining pretty lively. he was very hostile not being able to start his fire. after he gave up, I lighted it with one match. had tea, Salmon the ½ box from last night, Crackers and Lima beans. Everything is pretty wet but as it is the last day out, everybody is laughing at it. at 5:20 A.M. we started the ambulance. drove on and the Escort wagon was ordered to go with the teams, but should drive on as soon as in sight of town. This order created a good deal of dissatisfaction, but after [all] we made very good time. It was very misty weather and we all got pretty wet. After a while there came a great many gushes of rain, and it was sometimes at the very point of loosing all our tempers. All at once we could see, but far in [the] distance, Fort Dodge. Leny the Ex-Cook got "Grouse," Lt. Baldwins dog, up from the road up into the wagon, saying, "There is the Fort in sight, you S___ of a B___[,] now laugh. You can see your master." Our driver delighted in driving over the roughest ground he could find to give the boys a shake. Sergt. Lichtenberg got very hostile about it. At 12:15 P.M. we arrived in Dodge City and halted at the Dodge House. got a very good and ample dinner of which I was very much in need. The Dodge House is much improved[,] a new addition built. A great many guests are staying at the Hotel. The town has improved very much since my having been here. a great many new buildings have sprung up. new signs hung and houses and shops newly painted. Also a cattle yard laid out and partly finished. On top of the Calaboose (the City Prison) there is a new story, which I was informed is the City Hall. There is also a Church, with a small steeple. The Observers Office is transferred from the Dodge House to a new, and partly especially built, house and is quite an ornament to the town. Everybody is in high expectations about the Texas Cattle Trade, which, as the people living South of Wichita, try to prevent passing their land, may terminate here, where there are no settlements south of the town. Much more rain During the afternoon. started the Comparison of Instruments at 2:00 P.M. Our Mercurial Barometer would not work at first, and Lt. Woodruff had to let some mercury out. Mailed a Postal card to Mrs. Hunnius stating that I would start to-morrow evening for Leavenworth. Lent [borrowed] 10 dollars from Lt. Ruffner to defray my expenses here. During my prolonged stay here, bought a Scribners Monthly Magazine to keep me company during the night. Paid 50 cts. for it. The party except Dr. Mendenhall went to Fort Dodge to have the transportation papers made out. After supper saw Mr. Jacob Weil, who is clerking here at present for a dealers in skins and hides. After the 9:27 P.M. reading walked to the Depot to see the Party off[70] and get my transportation, which Dr. O'Brien was supposed to bring from the Fort Dodge. mine and Sergt. Lichtenbergs was on one and the same tickets, so the Sergeant had to stay back and will go to-morrow. After the train left walked to the U. S. Signal Office to stay up all night and take Observations every hour to make a set of 24. Sergt. Lichtenberg came up to the Office, started a big talk, but Observer Sergt. J. J. Weinberg, U. S. A., thinks that he is no success. The little gray kitten Mr. Weinberg lost the time I was here last, was, as he told me, taken out of his room by a lady. He has now as pets a Canary bird and two grey squirrels, which are pretty tame and very lively animals.

travelled 29 miles.

Thursday, June 29th 1876.

Between 5 and 6 o'clock this morning made sketch of the Signal Office. from 7 to 11 Sergt. Lichtenberg relieved me. [In the] Boot Hill (cemetary) N.W. of Dodge City, [there are] about 35 - 40 graves, all except 5 with a [cross drawn in manuscript] died in boots, no coffins. 3 children [with crosses] and 2 others [with crosses]. Made sketches of Calaboose and Church. The upper portion or story of Calaboose is the City Hall. Bought a Panama hat $1.50. it was very warm all forenoon. Sergt. Lichtenberg went to Fort Dodge to draw his commutation of rations. sent the letter by Lt. Ruffner, to the Acting Assistant Quartermaster with the Infantry Sergeant who carried Lichtenberg to the Fort. Dodge City has about 700 inhabitants at present. The Dodge House can furnish room for 90 guests. took the last reading at 3:02 P.M. 1990, 2000 are the numbers of the Signal Barometers. Office No. 232, 251. Lost my watch key. Paid my board bill $4.50 for 5 Meals and lodging April 26th and 5 meals $3.75 & 75¢. for lodging today. The Indian saddles I had to ship by express. Bought a piece of rope to tie together some of my bundles 20 cts. About 6 P.M. the Signal Sergt. Weinberg came up [to] me at the Hotel in a very excited manner showing me a telegram by Lt. Ruffner to him in which it was said that he should tell me to bring along the Chronometer he, Lt. Ruffner, forgot. Sergt. Weinberg was very indignant. he had to pay one dollar for the dispatch. he told me, he would prefer charges against Lt. R. He was going to state things to Gen'l. Pope, and report to Washington. I told him to do what he thought fit and fight it out. The dispatch reached me in good time. about 30 to 45 minutes later and the Chronometer would have run down. There is a talk here now of starting a bank sometime next week, as there is a great need for such an institution to pay off the Drivers of the Cattle herds. near evening some very large herds came up and forded the Arkansas River and most of them got loaded on cars. Such a Cattle herd is a great sight. all colors except green and blue. Turned over to Sergt. Lichtenberg 1 Thermometer, 2 Aneroid Barometers (B & C) and the Instrumental Observations Note Book, of which Lt. Ruffner by handing it to me yesterday said, that if I should loose it he would hang me. Got my baggage checked. 4 pieces [with] 1 pack with blankets, etc. 1 Buffalo robe with Indian relics and camp chair wrapped in it. 1 Hand valise and 1 box with eatables and the cactus. There were no Checks and they put labels to the packages. The report came that the train was three hours late; so we went back to the Hotel again. Slept a little, it being pretty chilly. at 12:15 the train arrived.

Friday, June 30th 1876.

Sergt. Lichtenberg had fallen asleep on a bench on the porch and could not find one of his gaiters. he was a pretty picture. after I found it he lost his pipe but picked it up somewhere on a place again. he got his eagles all right and takes care of the Mercurial Barometer. Slept a little, but [was] very uncomfortable. no room in the sleeping car. Woke as we halted a few moments at Hutchinson. this is quite a place. looks very pretty, 2 Churches and one handsome Public House, a court house or school it looks to be, but there is plenty more room left to build on. Burton (spelled Burrton on the Hotel) is a place the size of Dodge City. Wheat is all cut, standing on the fields. Corn pretty much back still. Grass very good looking. Arrived at Newton at 6:15. our train was trying to make up time lost and succeeded. They expected to be in Newton about 7 o'clock. we travelled a long while [at] 40 miles an hour, or 20 telegraph poles to the mile. Left Newton at 6:35. at 7:30 arrived at Florence and had breakfast, $0.75, very ample and good, Breakfast Green peas, fried potatoes, green Salad, Oysters, Salmon excellent, Coffee. Waiter girls all very decent looking and well dressed. 9:00 Cottonwood. 10:00 Emporia. Topeka 12:25. left Topeka at 12:55 on the Kansas City, Leavenworth & Topeka R. R. dinner in Topeka $0.75. Bought a pair of moccasins for Carl $1.00. Arrived in Lawrence at 2:00 P.M. The Lawrence bridge is still with the broken center span on Massachusetts Street[;] the R. R. bridge though is all right. Bought 1 rattle for Herman, 1 thimble & case for Bertha and 1 needle box for Anna. Arrived in Kansas City at 4:00 P.M. It is very hot. there must have been lately a heavy rain here as pretty nearly every deep laying place is under water. started at 4:40 [for Leavenworth].

NOTES

[1] E. H. Ruffner, "Annual Report of Lieutenant E. H. Ruffner, Corps of Engineers, for the Fiscal Year Ending June 30, 1877," U. S., Department of War, *Report of the Secretary of War*, vol. 2, part 2, in U. S., Congress, House Executive Document 1, part 2, 45th Cong., 2 Sess. (Washington, D. C.: Government Printing Office, 1877), 1399-1438. It should be noted that the published report of the survey of the headwaters of the Red River contains a number of editorial changes introduced to the manuscript official report, some of which are sufficiently substantial as to alter meanings.

[2] "Atlas of Detail Sheets of the Survey of the Head Waters, Red River, Texas[,] Conducted by First Lieutenant E. H. Ruffner, Corps of Engineers[,] Chief Engineer[,] Department of the Missouri[,] May and June 1876," File Mark Q 301 Flat, Record Group 77, Cartographic Division, National Archives, Washington, D. C.

[3] Francis B. Heitman, *Historical Register and Dictionary of the United States Army, from Its Organization, September 29, 1789, to March 2, 1903*, 2 vols. (Washington D. C.: Government Printing Office, 1903), 1: 850.

[4] E. H. Ruffner, "Annual Report of Lieutenant E. H. Ruffner, Corps of Engineers, for the Fiscal Year Ending June 30, 1876," U. S., Department of War, *Report of the Secretary of War*, vol. 2, part 2, in U. S., Congress, House Executive Document 1, part 2, 44th Cong., 2 Sess. (Washington, D. C.: Government Printing Office, 1876), 718-749.

[5] E. H. Ruffner, Headquarters, Department of the Missouri, Office of the Chief Engineer, Fort Leavenworth, Kansas, to Assistant Adjutant General, Department of the Missouri, [Fort Leavenworth, Kansas], 15 April 1876, U. S., Department of War, Army, Division of the Missouri, Office of the Chief of Engineers, Correspondence of the General Record Division Exclusive of Accounts and Returns, Letters Received 1871-86, General Records File 1254 (1876), Record Group 77, National Archives, hereafter cited as General Records File 1254 (1876).

[6] E. R. Platt, Assistant Adjutant General, Head Quarters, Department of the Missouri, Fort Leavenworth, Kansas, to E. H. Ruffner, Chief Engineer Office, Department of the Missouri, Fort Leavenworth, Kansas, 17 April 1876, General Records File 1254 (1876); E. H. Ruffner, Office of the Chief Engineer, Department of the Missouri, Fort Leavenworth, Kansas, to Chief of Engineers, U. S. Army, [Washington, D. C.], 16 July 1877, U. S., Department of War, Army, Division of the Missouri, Correspondence of General Records Division Exclusive of Accounts and Returns, Letters Received 1871-86, General Records File 2187 (1877), hereafter cited as General Records File 2187 (1877).

[7] "Atlas of Detail Sheets;" "Survey of the Headwaters of Red River[,] Tex.," General Records File 2187 (1877).

[8] Mary Alice Lange Jones. "Biography of Ado Hunnius," TS, n. d., 1-5, Carl Julius Adolph Hunnius Papers, PanhandlePlains Historical Museum, Canyon, Texas. The majority of Adolph Hunnius's surviving papers and literary remains are in the Carl Julius Adolph Hunnius Papers at the Manuscript Department of the Kansas State Historical Society, Topeka, Kansas.

[9]Carl Julius Adolph Hunnius, "Survey of the Sources of the Red River April 25th to June 30th[,] 1876," MS, Carl Julius Adolph Hunnius Collection, Kansas Collection, Kenneth Spencer Research Library, University of Kansas, Lawrence, Kansas.

[10]E. H. Ruffner, 1st. Lieut. Engineers, Office of the Chief Engineers, Fort Leavenworth, Kansas, to Assistant Adjutant General [E. R. Platt], Department of the Missouri, [Fort Leavenworth, Kansas], 15 April 1876, MS, General Records File 1254 (1876).

[11]The Leavenworth press reported to its readers that on the morning of 25 April 1876 "a Government surveying party under command of Lieut. Ruffner, left Fort Leavenworth for Texas." *The Leavenworth Daily Times* (Leavenworth, Kans.), 26 April 1876, 3.

[12]Charles Adam Hoke McCauley, a native of Maryland, was appointed from Pennsylvania to the United States Military Academy on 1 July 1866. Graduating twenty-second in his class, he became a second lieutenant in the Third Artillery on 15 June 1870. McCauley was still serving at this rank in the Third Artillery when he participated in the survey of the headwaters of the Red River in spring and summer 1876. He later advanced to the rank of colonel and became Assistant Quartermaster General on 24 February 1903. Heitman, *Historical Register*, 1: 655.

[13]Thomas Mayhew Woodruff, a native son of New York, was appointed from the District of Columbia to the United States Military Academy on 1 September 1867. Fifteenth in his graduating class, on 12 June 1871 he was appointed as second lieutenant in the 5th Infantry. Woodruff received a breveted rank of 1st lieutenant in recognition for his gallant service against hostile Indians at Bear Paw Mountain, Montana, on 30 September 1877. He advanced to the rank of major in 1890 and remained in the military service until 1899, the year of his death. Heitman, *Historical Register*, 1: 1058.

[14]Though the editor has searched for half a dozen years, Lt. McCauley's ornithology report has not been located. The Dr. Hayden mentioned is Ferdinand Vandiveer Hayden, who in 1876 was serving as Geologist under the direction of the Secretary of the Interior. U. S., Department of the Interior, Geological Survey, *Ninth Annual Report of the United States Geological Survey to the Secretary of the Interior, 1887-88* (Washington, D. C.: Government Printing Office, 1889), 31-38.

[15]Frank Dwight Baldwin, twice recipient of the Congressional Medal of Honor, was a native of Michigan who entered military service as a second lieutenant in the Michigan Horse Guards during the Civil War on 19 September 1861. A lifelong military man, he was serving as a first lieutenant in the 5th Infantry at Fort Elliott, Texas, when he commanded the military escort accompanying the survey of the headwaters of the Red River in 1876. Baldwin received his first Medal of Honor for distinguished bravery in fighting at Peach Tree Creek, Georgia, on 20 July 1864, while he won his second for gallantry in action against hostile Indians near McClellan Creek in the Texas Panhandle on 8 November 1874. Alice Blackwood Baldwin,

Memoirs of the Late Frank D. Baldwin[,] Major General, U. S. A. (Los Angeles: Wetzel Publishing Co., Inc., 1929, 3199; Heitman, *Historical Register*, 1: 185-186.

[16]Lt. Ruffner's use of the term Red River denotes the Prairie Dog Town Fork of the Red River.

[17]This camp lay on the north side of the Prairie Dog Town Fork of the Red River near what today is the Lake Tanglewood residential development.

[18]The confluence of Palo Duro Creek with Tierra Blanca Creek today marks the site of the town of Canyon, Texas.

[19]Col. John Irvin Gregg led a party consisting of 214 enlisted men and 11 officers from Fort Bascom, New Mexico, across the plains to the head of Tierra Blanca Creek and down it to its confluence with Palo Duro Creek, engaging a war party of Kiowas at that point on 15 August 1872, and then continuing to the southeast before returning to Fort Bascom. Gregg was a native of Pennsylvania who first entered military service during the Mexican War and who reached a breveted rank of brigadier general during the Civil War. Heitman, *Historical Register*, 1: 477; Charles L. Kenner, *A History of New Mexican-Plains Indian Relations* (Norman: University of Oklahoma Press, 1969), 197-199.

[20]Randolph B. Marcy and George B. McClellan, *Exploration of the Red River of Louisiana in the Year 1852*, U. S., Congress, House Executive Document [no number], 33 Cong., 1 Sess. (Washington, D. C.: A. O. P. Nicholson, Public Printer, 1954).

[21]This encampment by the surveying party was on the northwest side of South Ceta Creek in the area of the present-day church camps in Ceta Canyon.

[22]The pockets of waterworn fossils discovered by the surveying party and described also in the geological portion of the official report were identified and recorded by Curator of Paleontology Jack T. Hughes in 1953 and assigned Panhandle-Plains Historical Museum site number P-15. Jack T. Hughes, "Field Trip Record Wed., 4/15/53," TS, in Jack T. Hughes Field Notes (1953), 21, in Archeology Department, Panhandle-Plains Historical Museum.

[23]The New Mexicans here described were most likely *pastores*, sheep herders who entered the Panhandle from the west and who tended their flocks in the region until they were forced out by Anglo-American cattlemen. Other New Mexicans encountered by the expedition may have been *comancheros*, traders who came onto the plains to conduct commerce with the nomadic Plains Indian. Paul H. Carlson, "Panhandle Pastores: Early Sheepherding in the Texas Panhandle," *Panhandle-Plains Historical Review* 53 (1980): 1-16; J. Evetts Haley, "The Comanchero Trade," *Southwestern Historical Quarterly* 38 (January 1935): 157176; Kenner, *New Mexico-Plains Indian Relations,* 78-97; Frederick W. Rathjen, *The Texas Panhandle Frontier* (Austin: University of Texas Press, 1973), 94-96.

[24]Lt. Ruffner named this place Camp Cent, and Adolph Hunnius refers to it by this name in his diary. It was located near the head of Deer Creek,

a tributary of the Prairie Dog Town Fork of the Red River, approximately seven miles northwest of Tule Canyon, and was occupied on 7 June 1876.

[25]This camp, occupied on 8 June 1876, was on the north bank of Tule Creek just a short distance above its juncture with the Prairie Dog Town Fork of the Red River.

[26]This encounter, sometimes called "the First Battle of Palo Duro Canyon," is well described in Nelson A. Miles, Headquarters, Indian Territory Expedition, Camp on Right Bank of Red River, Texas, to Assistant Adjutant General, Headquarters, Department of the Missouri, Fort Leavenworth, Kansas, 1 September 1874, U. S., Department of War, Army, Office of the Adjutant General, Letters Received Relating to "Campaign against Hostile Indians in the Indian Territory," Consolidated File 2815-1874, Record Group 74, National Archives, and published in Joe F. Taylor, comp. and ed., "The Indian Campaign on the Staked Plains, 1874-1875: Military Correspondence from War Department Adjutant General's Office, File 2815-1874," *PanhandlePlains Historical Review* 34 (1961): 21-24.

[27]The stream Lt. Ruffner called "D" Company Creek today is known as Spring Creek.

[28]According to Adolph Hunnius in his diary, the bear was killed on 14 June 1876.

[29]According to Adolph Hunnius, the expedition reached this closing point on the survey on 16 June 1876.

[30]The map of the Indian Territory discussed here was prepared in the Office of the Chief Engineer at Fort Leavenworth over a period of three years and was published by that office in 1875 in four sheets with a scale of 1:500,000. Ruffner, "Annual Report 1876," 718-719.

[31]Red River here refers to the Prairie Dog Town Fork of the Red River.

[32]The stream that Lt. Thomas M. Woodruff knew as the Rio Piedroso today is called East Amarillo Creek.

[33]The stream which Lt. Thomas M. Woodruff called May Creek today is known as West Amarillo Creek.

[34]The site which Lt. Thomas M. Woodruff discovered, rather than being a burial, was the remains of a prehistoric Panhandle Aspect Indian slab house. The same site was identified from aerial photographs by Curator of Paleontology Jack T. Hughes in 1953, visited by him in 1954, and recorded as Panhandle-Plains Historical Museum site number A-133. Jack T. Hughes, "Field Trip Record Jan. 2, 1954," TS, in Jack T. Hughes Field Notes (1954), 1-2, in Archeology Department, Panhandle-Plains Historical Museum. Lt. Woodruff's digging and scraping with his sheath knife leading to the discovery of arrow points may merit recognition as the first known archeological excavation in the Texas Panhandle.

[35]This stream today is know as Bonita Creek. The hill on which this stadia station was placed is downstream a short distance from the present-day LX Ranch headquarters.

[36]Timothy Erastus Wilcox, a native of New York, served as a physician for the United States Army during most of his adult life beginning with Civil War service in 1865 and advancing to the rank of Chief Surgeon by 1898. Heitman, *Historical Register,* 1: 1034.

[37]The botanist identified in the report as Prof. Wood most likely was Alphonso Wood, who was born at Chesterfield, New Hampshire, in 1810. He was associated with Kimball Union Academy, the Ohio Female Seminary, and Terre Haute Female Seminary before retiring in 1867 to West Farms, New York, where he devoted the remainder of his life to the pursuit of botanical studies. He died there in 1881. *The National Cyclopaedia of American Biography* (New York: James T. White & Company, 1910), 14: 278.

[38]The following list of botanical specimens presents the scientific nomenclature as given in the manuscript official report of the survey. Many of these scientific names have changed, some of them multiple times, during the past century. With each specimen are given the original abbreviated citations for the authorities used in their identification.

[39]Alpheus Spring Packard, *Directions for Collecting and Preserving Insects,* Smithsonian Institution Miscellaneous Collections 11 (Washington, D. C.: Smithsonian Institution, 1873).

[40]Ferdinand Heinrich Herman Strecker was known during the nineteenth century both as a sculptor and as a naturalist. Born in Philadelphia in 1836, he lived in Reading, Pennsylvania, from 1845 until his death in 1901. During a lifetime of study, he gathered in his home perhaps the largest collection of butterflies and moths in North America, and he authored major books on Lepidoptera. *The National Cyclopaedia of American Biography* (New York: James T. White & Company, 1909), 10: 317-318; *Who Was Who in America,* 4 vols. (Chicago: Marquis–Who's Who Incorporated, 1943-68), 1: 1198.

[41]The following list of entomological specimens presents the scientific nomenclature as given in the manuscript official report of the survey. Many of these scientific names have changed, some of them multiple times, during the past century. With each specimen are given the original abbreviated citations for the authorities used in their identification.

[42]Ezra Townsend Cresson, a native of Philadelphia, was one of the leading nineteenth- and early twentieth-century authorities on Hymenoptera. After attending public schools, he worked first as a railway clerk and then in 1869 became associated with the Franklin Fire Insurance Company, which he served in executive positions until 1910. Cresson authored sixtyfive descriptive papers on North American Hymenoptera and was a prominent and active member of several American entomological societies. His personal collection of Hymenoptera, numbering over 85,000 specimens, was given to the American Entomological Society in 1901. He remained an active naturalist until his death in 1926. *The National Cyclopaedia of American Biography* (New York: James T. White & Company, 1933), 23: 225-226.

[43]Cyrus Thomas, known both as an entomologist and as an archeologist, was born at Kingsport, Tennessee, in 1825. Having studied in schools and

academies in eastern Tennessee, in 1849 he moved to Illinois, where he practiced law and served as a local official. From 1869 to 1874 he was an entomologist and botanist for the Geological Survey of the Territories under F. V. Hayden, from 1874 to 1876 taught at the newly opened Southern Illinois Normal University, and from 1876 to 1882 served as the Illinois State Entomologist. In 1882 he became archeologist to the Bureau of American Ethnology, devoting his latter years to the study of North American Indians and their prehistory. *The National Cyclopaedia of American Biography* (New York: James T. White & Company, 1906), 13: 528-529.

[44]For the standard study of the geology of Texas, including the Panhandle region, see E. H. Sellards, W. S. Atkins, and F. B. Plummer, *The Geology of Texas: Stratigraphy*, University of Texas Bulletin No. 3232 (Austin: University of Texas, 1932); E. H. Sellards and C. L. Baker, *The Geology of Texas: Structural and Economic Geology*, University of Texas Bulletin No. 3401 (Austin: University of Texas, 1934); and F. B. Plummer, Gayle Scott, Carl O. Dunbar, and John W. Skinner, *The Geology of Texas: Upper Paleozoic Ammonites and Fusulinids*, University of Texas Bulletin No. 3701 (Austin: University of Texas, 1937). For an account of the geology of the Palo Duro Canyon alone, see H. Charles Hood and James R. Underwood, Jr., "Geology of the Palo Duro Canyon," *Panhandle-Plains Historical Review* 51 (1978): 3-34.

[45]This site is identified in note 22.

[46]For a modern geologist's explanation of the formation of the Palo Duro Canyon, see William A. Matthews, III, *The Geologic Story of Palo Duro Canyon*, University of Texas at Austin Bureau of Economic Geology, Guidebook 8 (Austin: The University of Texas at Austin, 1969), 29-32.

[47]*Reports of Explorations and Surveys, to Ascertain the Most Practicable and Economical Route for a Railroad from the Mississippi River to the Pacific Ocean*, U. S., Congress, Senate Executive Document 78, 33 Cong., 2 Sess. (Washington, D. C.: Beverley Tucker Printer, 1856), 3, part 4: 19-25 and geology plate I.

[48]For a clear examination of the confusion of nineteenth-century geologists concerning the dating of strata in the Texas Panhandle and eastern New Mexico, see Barry S. Kues, "Early Geological Explorations in Northeastern and East-Central New Mexico, "*New Mexico Geological Society Thirty-Sixth Annual Field Conference, September 26-28, 1985, Santa RosaTucumcari Region*, ed. Spencer G. Lucas and Jiri Zidek (Socorro, N. M.: New Mexico Geological Society, 1985), 103118.

[49]Marcy and McClellan, *Exploration of the Red River.*

[50]Othniel Charles Marsh was one of the most noted paleontologists of nineteenth-century America. Born at Lockport, New York, in 1831, he studied at Yale University and at the universities of Berlin, Heidelberg, and Breslau in Germany. In 1866 he filled the Chair of Paleontology at Yale University, the first such position in America. Marsh secured from his uncle, George Peabody, $150,000 for the establishment of the Peabody Museum of Natural History at Yale, and for much of his life he was associated with that institution. As a paleontologist Marsh devoted much of his life

to collecting and studying fossil remains from the western United States, and he identified hundreds of theretofore unknown species. He died at New Haven in 1899. Charles Schuehert and Clare Mae Levene, *O. C. Marsh: Pioneer in Paleontology* (New Haven: Yale University Press, 1940). No record has been located to indicate that Marsh either received or identified the fossils sent to him.

[51]F. B. Meek, *A Report on the Invertebrate Cretaceous and Tertiary Fossils of the Upper Missouri Country,* Report of the United States Geological Survey of the Territories 9 (Washington, D. C.: Government Printing Office, 1876), 16-18 and plates 10-11.

[52]*Reports of Explorations and Surveys,* 99-100 and geology plate I.

[53]Marcy and McClellan, *Exploration of the Red River,* 188-215 and zoology plates 1-11.

[54]The saloon mentioned probably was the Opera House Saloon, owned by James H. "Dog" Kelley, one of the mayors of Dodge City. Kelley received his nickname from his large pack of hounds, which he raced for both pleasure and profit. Robert R. Dykstra, *The Cattle Towns* (New York: Alfred A. Knopf, 1968), 215-216, 219-220, 264-268; Ida Ellen Rath, *Early Ford County* (North Newton, Kans.: Mennonite Press, 1964), 35, 65, 174.

[55]The 5th Cavalry Band, with its headquarters at Fort Leavenworth, had already visited Fort Dodge, Kansas before moving to Camp Supply for a few days at that post. *The Leavenworth Daily Times,* 12 May 1876, 2.

[56]For accounts of Fort Elliott, Texas, which existed as a military post from 1875 to 1890, see M. L. Crimmins, "Notes on the Establishment of Fort Elliott and the Buffalo Wallow Fight," *Panhandle-Plains Historical Review* 25 (1952): 45-69; and James M. Oswald, "History of Fort Elliott," *PanhandlePlains Historical Review* 32 (1959): 1-59.

[57]The "Record of Events" in the post returns at Fort Elliott noted that on 6 May 1876 Lt. Ruffner and his party with an eight-man cavalry escort arrived at the post. U. S., Department of War, Army, Fort Elliott, Texas, Post Returns, May 1876, National Archives.

[58]The "upper town" discussed here was the successor to an earlier settlement on Sweetwater Creek, Hide Town. Known as Sweetwater, from the stream, at one time it had three saloons and a dance hall, but after Fort Elliott was established the business houses shifted location to another site nearer to the post, the site of Old Mobeetie today. Sallie B. Harris, *Hide Town in the Texas Panhandle* (Hereford, Tex.: Pioneer Book Publishers, Inc., 1968), 40-41.

[59]The "Record of Events" in the post returns at Fort Elliott noted that on 11 May 1876 the surveying party under the command of Lt. Ruffner departed the post "for H'dwaters Red River Tex." Fort Elliott Post Returns, May 1876.

[60]William Dixon, born in West Virginia in 1850, came to the west as an adolescent and during the 1870's became a buffalo hide hunter operating out of Dodge City, Kansas. After the 27 June 1874 Battle of Adobe Walls,

Dixon became a civilian scout for the U. S. Army. He died in Cimarron County, Oklahoma, in 1913. Olive King Dixon, "Early Days in Hutchinson County," *Frontier Times* 5 (April 1928), 316-317; Olive King Dixon, *Life and Adventures of "Billy" Dixon of Adobe Walls, Texas Panhandle,* ed. Frederick S. Barde (Guthrie, Okla.: Co-Operative Publishing Company, 1914); Mrs. Sam Isaacs, "Billy Dixon: Pioneer Plainsman," *Frontier Times* 16 (June 1939), 372-374.

[61]The cantonment mentioned here is the U. S. Army cantonment on what today is called Cantonment Creek, occupied by Major James Biddle and troops of the 6th Cavalry from February to May 1875 before the establishment of Fort Elliott. Oswald, "Fort Elliott," 3-4.

[62]This campsite was just northwest of the present-day town of Lefors.

[63]The Wilson noted as a guide for the surveying party was in all probability Lemnot I. Wilson, a former Kansas buffalo hide hunter who became a civilian scout for the U. S. Army during the 1874-75 Red River Indian Campaign. For traces of his life, see Frank D. Baldwin, Diary Transcript for 19-20 August 1874, MS, ca. 20 February 1890, "Adobe Walls" vertical file, historical files, Boot Hill Museum, Inc., Dodge City, Kansas; J. Wright Mooar, Snyder, Texas, to Andy Johnson, Dodge City, Kan[sas], 20 January 1923, MS, Andrew Johnson Papers, historical files, Boot Hill Museum, Inc.; J. Wright Mooar, "Buffalo Days," ed. James Winford Hunt, *Holland's, the Magazine of the South* 52 (February 1933): 10, 44; and *ibid.,* 52 (March 1933): 28.

[64]For accounts of the attack on the German family on 13 September 1874 and the rescue of Adelaide and Julia German by troops led by Lt. Frank D. Baldwin on 8 November 1874, see James L. Haley, *The Buffalo War: The History of the Red river Indian Uprising of 1874* (Garden City, N. Y.: Doubleday & Company, Inc., 1976), 143-146, 192-194; William H. Leckie, *The Military Conquest of the Southern Plains* (Norman: University of Oklahoma Press, 1963), 227-228; and Grace E. Meredith, *Girl Captives of the Cheyennes: A True Story of the Capture and Rescue of Four Pioneer Girls 1874* (Los Angeles: Gem Publishing Company, 1927), 1-123.

[65]Hunnius here refers to the flight of the Comanches after the 28 September 1874 Battle of the Palo Duro Canyon, in which Col. Ranald Slidell Mackenzie led U.S. troops against a large portion, if not the majority, of the Comanches then hostile. For accounts of the fight, see R. G. Carter, *On the Border with Mackenzie or Winning West Texas from the Comanches* (Washington, D. C.: Eynon Printing Company, Inc., 1935), 488-495; Haley, *Buffalo War,* 178-182; and Leckie, *Military Conquest,* 220-222.

[66]The Quitaque Mountains are several hills near the Quitaque Canyon in southeastern Briscoe County, an area of Comanchero trading with the Plains Indians for many years preceeding 1876. Kenner, *New Mexico-Plains Indian Relations,* 162-163.

[67]The "Record of Events" in the post returns at Fort Elliott confirms that "Lieut. Ruffner[']s surveying party and escort . . . left for Camp Supply I. T. on the 23rd." Fort Elliott Post Returns, June 1876.

[68]This original tintype photograph, reproduced in this book, is today preserved as item, RH, MS, 153:3.1a in the Carl Julius Adolph Hunnius Collection at the Kansas Collection, Spencer Research Library, University of Kansas, Lawrence, Kansas.

[69]For an account of the activities of W. M. D. Lee and Albert E. Reynolds as traders and contractors to the U. S. Army, see Donald F. Schofield, "W. M. D. Lee, Indian Trader," *Panhandle-Plains Historical Review* 54 (1981): 1113.

[70]The main party headed by Lt. Ruffner returned to Fort Leavenworth on 30 June 1876. *The Leavenworth Daily Times* (Leavenworth, Kans.), 1 July 1876, 4.

ATLAS OF

SURVEY of the HEAD WA

CON

First Lieutenant E. H

CHIEF ENGINEER DEF

MAY

AIL SHEETS

E

RS, RED RIVER, TEXAS

D BY

er, Corps of Engineers

NT OF THE MISSOURI

UNE

17 Sheets.
July 23. 1877

R o l l i

Rolling Prairie.

Sand Hills

Rolling Prairie.

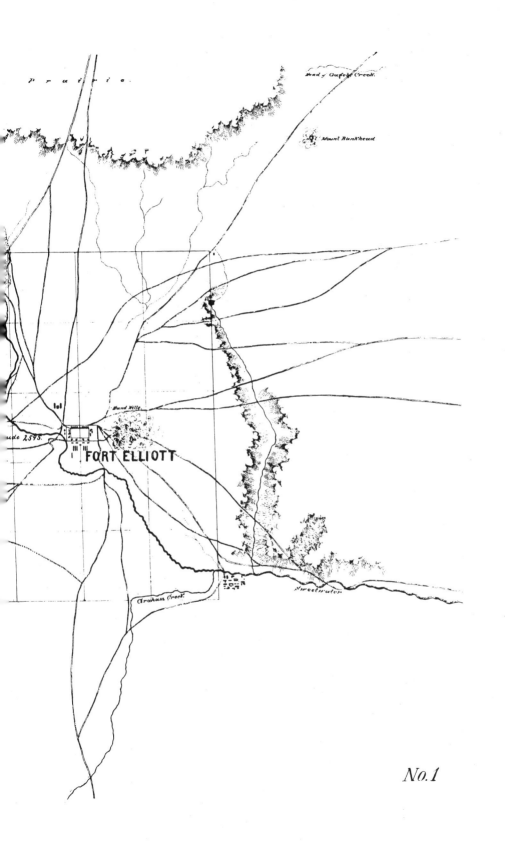

No.1

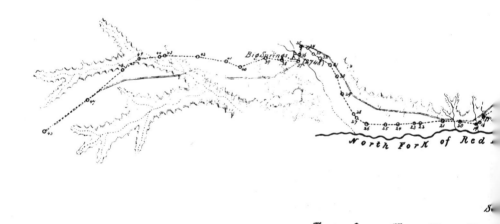

Big Springs Pass
(2740)

North Fork of Red

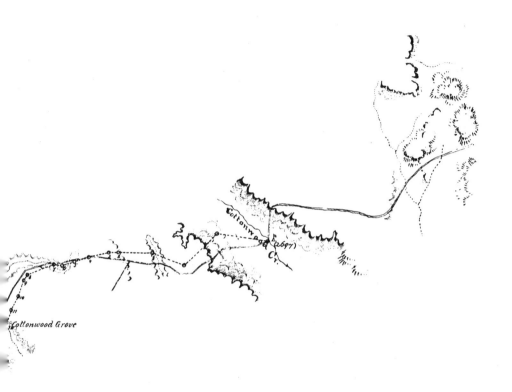

Cottonwood Cr.(1697)

Cottonwood Grove

rds

es

No.2

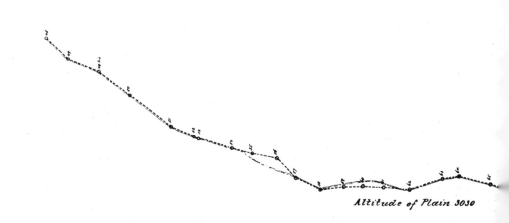

Altitude of Plain 3030

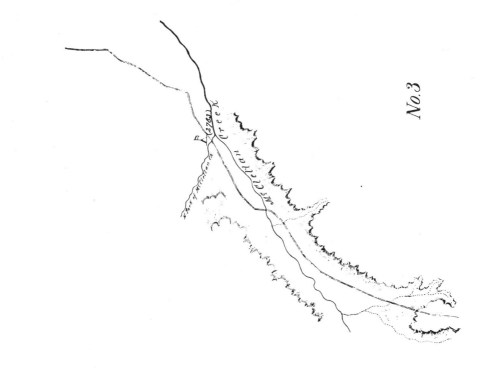

No.3

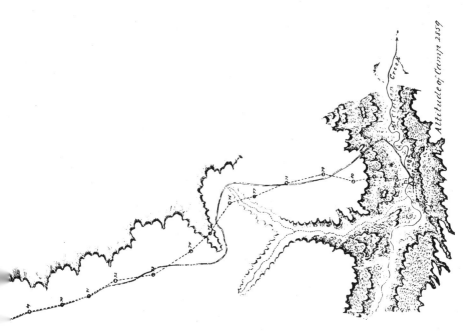

Altitude of Plain 3030

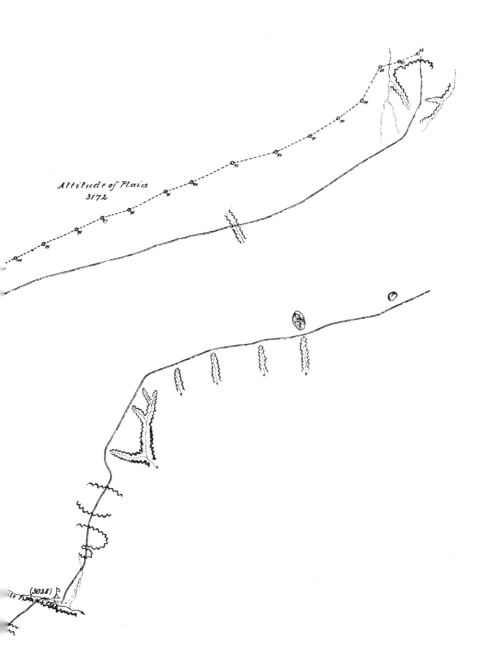

Altitude of Plain
3172

(3026)

No. 4

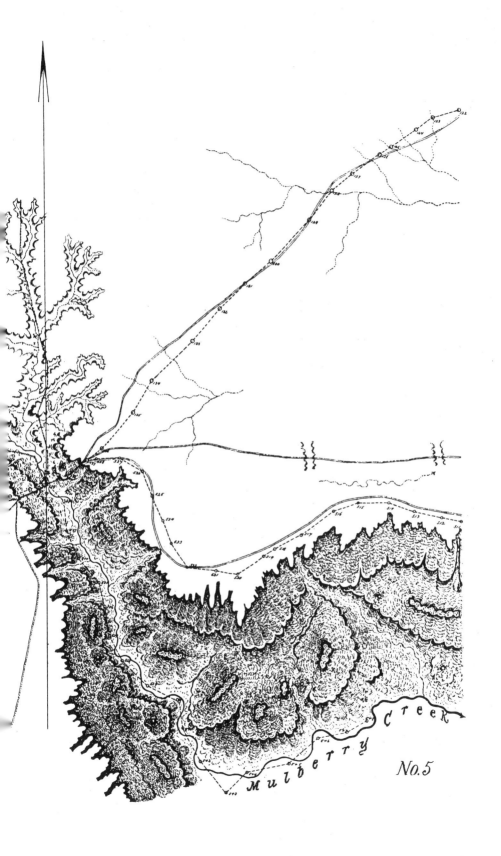

No.5

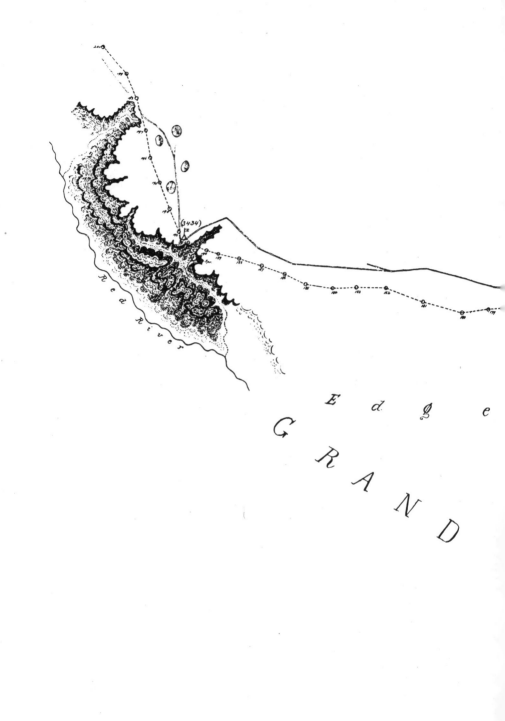

Red River

(1434)

E d g e

G R A N D

No.6

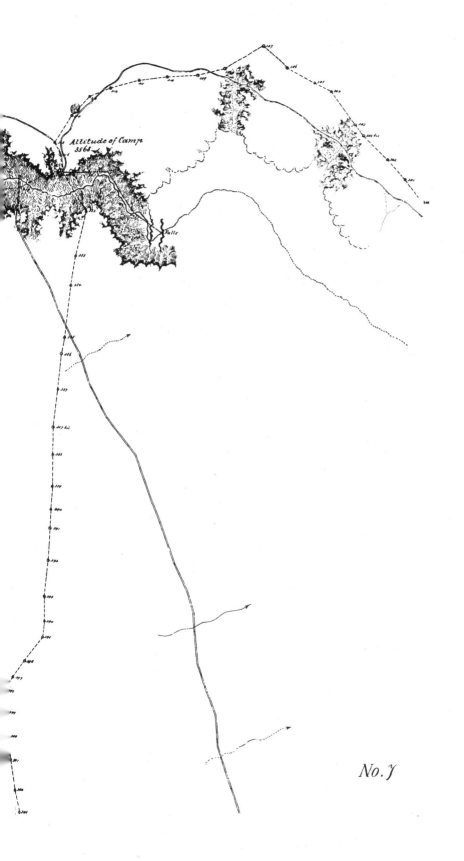

Altitude of Camp
3568

Falls

No. 7

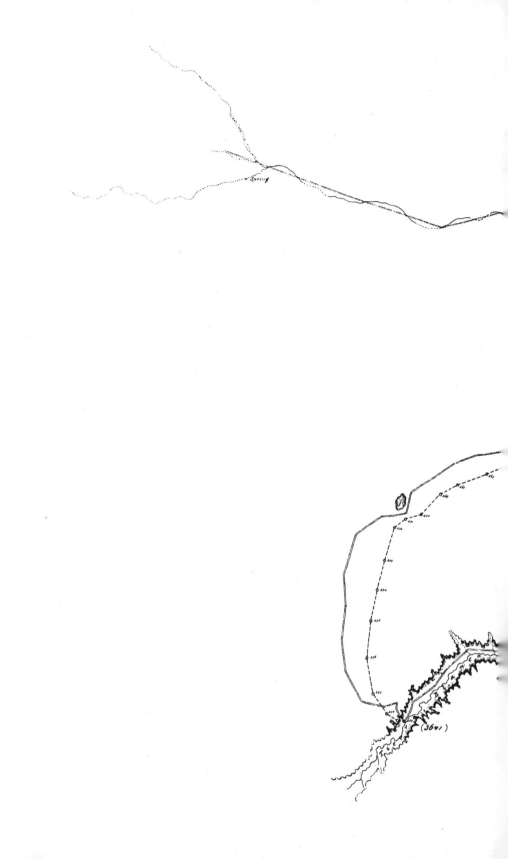

Spring

(3641)

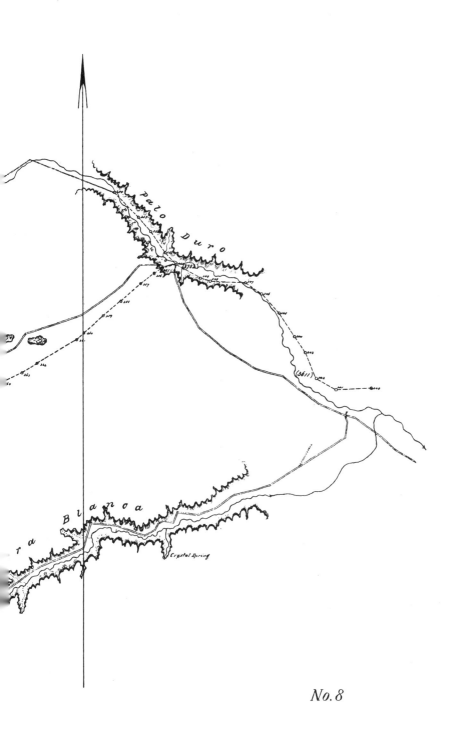

Palo Duro

ra Blanoa

Crystal Spring

No. 8

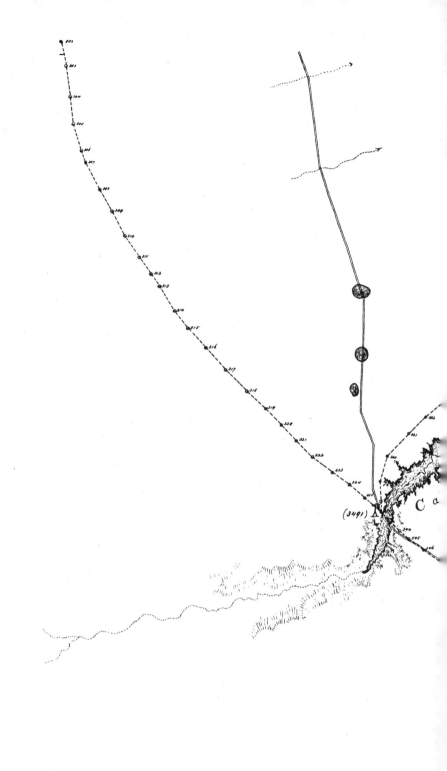

to Blanco

No. 9

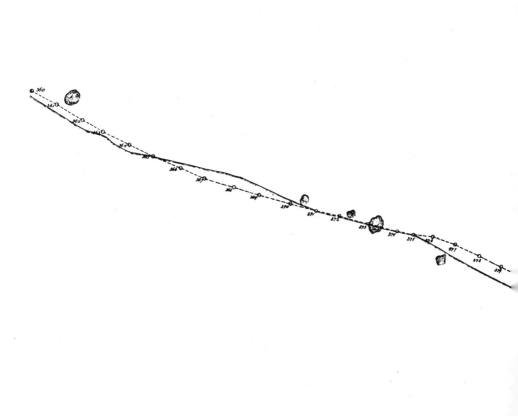

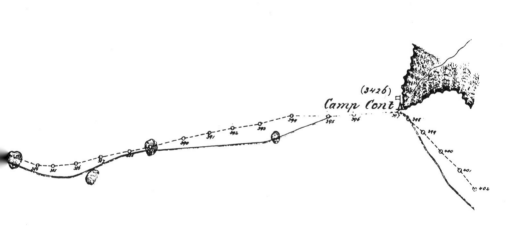

(3426)

Camp Cont

No. 10

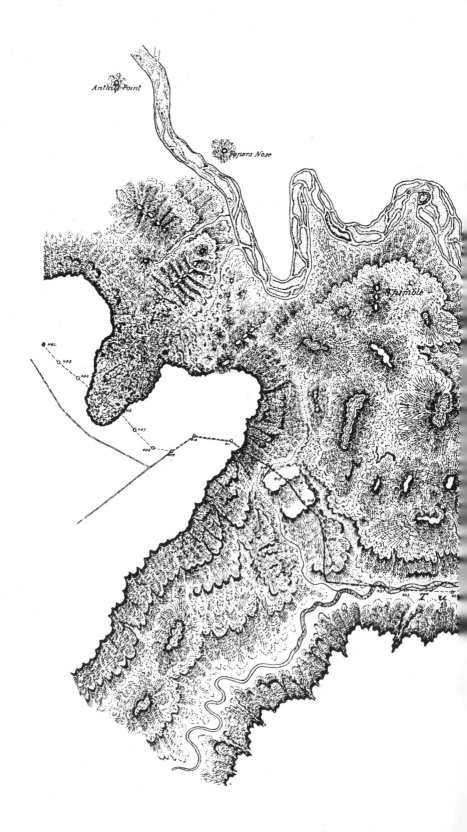

Anthill Point

Papers Nose

Thimble

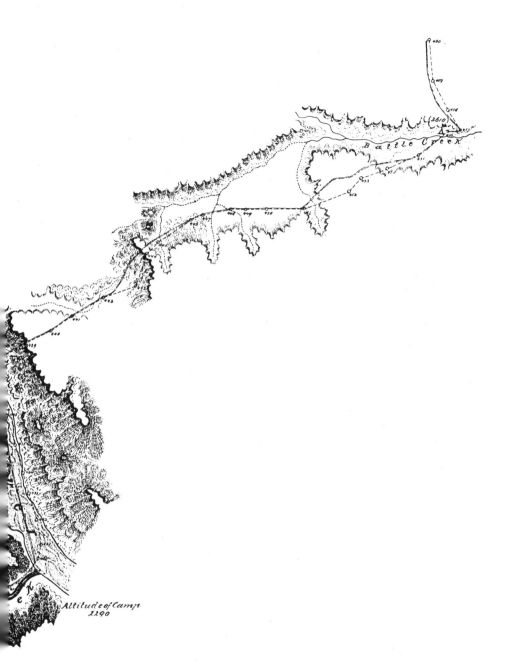

Battle Creek

(2610)

Altitude of Camp.
2290

No. 11

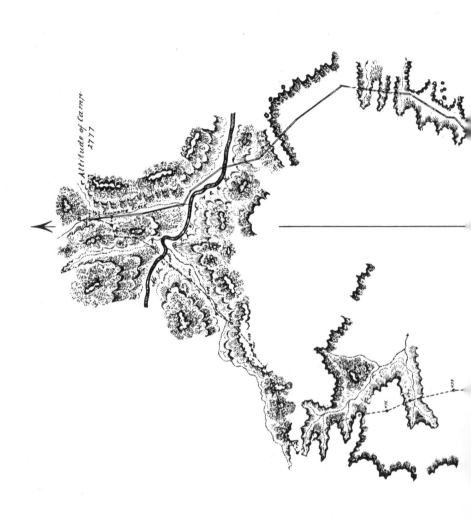

Altitude of Camp. 2777

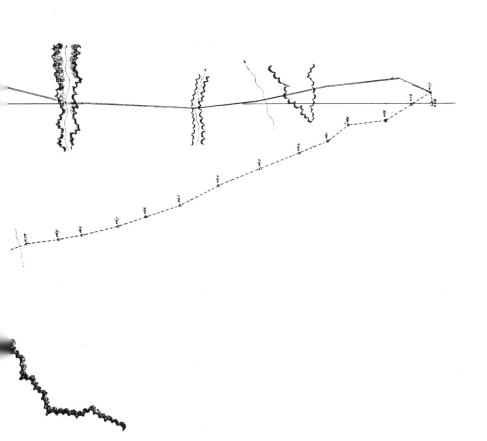

No.12

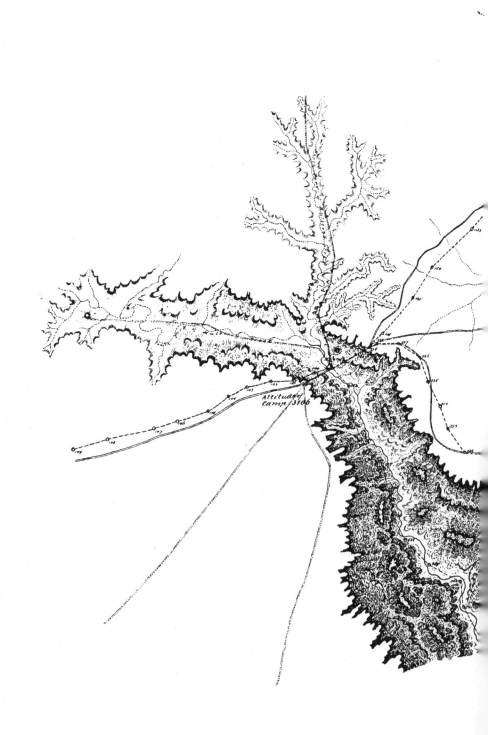

Altitude
Camp 3106

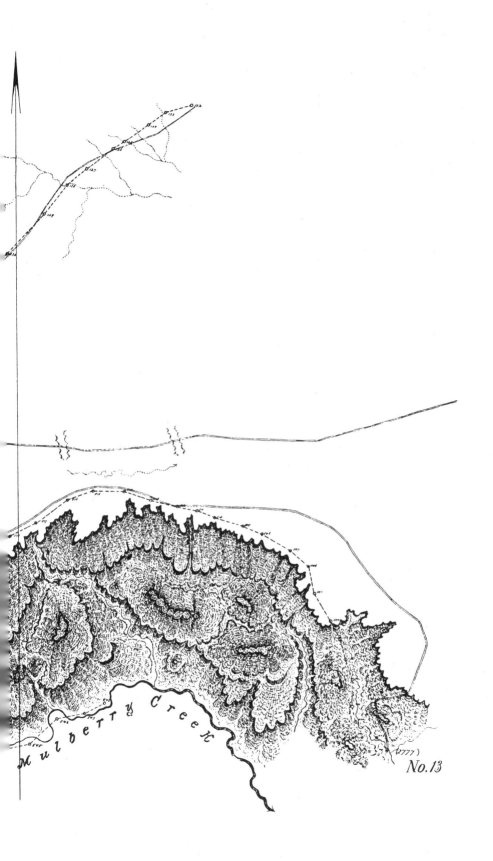

Mulberry Creek

No.13

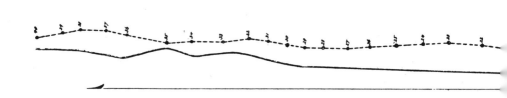

Dry Lake

(3566) PERMANENT CAMP ON RED RIVER.

Altitude of River
3254 Canadian River

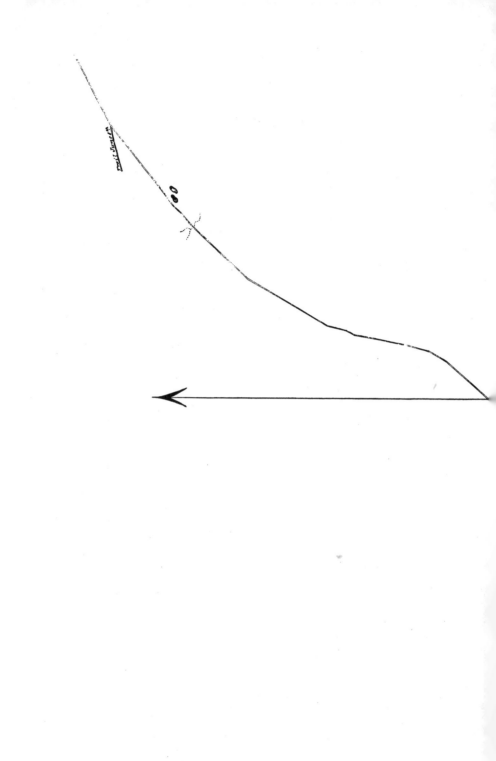

PRISMATIC COMPASS RECONNAISSANCE

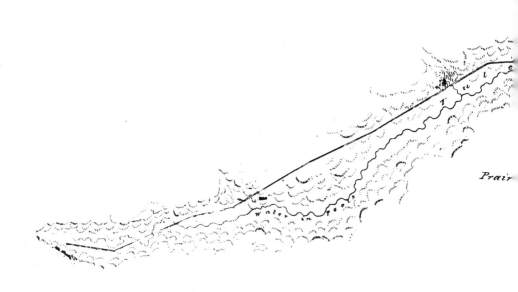

Water in pools

Tule

Prair

PRISMATIC COM

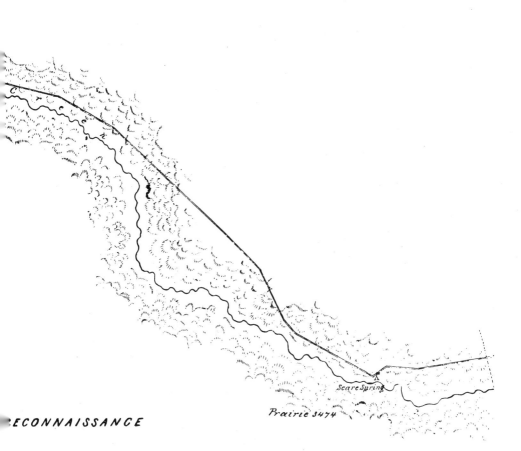

ECONNAISSANCE

Scare Spring

Prairie 3474

No.17

Personne

1st Lieut. E.H. Ruffner Corps of Engineers, in
1st Lieut. F.D. Baldwin 5th Infantry. In comme
2d Lieut. C.A.H. McCauley 3d Artillery, Ornitholog
2d Lieut. T.M.Woodruff 5th Infantry, Natural Histo
Ado Hunnius. Draughtsman, Assistant on Stadia Ti,
Sergt. C.A. Lichtenberg Co. II Engineers. Prismatic Con

Detail Sheets drawn by Lieut. T.M.Woodruff, Sergt. C

Table of Distances, Latitudes a

Stations	Distance in Yards	Latitude N. +		− S. E.	Departure +		−	W.	Stations	Distance in Yards	N.
South Base to 3	4.746		1822.6			4360.0		180	7052		
3 to 2	3.357	1161.8				3140.5		190	7061	10
2 to 5	7.740		1940.6			7484.5		200	6382	5.
5 to 7	4.403		2977.4			6450.0		210	8780	32
7 to 0	1.452		459.5			866.1		217	4590	
0 to 9 Station	918	322.2				189.4	252 to 290	9220		
10	3588		1077.5			3448.6		300	6409	
20	4203		2656.			2643.		310	6637	
30	3858	1121.				3269.6		320	6167	
40	2971	235.5				2471.3		324	3376	
50	9254		3566.			6574.	344 to 350	4405		
60	6840		6163.			2372.5		360	7784	
70	7155		6916.	576.				370	6757	
80	5769		4699	3190.5		2854.		380	5909	
90	5503		3529.					390	5933	
100	9716		3733.			6939.		400	6581	
110	7613		3262.			6464.		410	6431	
120	6419		2767.			5682.		420	6196	
130	7427		4241.			5928.5		430	6030	10
134	8182		5577.			5863.		440	6926	5
156	8604		2619.			8205.		450	7011	5
160	7011		1736.			6717.		460	8309	4
170	7231	1020.5				7196.		470	9535	5

...Expedition

...Stadia Line, Astronomy, Geology, Water Color Sketches

...Escort.

...cimens and Assistant in topography

...tions, Assistant on Stadia Line.

...with Meteorological Record

...ne, Meteorological Record

...rberg & Private H. Hartmann Co. C. 4th Cavalry

...artures.   Summary by tens.

	Departure				Distances	Latitude			Departure	
S. E.	+	−	W.	Stations	in Yards	N. +	−	S. E. +		− W.
		7048.	480	8066	7314.5				1809.
		6850.	490	5127	2640.		4128.		
		2895.	500	4984	3963.		773.		
		8999.	510	6647	4852.			3657.
...5		3328.	520	6856		1129.5		6335.
...		450.	531	6507	2316.			4900
...		1304.	328 to 343	Line down Colorado Canon 10544	5569.		7061.	
...	1834.		218 to 229	7649		5252.		3533.
...	3933.		240	8117		474.		
...	2573.5		250	7376	3434			2763
...	3451.		260	3451		4.		2710.
...	6077.		270	7671		3538.		663.
...	6160.5		280	6749		5669.		379.
...	5560.		10	6493	6432			533
...	5594.		20	6432	6103		1376.	
...	6006.5		30	6074	6656.		161.	
...	4753.5		40	6629	6464.		256.	
	4324.		50	7656	7240.			2403.
	5498.5		60	7945	6785.			3403.
	235.		70	5430	4277.			931.5
	5694.		75	7703	302.		6100	
	4203							
		3177.5						

NOTES ON THE ORNITHOLOGY OF THE REGION ABOUT THE SOURCE OF THE RED RIVER OF TEXAS, FROM OBSERVATIONS MADE DURING THE EXPLORATION CONDUCTED BY LIEUT. E. H. RUFFNER, CORPS OF ENGINEERS, U. S. A.

By C. A. H. McCauley,
Lieutenant Third United States Artillery.

Annotated by Dr. Elliott Coues, U. S. A.

LETTER OF TRANSMITTAL

Reading, Pa., July 29, 1876.

Sir: I have the honor to transmit herewith a copy of a report originally rendered to Lieut. E. H. Ruffner, Corps of Engineers, U. S. A., Chief Engineer of the Department of the Missouri, and also intended for publication in the Proceedings of an Eastern academy of science. Its appearance having been unavoidably delayed, the article is now offered for publication by the Survey with which you are connected, or for such other use as you may see fit to make of it; and I shall esteem it as a favor if you will assume the editorship of the paper.

In transmitting the following Notes upon the Ornithology of the region where were found the true sources of the Red River of Texas, and of the country traversed *en route,* it may be well to add a few prefatory remarks. Being on sick-leave in Southern New Mexico in March, 1876, and having made an application to the War Department for duty with the expedition, with the hope of improving my health, and having already joined the expedition when the application was disapproved, I continued as a volunteer. Though my duties mainly related to the survey proper, an effort was made, after each day's work and march had ended, to obtain and prepare as many specimens as possible, in order to gain some idea of the avi-fauna of the country. With very limited time, subsequently restricted by recurrence of sickness, my collection was necessarily meagre. This is the more to be regretted, since, as far as recollection serves me, a portion of the region surveyed had never before been visited in the interests of ornithology. [Marcy's well-known report on the Red River, covering the ground only in part, contains no ornithological matter among the several zöological papers which it comprises. — Ed. (Elliott Coues)]n

Leaving the railroad at Dodge City (five miles from Fort Dodge), Kansas, on the Arkansas River, longitude 100°, the route was by long marches to Camp Supply, Indian Territory, east of south, distant ninety-one miles, and thence to Fort Elliott, Texas, a new post on the Sweetwater, west of South, ninety-three miles distant, the latter, at which point the survey commenced, being less than fifteen minutes west of the meridian of Dodge City. South from Dodge, the road is over the characteristic western prairie, crossing the Cimarron River near the State line and the north fork of the Canadian above Supply, and below it Wolf Creek, along which the road runs for several miles, the Canadian itself, and the Washita River. Starting from Fort Elliott, from which we were absent but six weeks (during which time over 600 miles were traveled), returning June 22, the general course was southwest, striking the Red River about 100 miles distant, the main intermediate waters touched being north fork of Red River and its

Camp in Mulberry Creek, Texas, 17 and 18 May 1876.

main tributary, McClellan Creek, the Salt Fork, a branch called White Fish Creek, and Mulberry Creek, all emptying into the main river. Thence the scene of operations was that part of the Staked Plain (Llano Estacado) embraced between longitude 100°30' to 102° and latitude 34° to 35°30'. The surface of the great plain, the elevation of which is 4,000 feet above the sea, is one unvarying level, "flat beyond comparison," without an object on which to rest the eye of the traveler. The vegetation consists of short gramma-grass, here lower than usual, in accord with its desert surrounding, whilst at long intervals appears a small "soap-weed" *(Yucca angustifolia)*, so called from the use made of it by the natives in New and Old Mexico, or a prickly-pear cactus *(Opuntia mis-*

souriensis), both existing here in a dwarfed or depauperate condition compared with their size in more favored situations in the same or a higher latitude.

The sources of the Red River are two streams, the Tierra Blanca and Palo Duro, which, after their union, bear the river's name. Wearing for themselves, after proceeding a score or more of miles, deep beds by cutting through the resisting strata, these cañons are truly oases in the general surrounding waste.

The streams in their upper parts have fertile banks, with gently rolling land, which, covered with succulent grasses, are the famed resort of wild animals, timber-fringed everywhere, sparsely above, below more freely, with the trees of greater size and frequency. Birds are more frequently seen along these streams than elsewhere, the avi-fauna here finding its best expression.

In crossing the very barren Staked Plain, we miss even the dog-villages, so characteristic of the prairies, and consequently find no Burrowing Owls *(Speotyto cunicularia hypogoea Coues)*. In the rainy season, the slightest depressions of the surface, almost unnoticed by the ordinary traveler, become filled with water. Without these water-holes, the journey across the barren waste would be hazardous or impossible.

Many years ago, the Mexican scouts affirm a passage practicable in the rainy season from San Antonio to Santa Fé was staked out by some Mexicans, whence came the name "Llano Estacado," or Staked Plain. No stakes have ever been found by early or late explorers, but the tradition remains, and the name of that section has become established. It was after a heavy rain that the crossing from Fort Bascom, New Mexico, was safely made by General Gregg and his command in 1872.[o] Their longest march between water was 30 miles, a wearisome trip, indeed, with no living thing of any kind or nature in sight. How invaluable are the services of a guide on such an occasion may well be imagined. On encamping at water-holes, we found great numbers of birds, undoubtedly temporarily attracted by the water's presence. In the vicinity of the cañons, in which were the streams tributary to the Red River, the edge of the plain is cut up by short side-cañons, worn by the drainage during many successive rainy seasons. These are familiarly known as the "breaks" by the scouts, and are recognizable at great distances by the *mirages* that can be seen hanging above them. In the immediate vicinity on "breaks," and on short lines some miles away, are found the Southwestern Larks *(Eremophila alpestris chrysoloema)* in great numbers and Western Night Hawks *(Chordeiles virginianus henryi)* in abundance, and the only species I noticed venturing out upon the desert. No transition could be greater than that from the general level of the plain to the bottom of the cañons. The edges are steep and rocky, and the crossing by train often impossible save at long intervals. In these cañons, nature almost completely hides the streams with luxuriant vegetation, as if to make amends for her barrenness above, and fills the trees with life and song. As the streams descend, their cañon-beds gradually enlarge to that of the main stream, which at some places is several miles broad with a depth of 800 feet, whilst the river-bed itself is not over 500 yards wide. Seen from the plain above, the course of the river looks like a huge ribbon of white, incrusted as it is with alkali, glistening and reflecting hot rays. As the water, pure above, in its downward course passes over the gypsum strata, it becomes strongly impregnated. Among the species observed in such places were the Carolina Dove *(Zenaidura carolinenis)*, Killdeer *(Aegialitis vocifera)*, Mockingbird *(Mimus polyglottus)*, and a few Quail *(Ortyx virginiana)*. At long intervals are found, at the

View south from the cliff behind the camping place on Mulberry Creek, with Palo Duro Canyon shown in the distance, 17 May 1876.

head of some side cañon leading up from the main stream, little rills gushing out from near the summit of the plain, hundreds of feet above, looking like mountain-brooks as they descend, tumbling over rocks in mimic falls, with the water fresh and sparkling, all to be lost a mile or two from its source, sunken in the sand before reaching the river below. The localities in which the collector is best repaid for his pains are the upper parts of the Palo Duro, Tierra Blanca, and the lower and well-wooded portions of streams of good water, before they empty into the main river, such as the North Fork, McClellan and Mulberry Creeks, etc.

Should the paucity of species as presented in the report be deemed notable, it should be borne in mind that, owing to my extremely limited time and facilities, undoubtedly quite a number escaped attention; and that, owing to lack of any appropriation for such purpose, the expedition was without means for collecting specimens during a part of the trip; and that, after the necessary materials had been purchased with private funds, my arrangements were not complete until the arrival of a supply-train, June 2, our return to Fort Elliott being nineteen days later.

Besides the species herewith tabulated, my collection embraces a number of embryos and other alcoholic preparations. The classification and nomenclature adopted are those of your "Key to North American Birds".p [I make a few changes, with the author's permission, at my discretion.—Ed.] I have to acknowledge your kind assistance in identifying some of the specimens collected, and also the courteous attention received from Assistant Surgeon T. E. Wilcox,q United States Army, during the preparation of my report,

I am, Sir, with great respect, your obedient servant,

C. A. H. McCAULEY,

Lieutenant Third United States Artillery.

Asst. Surg. Elliott Coues, U. S. A.,

Secretary U. S. Geological and Geographical Survey.

TURDIDAE.

TURDUS MIGRATORIUS, L. — *Robin*.[1]

Though none were observed at headwaters in the Staked Plain, they were common along the wooden lower parts of streams, but lacking that friendliness they acquire on long acquaintance in populated districts. At ranches along the route and at the Army posts visited, they are upon the same terms of sociability as elsewhere in settled country.

MIMUS POLYGLOTTUS, (L.) Boie. — *Mockingbird*.[2]

All the timber-fringed streams, including those passed *en route* to and

[1] American Robin. *Turdus migratorius* Linnaeus. The American Robin is more common today as a breeding species than formerly. Its increased presence is a direct result of human settlement, for the planting of trees and shrubs in towns and around ranches and farms provided the necessary habitat requirements for nesting. T. V. and Luella Reeves, in "Birds Seen in the Panhandle of Texas, 1914, and Thereafter" (MS, West Texas University Library, Canyon), speak of robins rarely breeding in Canyon until "trees, shrubs, and lawns and available water increased," at which time it became more common. Even as late as 1945, Arthur Stuart Hawkins, in "Bird Life of the Texas Panhandle," *Panhandle-Plains Historical Review* 18 (1945):142-143, suggested that the species only occasionally nested. Although McCauley does not speak of finding nests, some of the birds he observed around ranches and Army posts were probably nesting, as the robin begins its nesting cycle in mid or late April.

[2] Northern Mockingbird. *Mimus polyglottos* (Linnaeus). There has been little change in the status of this bird, except that today, instead of being limited to the "timber-fringed streams," it has taken up residence around human habitations and on the plains where there are mesquite trees.

returning from Fort Elliott, Texas, and particularly Wolf Creek and the "Dry Washita," were melodious with the notes of this magnificent songster. At times it was exceedingly shy, especially when, perched on a low bush or sunflower-stalk, it discovered that it was being approached. On other occasions, the bird would allow an approach to within a few yards, and, continuing its song, occasionally jump into the air, fluttering its wings, and then alight upon the same twig. The songs were as varied and beautiful as those noted some years ago in the Carolinas and Georgia, and the birds were at places more numerous.

TABLE 1

Number of Collection.	Sex.	Locality.	Date.	Collector.	Collector's Name.	Length.	Extent.	Wing.	Tail.	Remarks.
11	♀ juv.	Red River Cañon	May 23	McCauley	186	9	13	4.2	4.5	Stomach con-
20	♂ ad.	Palo Duro	May 28	do	195	10	13	4.5	4.75	tained beetles,
24	— —	Red River	May 30	Sullivan	—	—	—	——	——	etc.
43	♂ ad.	White Fish Creek	June 19	McCauley	216	10	13	4.25	4.5	

A large number of nests were seen and examined, and in most instances left, as either the young were hatched or the embryos were very far advanced.

TABLE 2

Number of Collection.	Locality.	Date.	Collector.	Nests.	Eggs.	Remarks.
10	Cañoncito Blanco	June 6	Ruby	—	1	Two young in nest.
11	do	do	McCauley	1	2	
17	Battle Creek	June 13	Ruby	1	4	
28	White Fish Creek	June 19	McCauley	1	3	
29	do	June 20	do	—	1	Three young in nest.

SYLVIIDAE.

REGULUS CALENDULA, (L.) Licht.—*Ruby-crowned Kinglet.*[3]

A few individuals observed along the Washita and Canadian, evidently migrating.

REGULUS SATRAPA, Licht.—*Golden-crested Kinglet.*[4]

The only one of this species noted as at Cañoncito Blanco, June 4.

[3]Ruby-crowned Kinglet. *Regulus calendula* (Linnaeus). The Kinglet is still today a common migrant throughout the area. McCauley probably saw it on the outward journey, as it is normally not found later than the second or third week of May.

[4]Golden-crowned Kinglet. *Regulus satrapa* Lichtenstein. The surprising thing about this sighting is the late date, June 4. Thirty or more years of record keeping by members of the Texas Panhandle Audubon Society disclose the latest date of observation as 25 April, and rarely is it even reported past March. The site of the observation, Cañoncito Blanco (present-day Ceta Glen in southeastern Randall County) is an excellent place to observe it today in winter and migration. Probably the

TROGLODYTIDAE.

CATHERPES MEXICANUS CONSPERSUS, Ridgw.—*White-throated Wren.*[5]

Observed in the cañon region after a long day's ride over an alkali district. No water ever tasted as delicious as those fresh brooks that gush at intervals from the steep walls of the plain, to sink in the sand before reaching the river; and no singer's notes seemed brighter or more cheering than the warbling of this bird, which frequented these precipitous cañons, whose sides are thickly covered with cedars and undergrowth. This species was not observed elsewhere during the trip, but here it seemed particularly numerous.

The largest number of eggs observed in one nest was six.

TABLE 3

Number of Collection.	Locality.	Date.	Collector.	Nests.	Eggs.	Remarks.
32	Red River Cañon	June 12	McCauley	1	6	

ALAUDIDAE.

EREMOPHILA ALPESTRIS CHRYSOLAEMA, (Wagl.) Baird.—*Southwestern Lark.*[6]

This bright little songster was almost a constant companion in the daily surveys on the Staked Plain proper, being there especially noticeable and extremely abundant, and for a while numbers of nests were daily met with. Generally in company, flying to and fro in search of food, they showed but little signs of uneasiness, and allowed one to approach and pass unnoticed. One day, during a halt, the column happened to stop within a few yards of a bird upon her eggs, who, after flying to and fro in great solicitude, soon boldly approached, and resumed her place upon her nest with full confidence. The escort was directed to change its course to prevent riding over her, she meanwhile remaining as quiet as if she knew we were friends.

bird McCauley saw was an individual that opted not to make the journey to its nesting grounds in the western and northern parts of the continent.

5Canyon Wren. *Catherpes mexicanus* (Swainson). There has been no change in status. McCauley's lyrical description of its habitat and song is recognizable by anyone entering the canyonlands today.

6Horned Lark. *Eremophila alpestris* (Linnaeus). This is probably not as abundant a nesting species now as formerly because of widespread cultivation. Noteworthy in McCauley's account is the statement concerning the nests he found: "The usual number was five." This finding is contrary to that of later observers who speak of five eggs as the exception and three to four as the norm (Arthur Cleveland Bent, *Life Histories of North American Flycatchers, Larks, Swallows, and Their Allies* [1942; reprint, New York: Dover Publications, 1963], 173:325-356).

TABLE 4

Number of Collection.	Sex.	Locality.	Date.	Collector.	Collector's Name.	Length.	Extent.	Wing.	Tail.	Remarks.
10	♂ ad.	Staked Plain	May 20	McCauley	185	7	12.6	4.2	2.7	

With the whole surface of the plain unbroken in its clothing of short grass, and little to vary its monotonous vegetation save the Prickley-pear Cactus *(Opuntia missouriensis)* and Spanish Bayonet or "Soap-weed" *(Yucca angustifolia)*, the bird was limited in its nesting materials to the slender gramma-grass alone, of which its nest was built, concealed in a clump of unusual growth, the largest to be found, or beneath the shelter of a "Soap-weed." The usual number of eggs was five.

TABLE 5

Number of Collection.	Locality.	Date.	Collector.	Nests.	Eggs.	Remarks.
7	Staked Plains	June 2	McCauley	1	5	} Average 0.94
42	do	June 3	Ruffner	1	5	by 0.63 inches
43-49	do	June 4 to 10	McCauley	7	34	

SYLVICOLIDAE

PROTONOTARIA CITRAEA, (Bodd.) Bd. — *Prothonotary Warbler.*[7]

Frequenting Wolf Creek and the Canadian.

HELMITHERUS VERMIVORUS, (Gm.) Bp. — *Worm-eating Warbler.*[8]

Occasionally noted near the crossing of the Canadian.

[7]Prothonotary Warbler. *Protonotaria citrea* (Boddaert). Although his summation is terse, its implication is that the species was seen not too uncommonly. This is no longer the case as it has been reported in the Panhandle only four times since mid-century, with dates ranging from 29 April to 8 May (Texas Panhandle Audubon Society), all in Randall County. Today it is a rare to common summer resident in eastern Texas, west to about Tarrant and Brazos counties (Texas Ornithological Society, *Checklist of the Birds of Texas*, 2nd ed. [Austin: 1984], 111). In Oklahoma it breeds westward to Kay, Canadian, and Cleveland counties, with but few sightings west of there (George M. Sutton, *A Check-list of Oklahoma Birds* [Norman: Stovall Museum of Science & History, University of Oklahoma, 1974], 35).

[8]Worm-eating Warbler. *Helmitheros vermivorus* (Gmelin). What can be said of this species is much the same as in note 7 above. There have been only six reported sightings in the Panhandle since mid-century, five in Randall County and one in Hutchinson County (Texas Panhandle Audubon Society). It is a rare to uncommon summer resident in the Piney-Woods of east Texas, and it is rarely seen west of there in migration (T. O. S., *Checklist of Birds*, 111).

DENDROECA AESTIVA, (Gm.) Bd. — *Golden or Summer Warbler.*9

This bright, active songster was very common among the groves occurring near the upper part of Red River and heads of its tributaries, darting through the shrubbery, uttering its cheerful notes without cessation. The birds were nesting, and exhibited little or no shyness.

TABLE 6

Number of Collection.	Sex.	Locality.	Date.	Collector.	Collector's Name.	Length.	Extent.	Wing.	Tail.	Remarks.
5	♂ ad.	Mulberry Creek	May 17	McCauley	180	5	7½	2½	1½	Stomach contained small insects.
15	♀ ad.	Palo Duro	May 26	do	190	5	7¾	2⅓	1¾	
28	♂ ad.	Cañoncito Blanco	June 6	do	201	5	7¼	2½	1½	
54	♂ ad.	Cañoncito Blanco	June 6	do	227	5	7¼	2½	1½	

For beauty in constructing its home, this bird, as an architect, bore off the palm from all others whose nests were met with, No. 8 of the collection being particularly fine. As its European correspondent visits the farm to obtain the wool of the sheep and horse-hairs, so does this bird select the vicinity of the cottonwood grove to obtain the tree's cotton and near by the buffalo's wool, to build up and line, with the dexterity of a skilled weaver, the home for its young.

TABLE 7

Number of Collection.	Locality.	Date.	Collector.	Nests.	Eggs.	Remarks.
6	Red River Cañon	May 30	McCauley	1	3	Average 0.62 by 0.50 inch.
8	Cañoncito Blanco	June 3	Sullivan	1	2	

DEDROECA DOMINICA, (L.) Bd. — *Yellow-throated Warbler.*10

It is very probable that this species is not uncommon, though but few were noted in the localities of which *D. aestiva* seemed to have possession. More prevalent on Palo Duro than any other locality.

9Yellow Warbler. *Dendroica petechia* (Linnaeus). This is probably no longer a nesting species in the Panhandle, and certainly not where McCauley found his nests. The nest of 26 May along Palo Duro Creek, down-canyon from the expedition's Permanent Camp near present-day Lake Tanglewood, Randall County, is not far from the site of the last reported nesting in that area, which was the Palo Duro Club northeast of Canyon (10 June 1945) (Hawkins, "Bird Life", 144-145). The last reported nesting anywhere in the Panhandle was at Lake McClellan, Gray County, 23 June 1956 (Texas Panhandle Audubon Society). In recent years there have been scattered summer sightings in Hemphill and Lipscomb counties but with no confirmation of nesting. The species is still, however, a common migrant throughout the area.

10Yellow-throated Warbler. *Dendroica dominica* (Linnaeus). This is another unexpected observation, and one wonders if McCauley's identification is correct; latter-day observers have reported the species only five times since mid-century, with

ICTERIA VIRENS LONGICAUDA, (Lawr.) Coues. — *Long-tailed Chat.*[11]

Of all the streams that add to the volume of the Red River near its source, none are more pleasing than the Palo Duro at its head. The name signifies "hardwood," having been given to it by the Mexican hunters, who strike it far up in coming from New Mexico, in their journeys across the Staked Plain, to the buffalo hunting-grounds, or to the Indian reservations, for purposes of surreptitious trade in fire-water or arms. Fringed with brush-land [and] often high trees, with nutritious grass-land bordering it throughout, it is a favorite resort of various animals, and attractive to the hunter and naturalist. Here were found many Warblers, Thrushes, and Mockingbirds apparently engaged in rivalry of song, whilst the sprightly Scissor-tails darted to and fro, lording it even over the Kingbirds in the groves where they were neighbors. For a short distance, no place was found offering greater variety to the collector than this stream, which miles below its head passes through a beautiful cañon, from which it emerges to again wind through rolling country. Through here very abundant and more noticeable than elsewhere, this species inhabited the woodlands skirting the streams throughout nearly all the route. None, however, were observed in the regions strongly alkaline.

TABLE 8

Number of Collection.	Sex.	Locality.	Date.	Collector.	Collector's Name.	Length.	Extent.	Wing.	Tail.	Remarks.
21	♂ ad.	Palo Duro Creek	May 20	McCauley	196	7⅔	9⅔	3¼	3½	Stomachs contained chiefly *Coleoptera.*
22	♂	Red River Cañon	May 30	do	197	7½	9½	3¼	3¼	
33	♂	Mulberry Creek	June 15	do	206	7¾	9½	3⅛	3¼	
53	♂	Cañoncito Blanco	June 16	do	226	7¾	9	3¼	3¼	
56	♂	Palo Duro	June 17	do	229	7½	9	3¼	3¼	
57	♀	Palo Duro	June 17	do	230	7½	9⅓	3⅛	3¼	

dates ranging from 8 April to 3 May (Texas Panhandle Audubon Society). It is a rare to common summer resident in the eastern half of Texas, west to about Denton, Kerr, Bandera, and Victoria counties but is seldom reported west of there even in migration (T. O. S., *Checklist of Birds,* 109-110). Surprising as these reports of rare warbler species are, equally surprising is the absence of any mention of species that are common today and that one would expect McCauley to have seen: Orange-crowned Warbler *(Vermivora celata)*; Yellow-rumped Warbler *(Dendroica coronata)*; Common Yellowthroat *Geothlypis trichas)*; Wilson's Warbler *(Wilsonia pusilla).*

11Yellow-breasted Chat. *Icteria virens (Linnaeus).* One can only regret the disappearance of the wooded and brush-lined banks along the upper reaches of the Palo Duro and with them the removal of the chat as a nesting species. It is found there today only as a migrant, with an occasional summer sighting without confirmation of nesting. The habitat of these latter-day sightings is salt cedar stands *(Tamarix* sp.), an introduced shrub that has spread and become abundant since the Ruffner expedition (Robert A. Vines, *Trees, Shrubs, and Woody Vines of the Southwest* [Austin: University of Texas Press, 1960]: 760-761).

TANAGRIDAE.

PYRANGA AESTIVA, (L.) V. — *Summer Redbird.*[12]

Observed along Wolf Creek and the Canadian, always in pairs; too shy to permit me to secure specimens.

HIRUNDINIDAE.

HIRUNDO HORREORUM, Barton. — *Barn Swallow.*[13]

Frequenting settlements in Indian Territory; not as common as *P. lunifrons.*

PETROCHELIDON LUNIFRONS, (Say) Cab. — *Cliff or Eave Swallow.*[14]

A species very abundant in the cañon region of Red River and its tributaries. In descending a side-cañon leading down to the river, where the water only poured down in the rainy season, dashing over cliffs a hundred and at times three hundred feet high, I found occasionally the under side of the overhanging rocks covered with the mud nests of this species, curiously wrought and bottle-shaped as they often are. Some nests even then (the middle of May) contained young, whilst most of the other birds met with had scarcely as yet completed building. Also found building at ranches on the prairie near the streams.

COTYLE RIPARIA, (L.) Boie. — *Bank Swallow or Sand Martin.*[15]

Not uncommon along parts of Red River, where occasionally banks, of the most glaring red clay rise up perpendicularly for a hundred feet from the dry alkali bed below.

[12]Summer Tanager. *Piranga rubra* (Linnaeus). McCauley speaks of always seeing them in pairs, thus implying nesting, but breeding has yet to be confirmed. There are occasional summer sightings today along Wolf Creek and the Canadian River, but only of single birds; otherwise, its status is that of migrant. This tanager has been found nesting in Oklahoma as far west as Dewey and Woodward counties, so the possibility exists that it may also nest in the Panhandle (Sutton, *Check-list of Birds,* 41).

[13]Barn Swallow. *Hirundo rustica* Linnaeus. This is another species that has increased and spread with the coming of human settlement, and it is to be found commonly today throughout most of the area of McCauley's observations. Not only does it nest on buildings but frequently under over-passes and bridges, and in road culverts.

[14]Cliff Swallow. *Hirundo pyrrhonota* Vieillot. Not only is it still today an abundant nesting species in the habitat McCauley describes, it also exploits the same structures as the Barn Swallow (see note 13).

[15]Bank Swallow. *Riparia riparia* (Linnaeus). From the habitat described by McCauley along parts of the Red River, his observations were probably made in the lower reaches of the stream in Randall, Armstrong, and Briscoe counties; he was in those areas from mid-May to early June. His text does not state so explicitly, but he seems to imply that there is a direct correlation between the bank swallow and the presence of high banks of red clay, habitat this swallow might be expected to use for nesting. It is found there today, however, only as a migrant, with spring dates of 12 April to 19 May (Texas Panhandle Audubon Society). It is doubtful that the birds McCauley saw were nesting. Colonies are scarce and extremely

VIREONIDAE.

VIREO GILVUS, (V.) Bp. — *Warbling Vireo.*[16]

This exquisite little songster was frequently met with in the groves and thickets, except along alkali waters, where none were heard or observed. Very many specimens might have been obtained if desired, as they appeared to court familiarity, when no harm was suspected, in order to have their songs heard by all they could reach.

TABLE 9

Number of Collection.	Sex.	Locality	Date.	Collector.	Collector's Name.	Length.	Extent.	Wing.	Tail.	Remarks.
48	♂ ad.	McClellan Creek	June 20	McCauley	221	5.5	20	2.75	2	Stomach: seeds and grasses

VIREO SOLITARIUS, (Wils.) V. — *Blue-headed or Solitary Vireo.*[17]

Occasionally observed, but not as frequent as *V. gilvus*.

FRINGILLIDAE.

CHRYSOMITRIS TRISTIS, (L?) Bp. — *American Goldfinch or Yellowbird.*[18]

Observed along the Washita, and Wolf, McClellan, and Mulberry Creeks.

PASSERCULUS BAIRDI, (And.) Coues. — *Baird's Bunting.*[19]

Very few specimens noted. Personally all my searches for a nest of

local in Texas today, and the nearest to the Panhandle at which it has been found breeding is in Wilbarger County to the southeast (Harry C. Oberholser, *The Bird Life of Texas* [Austin: University of Texas Press, 1974], 2:575).

[16]Warbling Vireo. *Vireo gilvus* (Vieillot). Not as common now as formerly, in 1971 it was placed on the Blue List, a listing of those species which have recently or are currently giving indications of non-cyclical population declines or range contractions, either locally or widespread (Robert S. Arbib, Jr., "Announcing — the Blue List: an 'early warning system' for birds," *American Birds* 25 (1971): 948-949).

[17]Solitary Vireo. *Vireo solitarius* (Wilson). McCauley speaks of seeing only the "Blue-headed" or eastern race *(V. s. solitarius)*, whereas the western race (V. s. plumbeus) also migrates through the area. The latter is dark gray above with only a slight tinge of yellow on the flanks.

[18]American Gold finch. *Carduelis tristis* (Linnaeus). McCauley omits to say whether his observations were limited to either the outward or return legs of the journey, or if they included both. If while outward bound in mid-May, the species was probably a migrant, while if seen also on the return in early and mid-June, it may possibly have been nesting. It is not known as a nesting species today; however, there have been a number of summer sightings of late years in the Lake Marvin and Canadian River areas of eastern Hemphill County that are indicative of nesting.

[19]Baird's Sparrow. *Ammodramus bairdii* (Audubon). This observation is most likely

this species were unsuccessful, the one secured having been found by one of the escort, Private Ruby, of Company E, Nineteenth Infantry, a German, who was a very enthusiastic oölogist, having had in the "old country" a collection exceeding seven hundred sets of eggs of the European avi-fauna. The nest, found on the ground, is circular, apparently closely built, but withal very frail. Without, the bird had, after choosing its home, placed about a number of old leaves, chiefly good specimens of skeletonized ones, about which to build its nest. This was composed of slight pieces of the bark of grape-vines, which clustered in profusion about the trees near by, such grasses as were suitable, and an inner lining of finest rootlets or fiber. No horse-hair or parts of buffalo-wool were used in its building. It contained but three eggs, freshly laid, which averaged 0.80 by 0.66. The ground-color as a dull white, bespeckled very irregularly, but a little more closely at larger than smaller end, with markings of faint reddish-brown of a light and a darker shade.

TABLE 10

Number of Collection.	Locality.	Date.	Collector.	Nests.	Eggs.	Remarks.
12	Cañoncito Blanco	June 7	Ruby	1	3	

a case of misidentification, not of the species itself but of the alleged finding of its nest. Historically, it has never been known to nest as far south as the Panhandle. Presently it breeds (and probably always has) from southeastern Alberta, southern Saskatchewan and southern Manitoba south to central and eastern Montana, southern South Dakota, southeastern North Dakota and west-central Minnesota (American Ornithologists' Union, *Check-list of North American Birds*, 6th ed. (Washington, D. C.: 1983), 707).

Hoping to clarify the matter, I wrote Dr. Richard C. Banks of the National Museum of Natural History in Washington, D. C. where the McCauley collection was deposited. In his reply of 8 July 1986 he informed me that the National Museum did not have the nest and eggs of the Baird's Sparrow that McCauley supposedly collected: "In fact, as nearly as I can determine, we do not have any material taken by McCauley. I have no idea where his specimens are." Enlarging on the claim, he referred me to Robert Ridgway, *The Birds of North and Middle America* (U. S. National Museum Bull., 1901)50:203, wherein the author avers: "Two alleged breeding localities are so far outside the really established breeding range of this species that I can only refer to them as doubtful. These are, Camp Harney, eastern Oregon (Bendire, Proc. Bost. Sec. N. H., 1877, 118), and Cañoncito, northern Texas (McCauley, Bull. U. S. Geol. and Geog. Surv. Terr., iii, 1877, 663)." Undoubtedly the Baird's Sparrow was a migrant through the area of McCauley's travels, much more commonly then than now, as much of its preferred nesting habitat is now under cultivation. The recorded spring dates this century as 20 March — 17 May (Texas Panhandle Audubon Society).

The question remains, to what species did the nest McCauley collected belong? Could it have been that of the quite similar Grasshopper Sparrow *Ammodramis savannarum)*, congeneric with Baird's and a fairly common nesting grassland

PEUCAEA CASSINI, (Woodh.) Bd. — *Cassin's Finch.*[20]

First met with in the thickets along the Palo Duro. It was over an hour until, after crossing and recrossing the stream and following in its quick nervous flight, the author of the peculiarly attractive song, for which this warbler is noted, was first observed. Leaving camp at early dawn — absolutely necessary in long marches during the hot season — and traveling up the stream, the pleasant notes of these birds could be heard as we rode by the thickets everywhere skirting it. It was heard often afterward, and occasionally seen, chiefly in the dense underbrush along Red River, near where it enters its cañon. This begins abruptly, not far beyond the junction of the two streams by whose union it is formed.

TABLE 11

Number of Collection.	Sex.	Locality.	Date.	Collector.	Collector's Name.	Length.	Extent.	Wing.	Tail.	Remarks.
13	♀ ad.	Palo Duro	May 25	McCauley	188	6.75	8	2.4	2.5	

Like the Golden Warbler *(D. aestiva)*, as soon as alarmed, it darted through the shrubbery, often completely evading pursuit.

As the brooding birds would not return until the vicinity was free from any intruder, search for their nests was in general unsuccessful.

sparrow in the area today, but one he does not mention? Thinking that McCauley may have, indeed, misnamed his bird and had intended a reference to the Grasshopper Sparrow, I queried Dr. Jack D. Tyler, Department of Biological Sciences, Cameron University, Lawton, Oklahoma, concerning the synonymy of the two species. In his reply of 9 June 1986, he stated: "The enigma re the proper synonymy of Baird's Sparrow is quite interesting. Ridgway lists the taxonomic changes since the description by Audubon in 1843 through 1897, at which time the name was *Ammodramus bairdii,* and still is. The Grasshopper Sparrow, *A. savannarum,* on the other hand, though usually placed congenerically with Baird's, has had but three specific epithets: *passerina, savannarum,* and *australis* . . . Therefore, if McCauley had meant the Grasshopper Sparrow, he erred from the outset by calling it 1) by the wrong scientific name, and 2) the incorrect common name! In short, McCauley — based strictly on synonmy — *did* indeed mean Baird's Sparrow, *Ammodramus bairdii* (= *Passerculus bairdi)!*"

[20]Cassin's Finch. *Carpodacus cassinii* Baird. This is another probably misidentification. The Cassin's Finch is a species of the montane forests of western North America and is found only casually and irregularly as a winter dispersant in lower elevations to the east (A. O. U., *Check-list of N. A. Birds,* 745-746). The species McCauley most likely saw was the quite similar House Finch *(Carpodacus mexicanus),* still today a fairly common resident of the area but one he does not mention. Although he collected a female bird, the females of the two species are difficult to separate and it takes a certain degree of expertise to tell them apart.

TABLE 12

Number of Collection.	Locality.	Date.	Collector.	Nests.	Eggs.	Remarks.
6	Palo Duro	May 26	McCauley	1	3	

SPIZELLA PALLIDA BREWERI, (Cass.) Coues. — *Brewer's Sparrow.*21

Frequently seen, especially in those portions of prairie land that sloped down to streams that were tributary to Red River, and in the cañon bottom of that river itself.

TABLE 13

Number of Collection.	Locality.	Date.	Collector.	Nests.	Eggs.	Remarks.
2	Red River Cañon	May 21	McCauley	1	3	
3&4	do	May 23	do	2	6	
33-38	Palo Duro	May 25 to 27	do	6	20	
39-40	Camp's edge of Staked Plains	June 10 to 12	Ruby	2	6	

CHONDESTES GRAMMACA, (Say) Bp. — *Lark Finch.*22

Both along the prairies of Kansas and Indian Territory and on that arid waste, the Staked Plain, this sweet singer was not uncommon.

TABLE 14

Number of Collection.	Sex.	Locality.	Date.	Collector.	Collector's Name.	Length.	Extent.	Wing.	Tail.	Remarks.
42	♀ ad.	White Fish Creek	June 19	McCauley	215	—	—	3.4	3	

21Brewer's Sparrow. *Spizella breweri* Cassin. This is probably no longer a breeding bird of the Texas Panhandle as no evidence of nesting has been found here this century. More intensive searches in the northwestern sector might possibly identify some, however, for in 1957 a considerable number were found nesting in grazing land ten to twelve miles west of Boise City, Cimarron County, western Oklahoma (George M. Sutton, *Oklahoma Birds* [Norman: University of Oklahoma Press, 1967], 627-628). It also possibly nests yet today in northeastern New Mexico, as it is found occasionally in summer in Union County (John P. Hubbard, *Revised Check-list of the Birds of New Mexico* [Albuquerque: New Mexico Ornithological Society Publication No. 6, 1978], 100). The surprising thing about McCauley's observations is that he found the species nesting so far south; on 10-12 June the party was encamped on the edge of the Staked Plains, probably in present-day Briscoe County.

22Lark Sparrow. *Chondestes grammacus* (Say). The status of this species has not changed and it can be easily found throughout the area today. Although all the nests McCauley found were on the ground, it may also nest at higher elevations, particularly in cholla cactus *(Opuntia imbricata)*.

The nests were upon the ground, built more for comfort than for resistance to the winds that would test its firmness if placed aloft; the lower parts were coarse grasses, rootlets and dried leaves, whilst the eggs rested upon a soft cushion of buffalo-wool, fine hair and rootlets. One was in an open prairie situation, but to conceal it the birds had placed it beneath a huge buffalo hip-bone, entering by a small opening. In nest No. 24 was found an egg of the Cowbird [*Molothrus ater* of Gray, after Boddaert]. Their markings are odd and curious — nearer than any other perhaps to Chinese characters; they varied in color from a rich chocolate to dark sepia.

Of [t]he eggs, the greatest major axis noted was 0.82 inch, and smallest transverse 0.63.

TABLE 15

Number of Collection.	Locality.	Date.	Collector.	Nests.	Eggs.	Remarks.
16	Battle Creek	June 13	McCauley	1	2	} All eggs freshly
24	White Fish Creek	June 19	Ruby	1	d	} laid at this date.

CALAMOSPIZA BICOLOR, (Towns.) Bp. — *Lark Bunting or White-Winged Blackbird.*[23]

Very frequently observed, and not particularly shy.

EUSPIZA AMERICANA, (Gm.) Bp. — *Black-throated Bunting.*[24]

Whilst none of the districts traversed whose water was decidedly alkaline were entirely bare of inhabitants of the lower orders, as soon as they were passed and water fresh or passably good was met with, the difference in animal life was noticeable to the most casual observer. Leaving the mouth of the Tule, and passing up Red River, over its burning alkali bed, ten miles up, on a small island, quite a grove was found, with scarcely an inhabitant. Continuing on and up a side-cañon in search of water, I found it at last in abundance, most delightful and cool, a rapid brook rushing down in waterfalls, to sink, as usual, before reaching the river. In such places, bird life was abundant. There and in similar places were the Buntings and many others of the *Fringillidae*, whilst several of their natural enemies, the *Falconidae*, were almost always in view.

23Lark Bunting. *Calamospiza melanocorya* Stejneger. Today it is a very common to abundant migrant; if conditions are right, it will nest.

24Black-throated Sparrow. *Amphospiza bilineata* (Cassin). Small numbers are still resident in the Palo Duro Canyon system, with scattered sightings in other areas. It is at the northern edge of its range in Texas (T. O. S., *Checklist of Birds,* 123).

TABLE 16

Number of Collection.	Sex.	Locality.	Date.	Collector.	Collector's Name.	Length.	Extent.	Wing.	Tail.	Remarks.
38	♂	White Fish Creek	June 19	McCauley	211	6.5	10	3.25	2.5	

GONLAPHEA MELANOCEPHALA, (Sw.) Gray. — *Black-headed Grosbeak.*25

Occasionally noted in much the same localities, but not as often seen as *Guiraca caerulea.*

GUIRACA CAERULEA, (L.) Sw. — *Blue Grosbeak.*26

Very frequently met with along the Palo Duro and in parts of the Tierra Blanca; also found along McClellan, Mulberry, etc., Creeks, and during part of the trip in the Indian Territory. When noted on the Palo Duro, they were always in pairs, being busily engaged in finishing their nests. In the mouth and crop of the specimen obtained was found a large quantity of Prickly-pear Cactus *(Opuntia missouriensis)*, barbed bristles and all.

TABLE 17

Number of Collection.	Sex.	Locality.	Date.	Collector.	Collector's Name.	Length.	Extent.	Wing.	Tail.	Remarks.
16	♂ ad.	Palo Druo	May 26	McCauley	191	7.25	10	3.66	3	Stomach: insects and grass seed.

CYANOSPIZA CIRIS, (L.) Bd. — *Painted Finch; Nonpareil.*27

Contary to my expectations, I found this species during the course of the survey, obtaining a specimen on a small tributary of Mulberry Creek, about latitude 34° 50', being farther north than Wilmington, N. C., with an approximate elevation of 3,300 feet. Previous camps had been as far as thirty miles more southerly than this, in the vicinity of both fresh and alkali water, where, however, the species was not observed. The birds seen

25Black-headed Grosbeak. *Pheucticus melanocephalus* (Swainson). McCauley does not give dates but it can be found today during spring from late April to late May and occasionally into early June. The latter are late migrants as it does not nest in the Panhandle.

26Blue Grosbeak. *Guiraca caerulea* (Linnaeus). This is still a common breeding bird of the area.

27Painted Bunting. *Passerina ciris* (Linnaeus). Contrary to many people's expectations today, this most colorful of all North American birds is a fairly common summer resident of the Panhandle south of the Canadian River, particularly so in the Palo Duro Canyon. McCauley's inability to find a nest is one shared by most present-day observers.

were always in pairs, and appeared to be building. I was unable to find any nests, but do not doubt that they were breeding there. The colors of their plumage were as bright and exquisite as in Georgia and the Gulf States.

TABLE 18

Number of Collection.	Sex.	Locality.	Date.	Collector.	Collector's Name.	Length.	Extent.	Wing.	Tail.	Remarks.
69	♂	Mulberry Creek (tributary)	June 15	McCauley	240	5.5	—	2.7	2.5	

CYANOSPIZA CYANEA, (L.) Bd. — *Indigo-bird.*[28]

Occasionally seen, but not as often as *Guiraca caerulea.*

PYRRHULOXIA SINUATA, Bp. — *Texas Cardinal.*[29]

The only previous time I had seen this bird alive was during last March in Old Mexico. In the cities and plazas, it was at home among the vineyards or the shrubbery by the adobe wall about each yard or garden, where it appeared to be as undisturbed by passers by as the Robin *(T. migratorius)* in our towns. On the Staked Plain it was different, and though about half a dozen individuals were seen in Cañoncito Blanco and elsewhere, they were too shy to be secured.

CARDINALIS VIRGINIANUS, (Briss.) Bp. — *Cardinal Redbird or Virginia Nightingale.*[30]

Occasionally observed on the Canadian and the McClellan and Wolf Creeks; very shy. The birds were always in pairs, and could not be approached.

28Indigo Bunting. *Passerina cyanea* (Linnaeus). This bird may be more common today than formerly. It appears to have expanded its range westward along the Canadian River as far as northern Potter County, and it is found occasionally in summer on the Buffalo Lake National Wildlife Refuge and in the Palo Duro Canyon State Park, Randall County. At the latter location a pair feeding young was found 8 July 1979 (Frances Williams [compiler], "Southern Great Plains Region," *American Birds* 33 [1979]: 877).

29Pyrrhuloxia. *Cardinalis sinuatus* Bonaparte. Today this is only an occasional visitor in the southern parts of McCauley's survey; he speaks in particular of the Cañoncito Blanco area, site of present-day Ceta Glen in southeastern Randall County. It was at the church camps there that two female birds were found on 29 January 1978 and two males on 13 January 1983 (personal records). What is interesting is that McCauley found the birds in late spring; this is unexpected at that season as the species nests today much farther south. It is notorious for its sometimes peculiar habit of post-nesting dispersal northward in winter.

30Northern Cardinal. *Cardinalis cardinalis* (Linnaeus). This bird is evidently much more common now than formerly as McCauley speaks of seeing it only "occasionally." It has adapted well to human settlement and can be found frequently in towns.

ICTERIDAE.

MOLOTHRUS ATER, (Bodd.) Gray. *Cowbird.*31

[This species is so much better known as *M. pecoris* (Gm.) Sw., that it seems desirable to call special attention to the fact that a change in nomenclature is necessary. I have noted the case in my Checklist (p. 43),r and in the B. N. W. (p. 180)s; but ornithologists seem slow to recognize the requirements. In as far as my writings have any influence, I am myself to blame for this, for I think I have not hitherto followed Gray in formally recognizing Boddaert's unquestionable and legitimate priority. — Ed.]

A frequent visitor at our camps, especially when they partook of a permanent nature, or remained, as occurred in two cases, at the same place for five days or a week. During a day's march over the plain, a good-sized flock, perceiving our wagon-train, flew up to and followed it, keeping in rear of the last wagon, for a distance of eleven miles, when camp was reached. An egg of this species was found in a nest of a Lark Finch *(Chondestes grammaca)*, obtained at White Fish Creek.

AGELAEUS PHOENICEUS, (L.) V. — *Red-winged Blackbird.*32

This handsome member of the Blackbird family, though not infrequent, was not as common as *M. ater,* and, very sensibly, it evidently preferred the vicinity of ranches or an Army post to seeking a precarious existence in the wake of a buffalo herd on the Staked Plain. It was seen in largest flocks along the Sweetwater and other beautifully wooded creeks. In December and January last, I found this species wintering at Fort Garland, Colo., whose elevation is over 8,000 feet, and winter climate severe, with frequent cold and piercing winds blowing for days without cessation. Along the Sangre de Cristo Creek, flowing by the post, were flocks numbering hundreds.

XANTHOCEPHALUS ICTEROCEPHALUS, (Bp.) Bd. — *Yellow-headed Blackbird.*33

This uninvited visitor to the vicinity of the picket-line, generally in bands

31Brown-headed Cowbird. *Molothrus ater* (Boddaert). It is possibly more common today, for cowbirds prefer or even require modified environments such as towns and livestock for foraging (Jared Verner and Lyman V. Ritter, "Current Status of the Brown-headed Cowbird in the Sierra National Forest," *Auk* 100 [1983]: 355-368). The flock that followed the party's wagon train was no doubt feeding on the numerous insects that would have been disturbed by its passage, a habit the cowbird is noted for today when association with livestock.

32Red-winged Blackbird. *Agelaius phoeniceus* (Linnaeus). Found more commonly now than is the brown-headed cowbird *(Molothrus ater)*, it has spread from natural waterways where McCauley observed it most frequently to areas of water empoundments and irrigated lands where its required nesting habitats have developed.

33Yellow-headed Blackbird. *Xanthocephalus xanthocephalus* (Bonaparte). The fact that McCauley encountered few yellowheads is not surprising; although a of which half were Cowbirds, was only observed at a few places. They seemed, like *A. Phoeniceus,* to frequent but a few wooded creeks. Possessing habits that cause it to frequent the residence or surroundings of man and bring it under observation, it seems at times strange how long a journey may be made through a region which is part of its habitat without its being observed. While traveling last February over 500 miles with a portion of the Eighth Calvalry through the whole of new Mexico, *en route* from Fort Garland, Colo., to Texas, there was but a single point where this specics, popularly called in the regiment the "Ninth Cavalry Birds," was observed or to be seen. In the plaza of the Mexican town of Socorro, N. Mex., hundreds had chosen for their rendezvous some old shade trees on the side of the square, and had frequented them for many years, according to the traditions of the ever-lasting loafers and cigarette smokers that lounged around on every side. Two months later, on my return, the birds were there in immense numbers, as before. Nowhere else up the whole Rio Grande were they visible. A single nest of this species was found in the cañon of the Red River, where the stream, sometimes but a few feet wide, occasionally widens into good-sized marshy pools — the resort of ducks and other water-fowl. A few yards out from the edge, on a clump of thick, rank grass that rose five feet out of water, entwining about them to have them form a firm support, the birds had built their home. Without any mud plaster to hold the strands compactly, they had nicely woven together pieces of coarse, thick grass, and other material of a like nature, in abundance near by.

STURNELLA MAGNA NEGLECTA, (Aud.) All. — *Western Field Lark.*[34]

This variety of *Sturnella* was very abundant, except upon the sterile plain itself. Descending thence, however, to the cañon bottoms, or to

common to abundant migrant, migration would have been largely over by the time the party left Ft. Elliott on 11 May. The exact location of the nest he found in the canyon of the Red River is not clear. H. C. Oberholser in *Bird Life of Texas,* (2:808), places it in Armstrong County sometime between 18 and 30 May; however, the expedition first struck the canyon on 16 May and was in and out of it at various times before last ascending it on 13 June. These forays were made not only in Armstrong County but also in Randall and Briscoe Counties. The nest McCauley found represented the only definite record in the Panhandle until a colony of nesting yellowheads was found on a playa lake west of Hart, in Castro County, on 12 May 1978 (Frances Williams [compiler], "Southern Great Plains Region," *American Birds* 32 (1978): 1181). It appears to be an established breeder in that area today as nesting has been observed in subsequent years (Texas Panhandle Audubon Society, *et al.;* David H. Fischer, Michael D. Schibler, Richard J. Whyte, and Eric G. Bolen, "Checklist of Birds From the Playa Lakes of the Southern Texas Panhandle," *Bulletin of the Texas Ornithological Society* 15 (1982): 2-7).

34Western Meadowlark. *Sturnella neglecta* Audubon. McCauley makes reference to what was then considered to be the western subspecies of the meadowlark, *Sturnella magna neglecta,* and fails to mention the eastern subspecies *S. m. magna.* Unless there ranges have changed since his journey, he should have encountered them both, *S. m. neglecta* along the western and southern routes, and both it and some wooded stream, the songster is again heard greeting the marching column daily for several hours after the dawn has broken. This region is a part of its habitat, extending west through New Mexico, where I constantly saw it, during the past spring, in February, along the Rio Grande, below Albuquerque, and in April throughout the entire Territory. Whilst frequenting wooded sections, I have never observed one alight upon a tree or object higher than a sunflower stalk or low bush from which to sing. In New Mexico, they prefer the low adobe wall surrounding every house, or a grape-vine in the vineyards, and perch there to send forth those peculiarly exuberant songs, which are for the benefit of early risers alone, and with which, we may readily believe, the natives are unacquainted.

The nests were built of sage and thick grass, with fine grasses within. The exterior diameter above is 5½ inches, interior diameter 3½ inches, and depth 3½ inches. The eggs average 1.07 by 0.80 inches, one specimen being 1.00 by 0.80 inches. The ground-color is creamy-white, with markings of a faint and dark or reddish-brown, largest upon the great end.

TABLE 19

Number of Collection.	Locality.	Date.	Collector.	Nests.	Eggs.	Remarks.
9	Cañoncito Blanco	June 4	McCauley	1	6	
50	Red River Cañon	June 12	do	1	6	

ICTERUS SPURIUS, (L.) Bp. — *Orchard Oriole.*[35]

This beautiful and lovely songster was found frequenting most of the heavily wooded creeks, as Mulberry, McClellan, Etc., in Texas, and Wolf Creek above in the Indian Territory. Along the Dry Washita and Canadian, many were also seen and heard.

TABLE 20

Number of Collection.	Sex.	Locality.	Date.	Collector.	Collector's Name.	Length.	Extent.	Wing.	Tail.	Remarks.
39	♂ ad.	White Fish Creek	June 19	McCauley	212	6.75	9.6	3.25	3	
51	♂ ad.	Washita	June 23	do	224	7.00	9.5	3.25	3	

S. m. magna along the eastern and northern routes. It was not until 1908 that the two were recognized as separate species (Fourteenth Supplement to the American Ornithologists' Union Check-list of North American Birds. *Auk* 25 (1908): 343-399). Morphologically, the two are almost identical but can be told apart easily by their distinctive songs. The sound of singing meadowlarks is one of the glories of a Panhandle spring.

35Orchard Oriole. *Icterus spurius* (Linnaeus). The orchard oriole still frequents the areas McCauley names, but it is perhaps not as common now as formerly. In some parts of its range there is concern for its welfare.

ICTERUS BALTIMORE, (L.), Daud. — *Baltimore Oriole.*[36]

Occasionally noted along Wolf Creek and other beautifully wooded streams.

ICTERUS BULLOCKI, (Sw.) Bp. — *Bullock's Oriole.*

A very few specimens observed, same locality as last; neither species as numerous as *I. spurius.*

QUISCALUS MACRURUS, Sw. — *Great-tailed Grackle.*[37]

Several specimens observed along McClellan Creek and in other places. [I deem it prudent to prefix a query to this species, which is one of a group in which identifications are difficult, and a bird not known, I think, to occur in the United States except in maritime portions. The association of *Icterus bullocki* with the two eastern species of the same genus, as indicated by Lieutenant McCauley's determination of his specimens, would not, perhaps, have been anticipated.—Ed.]

CORVIDAE.

CORVUS CORAX, Linn. — *Raven.*[38]

As may be imagined, this most striking of the *Corvidae* was frequently seen. No place could be found that would better suit its preferences for a habitat than the great Llano Estacado. Fearfully monotonous, and with solitude as its main characteristic, rarely crossed by man, save in a few portions where the marchers may be made to strike water, it is perfectly congenial to the Raven, offering adequate sustenance in the carcasses of animals that are often too numerous to be pleasant to the traveler.

[36]Northern Oriole. *Icterus galbula* (Linnaeus). In 1973 the "Baltimore Oriole" *(I. galbula)* and the "Bullock's Oriole" *(I. bullockii)* were considered conspecific and combined into one species, the Northern Oriole ("Thirty-second Supplement to the American Ornithologists' Union Check-list of North American Birds," *Auk* 90 (1973): 417). McCauley would have encountered both subspecies in the eastern Panhandle (along with hybrids) and primarily the "Bullock's" in the western and southern sectors. That he did not encounter them with any frequency is surprising, as today the northern oriole is common throughout the area.

[37]Great-tailed Grackle. *Quiscalus mexicanus* (Gmelin). There is a question as to what species of grackle McCauley actually saw; the editor of the report, Elliott Coues, rightly questions his sightings. The great-tailed is a relatively recent addition to the avifauna of the Texas Panhandle. Reports of it only began to be recorded in the 1950's, and since that time it has steadily increased in numbers and expanded its range until it now occupies most of the area. Its concurrent expansion in Oklahoma has been well documented (W. Marvin Davis, "The Great-tailed Grackle in Oklahoma," *Bulletin of the Oklahoma Ornithological Society* 8 (1975): 9-15). The grackle McCauley saw was possibly the similar Common Grackle *(Q. quiscula)*, common to the area today but not mentioned by him.

[38]Common Raven *Corvus corax* Linnaeus. This raven is largely confined today to the extreme northwestern sector of the Panhandle, where it is uncommon. Its commoness in McCauley's day can probably be attributed to the abundant food supply provided by slaughtered buffalo.

CORVUS CRYPTOLEUCUS, Couch. — *White-necked Raven.*39

More abundant than any other of the *Corvidae.*

CORVUS AMERICANUS, Aud. — *Common Crow.*40

A few specimens observed along McClellan Creek, etc.

PICA MELANOLEUCA HUDSONICA, (Sab.) All. — *American Magpie.*41

Careful observations were made at different points for this species without success. I had observed them in great numbers about Garland, Colo., and in the Raton Range near Fort Union, N. Mex., and during a horseback trip in November last had met them along the Fontaine que Bouille at Pueblo, and frequently on the Saint Charles, south of that place. Having been recorded at altitudes lower than the Staked Plain, it was presumed that possibly the species might have extended down the Canadian from Fort Union and the Raton Range to the cañon region of the Llano Estacado, distant from the Canadian about twenty-five miles, for many localities visited possess all the characteristics of the Magpie's habitat in the Rocky Mountain region, save the characteristic dryness of the atmosphere. It is reported, however, in Eastern Kansas (Snow, B. Kans., 1873),t and in an atmosphere of much greater humidity than that of the Staked Plain. None were found on the route to Dodge City from the south.

TYRANNIDAE.

MILVULUS FORFICATUS, (Gm.) Sw. — *Swallow-tailed Fly-catcher; Scissor-tails.*42

This peculiarly beautiful and graceful bird was one of the specimens most frequently seen. They were especially active in the evening, just before dusk, skimming about in pursuit of insects with wonderful rapidity. As the males fly about the camp with their mates, in the twilight, you can single them out by the greater length of their tails. The two elegant feathery tines cross and open at volition, whence the ordinary simile to a pair of scissors. These birds are grace itself when on wing,

39Chihuahuan Raven. *Corvus cryptoleucus* Couch. While still fairly common today, this raven is not nearly so common as is the following species.

40American Crow. *Corvus brachyrhynchos* Brehm. Today a common species in the eastern Panhandle and to be encountered all along McCauley's route of march, it is another bird that has benefited by human settlement.

41Black-billed Magpie. *Pica pica* (Linnaeus). This bird was listed by McCauley because he expected to see it but did not. It is resident in nearby areas of western Oklahoma and northeastern New Mexico but its presence in the Panhandle as a wild bird has yet to be documented. Some claims for it have proved to be of escaped cage birds.

42Scissor-tailed Flycatcher. *Tyrannus forficatus* (Gmelin). Fortunately, this is still to be found all along McCauley's route. There is some evidence that it is being supplanted in parts of its range by the Western Kingbird *(T. verticalis).*

darting here and there as quick as thought, in bouyant sweeps and curves. The delicate crimson below their wings, as they go glancing by, glows in contrast with the beautiful hoary ash of their general plumage; and as the little heart ceases to palpitate, you pick up your specimen with a pang of remorse, and for once mentally agree with the friend beside you — visiting the Staked Plain in the "invalid" interest, and strongly an anti-collector — that, as he avers, "a bird-skinner *is* as bad as a butcher."[u] Even the teamsters call them "mighty pretty," and no one wonders that the "Texicans" (as our scouts, old buffalo hunters, title the natives) brag on their beauty, and call them "Birds of Paradise." In the evening, they were particularly shy, avoiding close proximity to camp; in the early morning, however, they seemed to be less suspicious of our presence. This was very noticeable in going up the Palo Duro, where they would sometimes fly closely by, or alight within a dozen yards and poise upon a branch of a small bush, like the Field-lark. They were found frequenting the fringe of timber bordering the streams as far as their headwaters in the Staked Plain, as well as along the streams in the Indian Territory — Wolf Creek, and others farther north emptying into the Cimarron — all draining portions of the Arkansas Basin. They ruled the wood wherever located, and not only repelled, but hotly pursued any Sparrow-hawk *(F. sparverius)* that ventured near their homes, and even maintained authority over the Kingbird *(T. carolinensis)*. The greatest tail-length in any of the species secured did not exceed 10 inches.

In the course of a trip last spring along the Rio Grande as far as Fort Bliss, Texas, and south 300 miles into old Mexico, where I frequently met with the Texas Cardinal *(P. sinuata)* at an elevation of 3,500 feet and below, the Scissor-tails were nowhere seen at any point, not even at the same altitude at which they occur in the Red River country.

TABLE 21

Number of Collection.	Sex.	Locality.	Date.	Collector.	Collector's Name.	Length.	Extent.	Wing.	Tail.	Remarks.
3	♂	Salt Fork, Red River	May 16	McCauley	178	10.2	14.5	4.6	6.3	
4	♂ ad.	do	May 16	do	179	13.6	14	5	9.3	
6		do	May 17	do	181	11.3	13	4.3	6.6	
23	♂ ad.	Palo Duro	May 29	do	198	13.5	15	5	8.6	
30	♂ ad.	Battle Creek	June 13	do	203	14.7	14.7	5.33	9.75	The stomachs
32	♀ ad.	Mulberry Creek (tributary)	June 15	do	205	9.75	14.50	4.67	5	contained more beetles
34	♀ ad.	Mulberry Creek	June 18	do	207	10.75	14.5	4.67	5.75	than flies.
47	♂ ad.	McClellan Creek	June 20	do	220	11.25	13	4.25	6.50	
62	♂ ad.	White Fish Creek	June 19	do	235	12.5	14	4.6	8.6	
63	♂ ad.	McClellan Creek	June 21	do	236	10.6	14	4.5	5.6	

Their nests were built well up, generally on cottonwood trees, and were very carefully constructed of small twigs, with the cotton from the trees well interwoven. The interior was made of fine woody fibre and roots, binding the innermost lining, invariably buffalo-wool, set in its place with all the cunning of a weaver's skill. They were circular; interior diameter at the top 3, and depth 2 inches.

The usual number of eggs observed was four, and their average size was 0.90 by 0.66. The ground-color was milk-white, uniform throughout; the markings, varying in size, of lavender and burnt-umber chiefly; some of sepia, at times very dark. They were irregularly scattered over the surface, mainly over the large end; sometimes large spots were found straying up to the small end, though that generally was free, save from a few specks. In none of the eggs examined were the blotches grouped thickly and closely about the great end, as in *T. carolinensis.*

TABLE 22

Number of Collection.	Locality.	Date.	Collector.	Nests.	Eggs.	Remarks.
30	White Fish Creek	June 19	McCauley	1	2	
31	do	June 19	Ruby	1	4	
51	McClellan Creek	June 20	McCauley	1	4	

TYRANNUS CAROLINENSIS, (L.) Bd. — *Kingbird; Bee Martin.*[43]

This species was generally found frequenting the same places where was seen *T. verticalis,* on the main creeks and rivers, except that part of Red River where the water was alkaline. Although not of the genus *Tyrannus,* the "Scissor-tails" evidently ruled over this bird in all the groves where they dwelled together, and appeared by their absolute control to better deserve the "Kingbird" appellation. The *Tyrannidae,* four species of which were frequently observed, held complete control in the wood during this their hatching season, as was evident from the fact that their nests were at times found close to those of *Falconidae.*

TABLE 23

Number of Collection.	Sex.	Locality.	Date.	Collector.	Collector's Name.	Length.	Extent.	Wing.	Tail.	Remarks.
40	♂ ad.	White Fish Creek	June 19	McCaul··	213	8.5	14.75	5.66	3.66	
41	♀ ad.	do	June 19	do	214	8.5	14.2	4.75	3.5	
46	♀ ad.	McClellan Creek	June 20	do	219	8.5	14.00	4.70	3.5	

For the purpose of securing an absolute identification of the eggs of this species, at a time (June 19) when none had been determined with certainty, a nest was found, both parents (Nos. 40 and 41) were secured, and from such as contained them the embryos were removed entire and preserved in alcohol.

The nest was situated well up, and generally placed among the smaller branches of a tree. Its materials were bits of sage *(Artemisia)* with small twigs and tinier ones above; rather rudely built below, but above better

43Eastern Kingbird. *Tyrannus tyrannus* (Linnaeus). Today this bird is largely confined to the eastern half of the Panhandle and only locally westward.

and more compact, using buffalo-wool with fine rootlets and threads to fasten it. As a piece of bird architecture or as a comfortable home, it does not equal that of the Scissor-tail or of the Arkansas Flycatcher *(T. verticalis)*. The nests were circular, with an interior diameter of above 3¼ inches and a depth of 1¼ inches, decidedly shallow, compared with those of the two species just mentioned.

TABLE 24

Number of Collection.	Locality.	Date.	Collector.	Nests.	Eggs.	Remarks.
22	White Fish Creek	June 19	Ruffner	1	3	
52	Mulberry Creek	June 20	McCauley	1	4	
54	McClellan Creek	June 21	do	1	3	
55	Sweetwater Creek	June 21	do	1	3	

TYRANNUS VERTICALIS, Say. — *Arkansas Flycatcher.*[44]

Observed in greatest abundance upon the Palo Duro and White Fish Creeks. This species was found frequenting all the streams flowing down from the brink of the great plain and in the Indian Territory, in localities of a like altitude and possessing the same general characteristics. None, however, were found along the Lower Tule, and other places where the water was excessively alkaline. Whilst searching for nests in a grove on the White Fish, I observed, upon a limb well up, one of this species, on which was sitting the mother bird. At that moment, down toward it, with its graceful swoop, came a Sparrow Hawk *(F. sparverius)*, which, from a distant tree, had been quietly observing the spot, and taken its bearings for attack. Quick as a flash, the mother jumped forward from her nest, with sharp shrieks and calls for aid, that promptly brought her mate from a neighboring tree to her assistance. The Hawk finding himself sorely mistaken in his calling, remembered pressing engagements elsewhere, and turned to leave, hotly pursued by the parents. Circling over and above him, relieving each other every foot as the Hawk flew on, they pecked his head so sharply that he gave a cry of pain, and took shelter in the nearest available tree. It was such a pretty instance of parental care and love that I determined to spare one bird's nest I would otherwise have taken.

Shortly after, although there appeared to be no enemy about, nor cause for alarm, after the departure of the Hawk, I was mystified by noticing the mother in the greatest distress, frequently jumping from her nest, all the while scolding and uttering cries that betokened extreme uneasiness and trouble. As this continued, whilst we were standing quietly under a neighboring cottonwood, one of the men was directed to go up and obtain the nest. As he was climbing up, and had gotten almost within

44Western Kingbird. *Tyrannus verticalis* Say. The most common flycatcher of the Panhandle, it has increased in both numbers and range in recent years. McCauley's account of it attacking a hawk is a common sight today.

reach, a tree-mouse shot by and ran down the tree, safely eluding capture. The nest safely gotten with its contents, all was clear. The rascally little mouse had made himself completely at home. Burrowing in the buffalo-wool, he had as warm and cosy a retreat as mouse ever dreamt of or wished for. When hungry, he quietly reached up, and his meal was ready and warm. It was purely a case of a "free lunch" in nature. He had eaten all the eggs but two, his retreat being full of fine pieces of egg-shells. Of those remaining, he had sucked out nearly all the contents of one, and upon the other he had also begun; a hole had been gnawed in the side of it, and the embryo, which had been well advanced, was lifeless.

TABLE 25

Number of Collection.	Sex.	Locality.	Date.	Collector.	Collector's Name.	Length.	Extent.	Wing.	Tail.	Remarks.
14	♂	Palo Duro	May 25	McCauley	189	8.25	15.75	4.9	3.5	Stomach contained *Orthroptera* and *Coleoptera.*
26	♂	Red River Cañon	May 31	do	199	9.00	16.00	5.1	3.75	
36	♂	White Fish Creek	June 19	do	209	9.00	16.25	5.25	4.00	
44	♀	McClellan Creek	June 20	do	217	9.00	14.25	4.00	4.00	
60	♂♀	Mulberry Creek	June 17	do	233	9.00	16.00	5.33	3.75	
61	♂	White Fish Creek	June 19	do	234	8.75	16.00	5.00	3.00	

The nests were built well up in the cottonwoods generally. The prettiest brought with me was on the outside 5 by 4.5 inches; the interior diameter was 3.5 by 3.25 inches, almost circular, and two inches deep, always deeper than those of *T. carolinensis*. Using large quantities of the fibrous, coarse cotton of the tree, they had matted this well for fully an inch about the limbs; through which, well interwoven, ran bits of sage-brush, coarse grasses, and fine twigs, with a few dried leaves. Above this part came finer grasses and small fibrous roots, whilst for the interior they had apparently carefully selected choice bits of cotton, at times arranged in strata, over which was buffalo-wool liberally placed and neatly fastened and bound with finest threads. The lining of the interior was unusually soft, being padded in a peculiar manner with the wool itself within. In the homes of the two preceeding species, the eggs ran upon the slender roots and threads which thickly cover and bind together the underlying wool; but this Flycatcher is more select; he fastens the tufts of wool below in such a way that the eggs have a resting-place almost as soft as down, and the intertwining threads are scarcely visible. Until we came, what a happy, fortunate mouse the little thief at White Fish was! The ground-color of the eggs was a light cream, uniform throughout, with lavender and purple blotches, with some of a darker purple, all disposed mainly nearest the larger end, but to be found over the whole surface. Occasionally some were scattered over the little end itself. It having been stated that the eggs of this and *carolinensis* were, with difficulty, or very frequently "not distinguishable," I made very careful comparisons of the two. Of the same family, and so closely allied, it might be supposed that they would build similar nests and of the same material. They do, but the nests are slightly different shape, more oval in most cases examined than the *T. carolinensis*, which is circular and averages 4½ inches diameter outer circumference, and 3¼ within, with almost twice the depth. The eggs of this species lie upon the wool itself, whilst the former's interior is a fine network of bark fibers matted above and within the wool. As to the eggs, which I found averaging 0.92 by 0.70 themselves, whilst there would be a great uncertainty in size, they may be distinguished as follows:—

1. *Shape.* — The egg of this species has its small end well rounded, being decidedly oval; that of *carolinensis* a decided point, although their lengths and greatest thickness are about the same.

2. *Color.* — The ground-color of the former being a richer cream color, more of a chrome-yellow tint than this. In all the specimens examined, this distinction was perceptible. To this may be added that the base or large end will at once determine the doubt, the ground-color in this species being uniform throughout, whilst, in the former's, the base has a wash of yellowish pink spread uniformly over it, and imperceptibly fading into the general color. No eggs were found unmarked in this respect, and, as a rule, it was found remarkably distinct.

3. *Markings.* — In this species, the markings are spots of reddish brown or burnt-umber, with scattering ones of a faint shade like lavender; whilst at the larger end occur decided sepias. The blotches are irregular in shape, but generally rounded, some eggs having nearly or quite all their spots elliptical. They are scattered irregularly over the surface, occurring everywhere, being frequently upon the small end, and of as large a size and the same intensity as elsewhere. Remembering that the grouping in *carolinensis* is entirely or almost wholly upon the great end, rarely passing the middle, and the opposite one always unspotted, the egg can be readily distinguished.

TABLE 26

Number of Collection.	Locality.	Date.	Collector.	Nests.	Eggs.	Remarks.
21	White Fish Creek	June 19	McCauley	1	2	
23	do	June 19	do	1	5	
53	McClellan Creek	June 20	Ruby	1	4	
56	do	June 21	McCauley	1	4	

MYIARCHUS CRINITUS, (L.) Cab. — *Great-crested Flycatcher.*[45]

Frequenting the thickets along some of the creeks and rivers, and part of the cañon of Red River.

[45]Great Crested Flycatcher. *Myiarchus crinitus* (Linnaeus). Today this is a bird of the eastern Panhandle and probably does not nest farther west than eastern Hutchinson County. It is seen occasionally in summer farther west but only as

The specimen secured gave evidence of quarreling propensities; of his having been engaged in many fights and having often been worsted.

TABLE 27

Number of Collection.	Sex.	Locality.	Date.	Collector.	Collector's Name.	Length.	Extent.	Wing.	Tail.	Remarks.
29	♀ ad.	Cañoncito Blanco	June 7	McCauley	202	8.5	12.5	4	3.75	

MYIARCHUS CINERASCENS, Lawr. — *Ash-throated Flycatcher.*[46]

Occasional; a few noted on McClellan Creek.

SAYORNIS SAYUS, (Bp.) Bd. — *Say's Flycatcher.*[47]

Several along McClellan Creek and a few other points.

CAPRIMULGIDAE.

ANTROSTOMUS NUTTALLI, (Aud.) Cass. — *Nuttall's Whippoorwill.*[48]

Night after night about our camps *en route* to and along Red River and its headwaters, seemingly half a mile off, or leaving you undecided whether it was but half as far, and often echoed from a distance by the cañon-walls of the streams, were heard the dismal, doleful cries of this *ignis fatuus* of birds to a collector. As twilight approached, they seemed to be plentiful in the neighboring ravine, but a search was generally useless; they could never be distinguished unless flushed, and then were gone like a flash, or else came up behind you on their quiet skimming wing amid tall chaparral, lost as soon as seen. The specimen obtained was the only one actually seen by me, and though it required a long tiresome tramp, searching and following for hours, it was worth it all. From my experience, I would rather engage to secure a dozen Chaparral Cocks *(G. californianus)*, with all their fleetness of foot and general shyness, than

a transient. This was possibly the status of the specimen McCauley collected in Cañoncito Blanco on 7 June.

[46]Ash-throated Flycatcher. *Myiarchus cinerascens* (Linnaeus). Evidently more common now than formerly as it can be found throughout the Panhandle, more so in the western half, and particularly in the Palo Duro Canyon.

[47]Say's Phoebe. *Sayornis saya* (Bonaparte). Today this bird is a common migrant with localized nesting.

[48]Common Poorwill. *Phalaenoptilus nutallii* (Audubon). The exact status of this elusive species in the Panhandle remains almost as unclear as McCauley found it. It is known principally as a migrant, with the extreme dates of 15 April to 25 November (Texas Panhandle Audubon Society). Calling night birds have been recorded in summer at scattered localities throughout the western half and particularly in the canyonlands and Canadian River breaks, but actual nesting remains unconfirmed. The nearest to the area at which nesting has been confirmed is Cimarron County, western Oklahoma (John S. Weske, "Nest of Poor-will in Cimarron County, Oklahoma," *Bulletin of the Oklahoma Ornithological Society* 6 (1973): 22).

another specimen of this species. Not as often noticed when camped upon the Staked Plain proper as when by its edge or in the cañons or ravines below, it evidently avoided the desert level, leaving that habitat to its relative, the Night-hawk. This species was also heard near the Canadian and the Cimarron, *en route* from Fort Elliott, Texas, to Fort Dodge, Kansas.[v]

TABLE 28

Number of Collection.	Sex.	Locality.	Date.	Collector.	Collector's Name.	Length.	Extent.	Wing.	Tail.	Remarks.
7	♀ juv.	Red River Cañon	May 18	McCauley		182	8	17	6	— —	Stomach contents: *Coleoptera* and *Lepidoptera*.

CHORDEILES VIRGINIANUS, (Briss.) Bp. — *Night-hawk.*[49]

Commonly known among the hunters and plainsmen as the "Bull-bat," from its attempts to rival the musical notes of the "bull-frog." These birds generally came about us several hours before sunset, whether camped on the summit of the Staked Plain or in a valley by the water. Along Red River they were particularly friendly, and flew about and through the camp, passing within a few feet of us here, there, and everywhere in search of insects.[w] In the daytime, they could be easily approached as they sat upon the prairie crouching and lying so close to the ground that even the merest bunch of the short grass seemed to protect them from the fine shot used. Whilst several of our party were riding across a desert stretch down from the head of the Palo Duro, one of the horses almost trod upon a mother on her eggs, when she jumped aside, fell, fluttered a few feet farther, and dropped utterly helpless; her wing was apparently too broken to use, and in her vain attempts to rise, she gave forth the most piercing, touching cries that wounded bird ever uttered. Altogether, it was one of the best decoys ever witnessed, quite surpassing the Quail's execution. Although aware of the trick, she was followed by one of the party; her delusion was continued in a zig-zag line, keeping not more than six to ten feet away, for a hundred yards, when, feeling that the original spot was surely lost, she flew away as happy as a mother bird could be after having saved her family.

One specimen differs slightly in appearance from the usual style of the species, and has white spots upon *six* of the outer primaries. Having been sent to Dr. Coues for his examination, he returned it, confirming its identification as *"virginianus,* although, as might be expected from the locality, it tends toward var. *henryi."* Other specimens seemd to be more decidedly like this variety.

[49]Common Nighthawk. *Chordeiles minor* (Forster). Though still a common resident and abundant migrant, it is probably not as much so as McCauley found it. This is another species that has been placed on the Blue List of birds (Arbib, "Announcing — the Blue List").

TABLE 29

Number of Collection.	Sex.	Locality.	Date.	Collector.	Collector's Name.	Length.	Extent.	Wing.	Tail.	Remarks.
12	♂	Red River	May 23	McCauley		187	9.5	22	7.75	4.5	} Stomach contents: *Coleoptera* and *Lepidoptera.*
18	♀	Palo Duro	May 26	do		193	9.0	22	8.00	4.5	
55	♀	Cañoncito Blanco	June 6	do		228	—	—	——	——	

One of the specimens obtained was secured in the act of entering the hole of a Prairie Dog *(Cynomys ludovicianus)*, another of the same brood having succeeded in taking refuge in it before the "rear guard" was cut off.

ALCEDINIDAE.

CERYLE ALCYON, (L.) Boie. — *Belted Kingfisher.*[50]

Red River and its headwaters, with the streams in many places abounding in fish, and the pools, the haunts of many of the *Anatinae,* were apparently without any of this species. They were, however, found very abundant on McClellan Creek, the Canadian, etc.

TABLE 30

Number of Collection.	Sex.	Locality.	Date.	Collector.	Collector's Name.	Length.	Extent.	Wing.	Tail.	Remarks
45	♀	McClellan Creek	June 20	McCauley		218	11.75	18.00	6.20	4	
65	♂	do	June 21	do		238	12.00	18.75	6.25	4	

GEOCOCCYX CALIFORNIANUS, (Less.) Bd. — *Chaparral Cock; Ground Cuckoo.*[51]

This odd-looking bird, so striking in its appearance, was first observed in the Cañon of Red River, below the summit of the plain, where the chaparral surrounded us. It was noticed frequently by one of the escort whilst guarding the stock, and seemed so little to fear harm that it ran several times within a few feet of him. It required, however, hard work for a day to find the specimens secured, and then their position was only known by the harsh call they uttered, when perseverance in calling them was rewarded at last by securing the pair. The curiosity of this

[50]Belted Kingfisher. *Ceryle alcyon* (Linnaeus). This bird is more often found today around empoundments than along waterways.

[51]Greater Roadrunner. *Geococcyx californianus* (Linnaeus). One of the most commonly recognized birds of the area, even by those with little interest in bird life, it can be seen frequently throughout, more so in the canyonlands and river breaks.

bird is exceeding, and he never fails to gratify it. If there is any unfamiliar sound over the ridge above him, up comes his head over the top, and he stops for a moment to stare. That suffices, however, and if the object be strange and apparently unfriendly or in purusit, he is off like a flash. Frequenting the chaparral or scrub-oak only, and the rough ravines they cover, he travels on foot, and the celerity of his movements in such a mass of tangle-brush is wonderful.

The species was frequently observed subsequently whenever we descended from the top of the plain to the cañons of the streams.

Once near Battle Creek I observed one flying; it had, however, been alarmed by one of the scouts ahead of the column, and only used its wings to cross a wide ravine, when it immediatley ran out of sight some hundreds of yards with the swiftness of a deer. From the locality they prefer, they get part of their name; to the notes they utter is due the other, a coarse *cuckoo* at the best. It is no prettier than the bird; a succession of low chuckles, grating harshly at first, softening at the end, and repeated often if you get near a pair. A few of the notes bring to mind the call of a barn-yard cock to his hen. In the quiet of an early morning, the *cuckoo,* or call, may be distinctly heard two hundred yards away across a ravine; once heard and fairly caught, you will always remember it. This time of the day is the best to secure them; easiest done by arousing their curiosity. Approaching the neighborhood of the Cuckoo's call, which you can only do by listening, as you go on, you stoop low in the chaparral and imitate their notes, or that of a mating bird. As soon as he catches the unusual sound, if on the alert, you will see him in a second before you. A friend who for a long time resided at Brownsville, Texas, informed me that there and generally along the Lower Rio Grande the Mexican name for this species is "Cha-cha-la-ca," [It may be worth while to remember that this name, under various spellings, is generally applied, or supposed to apply, to a very different bird, namely, *Ortalida retula.* —Ed.] which they say are the *bona-fide* notes uttered by the Cuckoo, being ordinarily known among the Texans as the Road-runner; and that several had been taken while young from a nest and had grown perfectly tame under the care of one of the natives, when they greatly resembled the Magpie *(P. malanoleuca* var. *hudsonica)* in the traits which become prominent on changing their wild nature to that of a domestic bird. For bright buttons, or anything of brass or glittering, they had an insatiable craving, and would sacrifice the interests of their best friends to satisfy their unnatural appetites. One of the pet "Cha-cha-la-cas" unfortunately, at a favorable opportunity, got his eye upon a breast-pin within reach, belonging to his owner, a fair Mexican belle, promptly "went for it," and bolted it whole. The Mexican love for jewelry, brass-plated or genuine, was, however, too powerful, and the pet Cuckoo was sacrificed.

In New Mexico, I found them called by the native inhabitants *Paisano,* by which, too, he is known farther up the Rio Grande in Western Texas. It signifies a "countryman," and is said to arise from his wildness, frequenting only unsettled places, and keeping away from the sight of man. It is traditional among them that he not only have a natural antipathy for all sorts of small snakes, devouring them with much gusto, but that he does not hesitate to attack the Rattler *(Crotalus confluentus)*, and gets the best of him in the fight.

The examination of the stomachs of the pair showed in the male Dragonflies *(Neuroptera)*, Grasshoppers *(Orthoptera)*, and a good quantity of hemplike woody fibre similar to the scrub-oak. The females showed a Lizard *(Cnemidophorus gularis)* and a great quantity of similar fibre, of which at times they must partake largely.

TABLE 31

Number of Collection.	Sex.	Locality.	Date.	Collector.	Collector's Name.	Length.	Extent.	Wing.	Tail.	Remarks.
8	♂ ad.	Red River Cañon	May 20	McCauley	183	24.0	20.0	7.5	13.1	Tarsi 2.6 ( ) and 2.5 ( ).
9	♀ ad.	do	May 20	do	184	20.8	19.8	7.2	12.0	Bill each 2.1.

COCCYZUS AMERICANUS, (L.) Bp. — *Yellow-billed Cuckoo.*[52]

Found frequently on Mulberry, McClellan, and other creeks, some distance from their heads, where the scant timber-fringe at their upper parts had developed into fine shady groves. They were decidedly shy and preferred to perch among high branches, often alighting, where they could have an extended view, upon the bark of a tree, clinging in the most approved Woodpecker style. Occasionally dashing about, with their bright, lustrous plumage flashing through the trees, they would venture down to a common-place sunflower or reed in search of insects. Like many of their kind, the Cuckoos were relying chiefly upon grasshoppers for their food.

TABLE 32

Number of Collection.	Sex.	Locality.	Date.	Collector.	Collector's Name.	Length.	Extent.	Wing.	Tail.	Remarks.
35	♀ ad.	Mulberry Creek	June 18	McCauley	208	12.5	17.5	6	6.5	

But one nest was found, which contained a single egg, June 17. No young were observed in it or near by. The egg, a pretty pale green and decidedly oval, measured 1.2 inches by 0.83 in diameter.

52Yellow-billed Cuckoo. *Coccyzus americanus* (Linnaeus). Although placed on the Blue List in 1973 and retained there each year since, it is considered by most local observers to be holding its own in the Panhandle (Arbib, "Announcing — the Blue List").

TABLE 33

Number of Collection.	Locality.	Date.	Collector.	Nests.	Eggs.	Remarks.
19	Mulberry Creek	June 17	McCauley	1	1	

PICIDAE.

PICUS SCALARIS, Wagler. — *Texas Woodpecker*.[53]

Several specimens noted on McClellan, Mulberry Creeks, etc. Not as frequent as *M. erythrocephalus*.

MELANERPES ERYTHROCEPHALUS, (L.) Sw. — *Red-headed Woodpecker*.[54]

Very abundant on McClellan, Mulberry, and other wooded creeks, except at their headwaters, where they were, however, found occasionally. Specimens obtained showed slight yellowish tinge, with a few faint crimson-tipped feathers on the belly.

On submitting one of them to Dr. Coues for his examination, he confirmed its identification, pronouncing it an undoubted *M. erythrocephalus*.

For comparison with the Kansas varieties, I obtained one of the latter, and found the difference marked, if not distinctive. In place of the strong yellowish wash, the belly was pure white, save a few feather-tips, with a faint tinge of lemon. The Texan ones contained much less white upon the tail, on both rectrices and coverts; had feet and tarsi more bluish than the latter, whilst their bills, black-tipped, were horn-blue throughout, the Kansas variety grading to ashy-white at the base.

TABLE 34

Number of Collection.	Sex.	Locality.	Date.	Collector.	Collector's Name.	Length.	Extent.	Wing.	Tail.	Remarks.
2	♂ ad.	Sweetwater Creek	May 12	McCauley		177	9.25	11.6	5.4	3.6
25	— —	Red River Cañon	May 29	Lt. Baldwin		— —	— —	— —	— —	— —

[53]Ladder-backed Woodpecker. *Picoides scalaris* (Wagler). Today this is the most widespread and common woodpecker of the area, the one you would most likely encounter on any given day afield. This change in status was possible brought about by the spread of mesquite trees and yuccas as they are plant associations to the bird's liking. McCauley's assertion that it was seen less frequently than the Red-headed Woodpecker [*Melanerpes erythrocephalus*] would probably hold true today only in the more heavily wooded portions of the eastern Panhandle.

[54]Red-headed Woodpecker. *Melanerpes erythrocephalus* (Linnaeus). Common in the eastern Panhandle and locally westward, today one would hardly call it "abundant."

STRIGIDAE.

BRACHYOTUS PALUSTRIS, Auct. — *Short-eared Owl.*[55]

McClellan Creek and other streams, in their well-wooded parts, with marshy banks and here and there large pools, the delight of the buffalo, possess their quota of inhabitants of the *Strigidae*. The specimen secured was shot in a grove immediately by the camp, and being brought in not quite dead and shown to one of the captive Falcons *(F. mexicanus)* kept as pets, they at once engaged in a combat, and could not be separated until the last breath of the Owl had loosened her grip.

TABLE 35

Number of Collection.	Sex.	Locality.	Date.	Collector.	Collector's Name.	Length.	Extent.	Wing.	Tail.	Remarks.
49	♀ ad.	McClellan Creek	June 21	McCauley	222	16.75	38.75	11.5	6	Stomach contained a Gopher *(Geomys bursarius?)*

? SYRNIUM NEBULOSUM, (Forst.) Boie. — *Barred Owl.*[56]

This specimen was secured in one of the deeply-shaded groves along Lower McClellan Creek, sitting lengthwise upon a great high limb. None were noticed at any headwaters of streams, which point they doubtless never frequent, owing to the smaller size of the timber.

TABLE 36

Number of Collection.	Sex.	Locality.	Date.	Collector.	Collector's Name.	Length.	Extent.	Wing.	Tail.	Remarks.
50	♀ ad.	McClellan Creek	June 21	McCauley	223	24.0	52.0	14.75	8.75	Stomach contained a Gopher *(Geomys bursarius?)*

[55]Short-eared Owl. *Asio flammeus* (Pontoppidan). The surprising thing in this account is the collection of a specimen on 21 June. The species is not known as a summer resident today as it is found only from late fall to early spring. The only reported summer sighting in this century is that of Kenneth Carlander, noted in "The Final Report of the Summer Survey of the Birds of the Panhandle of Texas" (Manuscript, Research Center, Panhandle-Plains Historical Museum, Canyon, Texas). The single instance of nesting anywhere near the Panhandle took place in Woods County, northwestern Oklahoma, "many years ago" (Sutton, *Checklist of Birds,* 21). This is a bird of open grassland, rarely alighting anywhere except on the ground or fence posts, and one would not expect to collect a specimen from a "grove" as McCauley did.

[56]Barred Owl. *Strix varia* Barton. This is a bird of dense woodland, and its only reported presence today is in the Lake Marvin area of eastern Hemphill County. A diligent search would possibly still disclose it along McClellan Creek where McCauley collected one.

SPEOTYTO CUNICULARIA HYPOGAEA, (Bp.) Coues. —
Burrowing Owl.[57]

Both upon the great plain itself and on the rolling prairies from Dodge, Kansas, to the south, up to its edge, scarcely a town of Prairie Dogs *(C. ludovicanus)* was without its owlish sentinel. In many of them, they seemed to outnumber the other inhabitants, the road south of the Cimarron being still remembered for its large number of the birds. Their shyness seemed to vary with the sun; at midday or afternoon exceedingly wary generally; in the early morning the reverse. It may have been a morning nap, or a delusive idea that they alone had eyes. Be that as it may, before the sun was well up, they showed the utmost indifference to our approach, and never moved until we were almost upon them. It was particularly so upon a damp and drizzly morning; and as we drove by the dog's town, we merely caught a glimpse of the hind legs and tail of the dog himself scampering into his hole, intent upon the interest of his family; whilst nearer, upon a small sunflower or reed, perched the owl, as immovable as a supreme-court judge. The owl was always apparently lost in thought, had nothing to do in particular, and more time at his disposal than anything else in the world, whilst the dog was always busy and without a moment to spare. The other member of the trio which leads the traditional life of peace in the same dwelling, constituting the "Happy Family" of the boundless prairie and the Far West, the Rattlesnake *(Crotalus confluentus)*, was also noted, often in their vicinity. The oft-told tale of their social life having been related by distinguished naturalists, had always been received without the grain of allowance necessary for snake stories, although an actual instance had never been met with. Last spring, however, I witnessed an occurrence which showed that the dogs and the snakes may be found in the same holes, whatever the nature of their association may be.

Marching along in Texas, near the Rio Grande, one day, through a dog town, one of the finest pack of hounds belonging to Lieutenant Goodwin, Ninth Cavalry, took after one of the dogs, that, perched on the top of his mound, was barking in a manner peculiarly aggravating. The hound of course got there a second too late — what was ever in time for a prairie dog? — but put his nose in the hole as far as possible, and drew forth a live rattlesnake. The column went on, but the poor hound was left behind.

We were upon the Staked Plain when the owlets were just the size for a delicious morsel; the rattlesnakes were also plentiful, and, as I naturally killed every one I met with, I made it a point to often examine to see whether any of the young birds had fallen a prey to their

[57]Burrowing Owl. *Athene cunicularia* (Molina). The fate of this species is closely connected with that of the black-tailed prairie dog *(Cynomys ludovicianus)*. Though still common, the burrowing owl is not nearly as much so as when "dog towns" stretched for miles across the prairie, as in McCauley's day.

next-room neighbors, but without success. This, however, was not conclusive that they sometimes did not; merely that none had been detected
in the act.

No hole was examined to get down as far as the eggs, simply for want
of time; we frequently saw them apparently paired, at the same hole,
and, without doubt, nidification was in process, from the general size
and age of young seen later. The number of eggs has been differently
stated, but, although variable, it must often be at least six, for I have seen
broods of as many young, well fledged, to which may be added possibly
one or more sacrificed to appease the hunger of the snakes, either as
a developed embryo or before. All of the broods referred to were too
young to have gone many yards from home; there were none of their
kind for a long distance, and the extreme solicitude displayed by the
mothers was conclusive that they belonged to one clutch.

During a day's march across the country near McClellan Creek, when
we had seen no owls for a long distance, one of the scouts with our party
espied, a short distance ahead, a mother with her family, giving them an
airing in the morning sun, perhaps ten or fifteen yards from their home.
Putting spurs to his horse, he bore down upon them, the frightened mother
scrambling for home, anxiously calling her young. Unfortunately for the
interest of the family, they were only equal to a fair toddle, and in their
confusion two of them were cut off and captured, one of which was set
at liberty, at once going for his hole with a lively step. There were six
or seven in all, and undoubtedly were from the same hatch; they were
in their pin-feathers (June 19). The captive was taken to camp, and such
an exceedingly comical object was he, with his little body and huge yellow
eyes, that he turned out to be the prime pet of our party, furnishing more
amusement than all the others together.

TABLE 37

Number of Collection.	Sex.	Locality.	Date.	Collector.	Collector's Name.	Length.	Extent.	Wing.	Tail.	Remarks.
52	♂ ad.	Staked Plain	June 18	McCauley		225	9.6	28.8	7.3	3.1	Stomachs con-
64	♀ ad.	Staked Plain	June 21	do		237	9.5	28.0	7.0	3.0	tained *Coleoptera*,
69	⚥ ad.	Cimarron River	June 24	do		242	9.6	28.4	7.1	3.0	etc.
70	♂ ad.	Bluff Creek, Kans.	June 27	do		243	9.8	28.5	7.2	3.5	

FALCONIDAE.

NAUCLERUS FURCATUS, (L.) Vig. — *Swallow-tailed Kite.*[58]

A specimen noted, going along Wolf Creek, Indian Territory.

[58]Swallow-tailed Kite. *Elanoides forficatus* (Linnaeus). This was an unlooked-
for sighting. This is a species that today breeds in the United States only from
South Carolina south to Florida, and west to Louisiana (A. O. U., *Check-list of
N. A. Birds,* 102). Observations beyond that range are rare. Formerly the

FALCO MEXICANUS, Licht. — *Lanner Falcon.*[59]

Occasionally observed in open country to Red River region, and thence in cañon localities. At Cañoncito Blanco, after obtaining one of the parent birds, an attempt was made to secure the nest, admirably situated in a crevice, about fifteen feet below the top of the vertical cañon-wall. Its height was nearly a hundred feet from the stream's bed, and the wall could not be scaled from below, the top jutted out, a great rock overhanging, preventing any one from getting down from its edge. After shooting one of the brood, which, older and much larger than the others, was advanced enough to fly, the rest were secured by one of the scouts in a decidedly novel manner. Tying a fish-hook to a short rag, fastened at the end of a long pole, he thrust it down into the nest, lying down on the overhanging edge of the rock. True to their instincts, the young, unable to walk or fly, were ready for a flight; they pecked at the "intruder" one by one, and were rudely fished out in succession. The total number of the young was four, [As this species, perhaps, lays but three eggs, may not the larger bird observed in this case have been one of the parents? — Ed.] and from their relative size the three last eggs laid must have been hatched out at or nearly the same time. The captives were thereafter the pets of the camp, and thrived wonderfully, showing their remarkable pugnacity and spirit on every possible occasion, regardless of the size of the opponent. No amount of kindness could ever induce them to forget the use of their claws against their best friend; all efforts of taming them were fruitless. When given, for the first time, a bird, a Killdeer Plover, shot for their benefit, they scrambled over it, and, after a rough diversion, settled down in opposite directions at the end of their lariats, which were used to keep them attached to their owner's tent. Holding on by their claws to their prize, they pulled out the feathers carefully with skill of experts, and then swallowed both flesh and bones.[x]

TABLE 38

Number of Collection.	Sex.	Locality.	Date.	Collector.	Collector's Name.	Length.	Extent.	Wing.	Tail.	Remarks.
27 66	♀ ad. ♂ ad.	Cañoncito Blanco do	June 3 June 4	McCauley do	200 239	19 —	43 —	14 ——	9.25 ——	The stomach contained a Gopher (*G. bursarius?*).

swallow-tailed kite was a transient and summer resident throughout the well-wooded parts of eastern and central Oklahoma (Sutton, *Oklahoma Birds*, 96). What is surprising is that McCauley did not record seeing the common kite species of that area today, the Mississippi kite (*Ictinia mississippiensis*). He could hardly have confused the two, however, as the deeply forked tail of the swallow-tailed is quite striking.

59Prairie Falcon. *Falco mexicanus* Schlegel. The status of this species has changed dramatically since McCauley's day; it no longer breeds where he found it in

FALCO RICHARDSONI, Ridg. — *Richardson's Falcon.*[60]

This handsome Falcon was found very abundant, chiefly in the cañon region of Red River. Ascending any of the side-cañons running from the river up to and against the almost vertical wall of the plain, one was almost sure of having several in sight. They were also common, though not in the same abundance, in the lower heavily wooded parts of Mulberry and other creeks, where they were not so extremely shy and wary. None were observed whilst passing through the Indian Territory. As the Red River tributaries were ascended, the large and beautiful groves grew smaller proportionally, until even the scant timber-fringe dwindled to low brush along the bank, with simply an occasional tree. Here various birds, deadly foes by nature, would of necessity apparently forge their enmity, and built in such proximity as could nowhere else be found. One of the parties which ascended the Tule to its headwaters, finding no trees of the highest permanent water, and noticing a solitary one beyond, visited it. It was found three miles higher up, without water, and upon it were several nests. Of these, one belonging to a species of *Falconidae* and another to one of the *Corvinae*, were

Cañoncito Blanco, and it is questionable that it does so anywhere in the Panhandle. At the turn of the century it was yet a resident along the edge of the plains (John K. Strecker, Jr., *The Birds of Texas: an Annotated Check-list* [Waco: Baylor University Bulletin, 1912], 15:28). Still later, it was classified as a permanent resident and found nesting in the Palo Duro Canyon (Kenneth Carlander, "Birds of the Palo Duro," *Amarillo Daily News*, 15 December 1934; James O. Stevenson, "Birds of the Central Panhandle of Texas," *Condor* 44 (1942): 110). By mid-century a few were being seen in summer but nesting was not discovered (Hawkins, "Bird Life," 125-126). Today it is known primarily as a winter resident with only an occasional summer sighting.

60Merlin. *Falco columbarius* Linnaeus. This must be yet another case of misidentification as the merlin has never been known to nest in the southern Great Plains, and for McCauley to refer to it as "very abundant" is cause for wonder. Oberholser, who was familiar with McCauley's work, omits referring to any possible Panhandle nesting, thus dismissing such a claim (Oberholser, *Bird Life of Texas*, 1:258-260). The pale race of the merlin that McCauley refers to (*F. c. richardsoni*) breeds today in the Great plains from central Alberta and Saskatchewan to Wyoming and Dakota (Leslie Brown and Dean Amadon, *Eagles, Hawks and Falcons of the World* [New York: McGraw-Hill, 1968], 2:803). There have been recent (1975 and 1978) isolated instances of it nesting in extreme northwestern Nebraska (Paul A. Johnsgard, *Birds of the Great Plains* [Lincoln: University of Nebraska Press, 1979], 103). One must conclude that McCauley confused this race of the merlin with the similar American Kestrel (*F. sparverius*), which he also found common. Disturbing about his report, however, is the alleged finding of two nests in trees; one an exposed nest near that of a raven or crow (Corvinae = Corvidae), the other a twig nest placed in the crotch of a tree. The merlin is known for nesting in the old abandoned nests of other species, particularly of crows, whereas kestrel nests, when in trees, are located in cavities (Arthur Cleveland Bent, *Life Histories of North American Birds of Prey* [1937: reprint, New York: Dover Publications, 1961], 170:70-127). Today the merlin is a rare migrant and winter resident and has been recorded no later in the spring than 20 April (Texas Panhandle Audubon Society).

within 6 feet of each other. At a grove on White Fish Creek, where, within
500 yards were over forty nests of various kinds of birds, the nest obtained was taken from a small cottonwood with nests of *Tyrannidae* upon
the one adjoining. It was placed in a crotch of a tree, 20 or 25 feet up.
The twigs used in building varied from one-fourth of an inch to a tenth,
mainly of small size; the whole structure being 6 inches high, with an
outside diameter above of 8 inches. After having built up 2 inches from
below, and considering this foundation firm and secure, the birds began
the building of a high and hollow nest with a well-filled leafy interior.
An outer circle being completed in the usual way, well braced to the
part below, they broke off the tip ends of tiny branches of the cottonwood, leaving an inch or two of the stem, with as many leaves as possible. The ends of these were carefully placed through and twining about
the outside circle, and continued until the layer of leaves was as high
as the row of sticks without. Keeping each successive row the same,
they arrived within an inch of the top, when, deciding that the interior
must be made still softer for their young, they selected twigs with the
bursting buds of cotton, which were carefully arranged and intertwined.
Above, covering the cushion of cotton, were placed a number of leaves,
making the whole interior or leafy diameter 5 inches, upon which the
eggs were laid. They were of the nearly subspherical shape common
to birds of prey, and of a dirty white, with considerable discoloration;
of unequal size, with the same length, one exceeded the other in transverse diameter by a tenth of an inch.

TABLE 39

Number of Collection.	Locality.	Date.	Collector.	Nests.	Eggs.	Remarks.
20	White Fish Creek	June 19	McCauley	1	2	

FALCO SPARVERIUS, L. — *Sparrow Hawk*.[61]

This elegant, plucky little Falcon flourishes, as he everywhere does,
throughout the section visited, except upon the Great Plain. Every wooded stream had its quota, and as, in seeking food, they descend from
feathered prey to the insect world, they must have all been rolling in
fat, judging from the great abundance of grasshoppers, of various sizes
and hues. They were at all events, wherever we met them, the very
picture of laziness, and rarely made the effort necessary to capture a
Sparrow. They managed, however, to keep up their natural distrust,
and were wary of us whenever we passed. Occasionally venturing to

61American Kestrel. *Falco sparverius* Linnaeus. There has been little change
in its status, except that today it is found also upon the Great Plain in the vicinity
of human settlements.

attack one of the *Tyrannidae,* and invariably getting the worst of it, with a crest-fallen look he kept his enforced and secluded retreat, until, detecting one of us attempting to approach, he left disgusted with things in general. They and larger *Falconidae* seemed to be living at perfect peace with the doves *(Z. carolinensis),* of which hundreds were about; in fact, it would be a difficult matter for any of them, desirous of such prey, to find a locality where they could be as well suited.

BUTEO BOREALIS, (Gm.) V. — *Red-tailed Buzzard or Hen Hawk.*[62]

One of the species observed whilst *en route* near the Canadian.

BUTEO SWAINSONI, Bp. — *Swainson's Buzzard.*[63]

This magnificent Hawk was frequently seen along streams passed, and both in Red River Cañon and at the very origin of the waters, far up in the Staked Plain. At other times they were noted out on the level of the plain, miles from timber.

During a reconnaissance up the Palo Duro, at its very source, a small spring, were found a few trees, on one of which, about fifteen feet high and overhanging the water, was a nest of this Hawk with one of the parent birds upon it. As we rode up, the bird quietly withdrew; but being interested in our visit, perched upon a cliff near by, where there was a commanding view, distant about 300 yards. After an attempt to get within range, which was unsuccessful, the bird left at once. Instead of circling about and descending to some other and more distant point of view, nothing was seen of the Hawk during an hour, occupied in rest and a lunch, and it seemed likely that we must wait for several hours at the least for its return. The nest at the top of the tree, where it was well exposed to view, was then rifled of its contents, a single egg. Desirous of obtaining the parent by fair or foul means, a stone of the same size wrapped in white paper was left in its place. One of the party, with his carbine, being concealed in the undergrowth by the water and below the nest, all the others with the horses were withdrawn the distance of over a mile. Shortly, both the old birds appeared at an immense height, and soon came nearer, sweeping around in graceful circles. After gradual descent, and an apparent consultation, the proprietor of the original egg, deceived by appearances, and influenced by parental feelings, took place cautionsly upon the nest, and was secured by a carbine shot.y

62Red-tailed Hawk. *Buteo jamaicensis* Gmelin). It is widespread in the Panhandle but more so in the area where McCauley observed it near the Canadian River.

63Swainson's Hawk. *Buteo swainsoni* Bonaparte. A common buteo of the plains, its declining numbers is cause for concern, and it is now on the "Blue List" (Arbib, "Announcing — the Blue List"). It can be observed in flocks of hundreds during migration, particularly in late September and early October.

TABLE 40

Number of Collection.	Sex.	Locality.	Date.	Collector.	Collector's Name.	Length.	Extent.	Wing.	Tail.	Remarks.
19	♂ ad.	Palo Duro	May 26	McCauley	194	19	50	15.3	8	Tarsus 2.8; bill 1.5.

The nest was built in the usual style of large rapacious birds, in one of the main crotches of the tree, and of twigs from one-fourth to one-third of an inch in thickness; above was a scant layer of leaves taken from the tree. The egg is of a slightly bluish or a very dull white, with spots of a rusty brown; the major and transverse axes 2.24 by 1.73 inches.

TABLE 41

Number of Collection.	Locality.	Date.	Collector.	Nests.	Eggs.	Remarks.
5	Palo Duro	May 26	McCauley	1	1	

PANDION HALIAËTUS, (L.) Savigny — *Fish Hawk or Osprey.*[64]

A very few noted, chiefly on the Canadian. In connection with the well-known parasitism of the Bald Eagle and the Osprey, an occurrence of the kind may be here noticed without being deemed irrelevant, inasmuch as it shows how illy disposed is the Hawk to furnishing unrewarded the Bird of Liberty's provender. A friend who resides near Baltimore, upon one of the small inlets of the Chesapeake Bay, was recently taking a walk near the water's edge, when he noticed a Fish Hawk rise from the water with a prize in his mouth, and, after getting a short distance inland, beset upon by an Eagle, evidently waiting for a meal, and a quiet spectator of the fishing. Being attacked and compelled to give it up, he dropped it, which the Eagle, catching in the air, flew away with, apparently disregarding the pangs of a guilty conscience. The next day he noticed a repetition of the fishing operation by the Hawk, and on the Eagle's approach as before, he promptly dropped it again, and quickly disappeared. The Eagle caught it as before in the air; but, strangely, as he thought, let it go, and it fell to the ground. Being generally interested in nature, the gentleman

64Osprey. *Pandion haliaetus* (Linnaeus). A migrant throughout the area, its numbers are gradually increasing following an alarming postwar decline due to the widespread and indiscriminate use of DDT and other harmful pesticides that are now banned or controlled. McCauley must have seen his birds while outward bound in early May as the species has been reported only once in this century past mid-May — 18 June 1942 (Phillip F. Allan and Palmer R. Sime, "A Hawk Census on Texas Panhandle Highways," *Wilson Bulletin* 55 (1943): 35).

concluded to go up and examine the cause of the unusual conduct of the thieving "Emblem of Freedom," our Great North American Bird. He did so, and, reaching the spot, found the supposed fish a piece of dried manure. It was the old story of "Revenge is sweet," etc., but at once suggests the conundrum, "Is there naught save mere instinct granted by nature to her creatures?"

HALIAËTUS LEUCOCEPHALUS, (L.) Savigny. —
White-headed or Bald Eagle.[65]

Met with several times in the cañon of Red River. On Mulberry Creek, June 17, a nest of this species was found containing two young about a week old. They were taken to camp, added to the list of pets of the soldiers, and brought in on our return. It was over a month before they acquired the necessary strength or learned to use their legs. Of a generally uncouth appearance, their awkward look was heightened by squatting in the most ungraceful manner upon their "elbows," as the soldiers remarked, the whole tarsus resting on the ground, and their toes and claws continually in their way, for they were evidently conscious of having no place to put them so as to be of ease.[z] This is one of all the feathered tribe most valuable to the red men. The birds seen were consequently and naturally, to no small degree, mistrustful on our approach. Every chief and young buck of a tribe must needs have his war-bonnet; and as the quills of the Eagle alone will suffice for such purpose, they are always in demand and eagerly sought for. The purchaser of Indian trophies and things has consequently to pay well on his adding this curiosity to his collection.

POLYBORUS THARUS AUDUBONI, (Cass.) Ridg. —
Audubon's Caracara.[66]

But a single one of the species observed near Lower Mulberry Creek, though a large number of buffalo carcasses were passed. This is almost the extreme northern limit of its range, and doubtless over the southeastern portion of the plain it will be found very common.

[65]Bald Eagle. *Haliaeetus leucocephalus* (Linnaeus). No longer a breeding species in the Panhandle, its last known nesting took place in 1916 when eggs were collected in Potter County (Oberholser, *Bird Life of Texas,* 1:246). Periodically there are reports of summer birds with possible nesting, but none have been verified. The last firm sighting was of an adult bird along White Deer Creek in southeastern Hutchinson County on 25 June 1955 (Texas Panhandle Audubon Society). The McCauley nest on Mulberry Creek was in present-day Armstrong County.

[66]Crested Caracara. *Polyborus plancus* (Miller). Today the range of the caracara in Texas is from the Lower Rio Grande Valley north along the eastern edge of the Edwards Plateau to Hood, Kaufman, Van Zandt and Johnson counties, and south to Brazos County (T. O. S., *Checklist of Birds,* 33-34). That McCauley saw it so far north of this range, in present-day Armstrong County, is probably attributable to the large number of buffalo carcasses he speaks of, for the species is a carrion feeder. There have been two possible but unconfirmed sightings this century: 19 April 1953 in Randall County and 11 May 1983 in Hutchinson County (Texas Panhandle Audubon Society).

CATHARTIDAE.

CATHARTES AURA, (L.), Illiger. — *Turkey Buzzard.*[67]

Common; seen in almost every section visited. Observed also feeding upon carrion in company with *C. atratus.*

CATHARTES ATRATUS, (Bartr.) Less. — *Black Vulture or Carrion Crow.*[68]

The most numerous of the *Cathartidae* observed.

On our return, in June, to Mulberry, McClellan, and other creeks, which the buffalo, in their northern migration, reached after our first visit, we found many carcasses of animals slain by hunters, generally for their hides alone, very little of the meat being used. This had attracted the Vultures in considerable numbers, compared with the quantity observed whilst going in May to the south and west.

COLUMBIDAE.

ZENAEDURA CAROLINENSIS, (L.) Bp. — *Carolina* or *Common Dove.*[69]

At several small groves of young cottonwoods, near McClellan and other creeks, the number seemed to be limitless, every bush or tree having tenants of this species. Passing one day down McClellan Creek, as we were riding underneath trees, a Dove suddenly fell to the ground, and, struggling to rise without success, went through the usual various gymnastic feats essential to attain their object. The soldier with me called my attention to it, and starting off to "catch the lame bird," followed through the brush, frequently on the point of getting it, and was much astonished when the Dove rose up and flew off, after having drawn him a hundred yards away. I have frequently during the trip noted that if you suddenly come upon a nest and surprise the mother there, after sitting until she becomes aware that you are staring her out of countenance, and there is no room for hoping that you have missed her, or of saving her eggs, she will be up and off. If, however, she observes your approach, she will generally attempt the well-known fraud described. Near the lower bed of Red River and other alkali grounds traversed, they were also found, but not in the profusion [in which] they exist along McClellan, Mulberry, and other creeks containing good water, where it very naturally became a little monotonous to meet three Doves to one of any other species.

67Turkey Vulture. *Cathartes aura* (Linnaeus). Abundant in McCauley's day because of the large food source provided by dead buffalo, it is no longer found in great numbers. More sanitary range practices today have no doubt further reduced its population by the removal of significant numbers of dead cattle; "buzzards," however, are still fairly common.

68Black Vulture. *Coragyps atratus* (Bechstein). This vulture is no longer to be found in the Panhandle. It was another carrion feeder that was exploiting an abundant food source; McCauley's assertion, however, that he found it more numerous than the turkey vulture is unexpected. Subsequent sightings have been rare, the last being in 1958 (Texas Panhandle Audubon Society).

69Mourning Dove. *Zenaida macroura* (Linnaeus). Still abundant today. McCauley's assertion that no ground nests were found because of reptiles is partially true. It commonly nests on the ground early in the season (March-April) before the vegetation has grown too high and dense.

TABLE 42

Number of Collection.	Sex.	Locality.	Date.	Collector.	Collector's Name.	Length.	Extent.	Wing.	Tail.	Remarks.
17	♀ ad.	Palo Duro	May 26	McCauley		192	9	16	6	3.5	Stomach: seeds, etc.

A very large number of nests could have been secured if desired, as nidification was going on (June 5-19). As a natural result of the existence in large numbers of various reptiles, none of the nests were upon the ground, being invariably on the lower limbs, or if they were well up, in the cluster of the grape-vines that often luxuriantly encircled the trees. The nests were flimsy affairs, and of the eggs, as ordinarily found, the two differed slightly in size. The greatest major axis was 1.14 inches, from which it decreased to 1.08; the extreme variation of the transverse being 0.84 to 0.80, and the general average of all measured being 1.11 by 0.813.

TABLE 43

Number of Collection.	Locality.	Date.	Collector.	Nests.	Eggs.	Remarks.
13	Tule Creek	June 9	McCauley	1	2	
25	White Fish Creek	June 19	do	1	2	
26	McClellan Creek	June 20	do	1	2	

MELOPELIA LEUCOPTERA, (L.) Bp. — *White-winged Dove.*[70]

A single specimen noted along one of the southern creeks. None of *C. passerina* met with during the trip.

MELEAGRIDAE.

MELEAGRIS GALLOPAVO AMERICANA, (Bartr.) Coues. — *Common Wild Turkey.*[71]

This species was first met with at Wolf Creek, Indian Territory, where numbers were observed, but not in the abundance in which it was

[70]White-winged Dove. *Zenaida asiatica* (Linnaeus). There have been only six reported sightings in the Panhandle since this one. Color slides taken of one found on the Buffalo Lake National Wildlife Refuge in Randall County 19-21 May 1973 were deposited in the Texas Photo-Record File at Texas A&M University. It is a common summer resident in the South Texas Plains and can be found no nearer to the Panhandle than Bexar and Jeff Davis counties (T. O. S., *Checklist of Birds,* 55). McCauley speaks of not seeing the common ground-dove *(Columbina passerina),* as though he expected to. It, too, is a resident of south Texas with only occasional sightings as far north as Crosby and Lubbock counties (ibid., 56).

[71]Wild Turkey. *Meleagris gallopavo* Linnaeus. McCauley's account bears testimony to the rapid decline of the wild turkey in the Panhandle from its former status of

found as lately as two years ago. It may be said to be common throughout the whole section visited save in the alkali region of Red River proper. The decrease or disappearance of this game bird from this section, particularly from the Palo Duro and the Washita regions, has been very marked during the last few years.aa

The young were hatched and able to fly into low trees, June 15, at which time the mothers showed comparative indifference to our approach, all their efforts being combined to get their broods away. Some of the gobblers killed were of large size and great weight, reminding us of well fattened "Christmas turkeys."

An egg taken from a nest, just starting, was 2.28 by 1.70 inches; ground-color faint sienna, with small spots, various in size, of a darker shade.

TABLE 44

Number of Collection.	Locality.	Date.	Collector.	Nests.	Eggs.	Remarks.
1	McClellan Creek	May 15	McCauley	—	1	

TETRAONIDAE.

CUPIDONIA CUPIDO PALLIDICINCTUS, Ridgw. — *Southern Pinnated Grouse or Prairie Hen.*[72]

This magnificent game bird was first observed in traveling along the road south from Fort Dodge, between the Cimarron and north fork of the Canadian. It was abundant in coveys of from twenty to thirty; south of that less frequently seen.bb Beyond the Sweetwater, they were not

abundance. That abundance was recorded on numerous occasions by Abert during his exploration through the region in 1845. (H. Bailey Carroll, "The Journal of Lieutenant J. W. Abert from Bent's Fort to St. Louis in 1845," *Panhandle-Plains Historical Review* 14 [1941]). By 1905 the last wild turkey had been eradicated from northwest Texas (Oberholser, *Bird Life of Texas,* 1:283). The presence of the species in the Panhandle today is the result of restockings that began near mid-century with releases on Horse Creek; at two places on the Canadian, in Oldham County; on Mustang Creek, in Hartley County; on the South Palo Duro, in northeastern Moore County; and along the Canadian, in Potter County (A. W. Schorger, *The Wild Turkey* [Norman: University of Oklahoma Press, 1966], 459). These releases were of the subspecies *M. E. intermedia,* the Rio Grande turkey; originally, both the Rio Grande and Merriam's turkey *(M. g. merriami)* occupied the Panhandle, meeting along the Canadian River in what is probably now Carson County.

72Lesser Prairie-Chicken. *Tympanuchus pallidicinctus* (Ridgway). Today the bulk of lesser prairie chickens in the Panhandle are confined to Lipscomb, Hemphill, and Wheeler counties where McCauley found them (A. S. Jackson and Richard DeArment, "The Lesser Prairie Chicken in the Texas Panhandle," *Journal of Wildlife Management* 27 (1963): 733-737). This remnant population has been under considerable stress from habitat destruction, hunting, and indiscriminate aerial spraying of harmful pesticides.

found, nor were they seen in any part of the lower sections visited, until, on our return, we reached the rolling land north of McClellan Creek. This, the only one of the Grouse family proper we met with, avoids the Staked Plain, and ventures near it only where all the conditions of its prairie-life may be fulfilled.

ORTYX VIRGINIANA, (L.) Bp. — *Virginia Partridge or Quail.*73

The habitat of this variety of the finest of game birds, extending over the great western plains, reaches through that part of the Indian Territory we traversed and across the Pan Handle to the Upper Cañon region. Strictly avoiding the Staked Plain, their range is south through Texas, touching the eastern border of the plain itself, and thence down to some point, perhaps as yet a matter of conjecture, where is found the northern limit of var. *texanus.*

At the most western part of Mulberry Creek, about longitude 101°, two specimens were secured; ten miles or more farther to the west, in the bed of Red River itself, several hundred feet below the level of the plain, I found them with young, well fledged, and as lively as crickets, June 11. In this latter place, the water was as vile and unwholesome as an alkali drink, for a steady thing, is generally acknowledged to be. Sixty miles farther up the river, our camps were by the stream in the cañon; and up beyond, on rolling land along the Palo Duro and Tierra Blanca, fine fresh water and rich grassy lands; but in these sections we never flushed a Quail, nor did we ever hear the "bob-white," so familiar farther east, during our incoming and return. The fine execution of the familiar trick of the mother bird during nidification, when an intruder approaches her home, is too well known to required repetition. It was interesting, however, to watch her movements when she found her decoy unsuccessful. Walking one day through a cluster of young cottonwoods, suddenly up jumped a hen, a half-dozen yards ahead of me, and took sharply to

---

73Northern Bobwhite. *Colinus virginianus* (Linnaeus). This bird is today a common resident throughout most of the area, more so in the eastern half. McCauley speaks of three other species of quail he did not see but seemed to anticipate seeing. The scaled, or "Blue," quail *(Callipepla squamata)* is a common resident of the Panhandle. Its range is complimentary to that of the bobwhite, although range overlap occurs. The scaled quail is typically found in mesquite or juniper savanna habitats, while the bobwhite typically occurs in woodland or riparian woodland habitats (Paul A. Johnsgard, *Grouse and Quails of North America* [Lincoln: University of Nebraska Press, 1973], 358-360). It is hard to believe that McCauley did not encounter the scaled quail for it is today quite common in the Red River canyon. The Montezuma Quail *(Cyrtonyx montezumas = Cyrtonya massena)* was never a resident of the Panhandle. Its Texas range today is confined to the higher elevations of Trans-Pecos and on the western edge of the Edwards Plateau; likewise, Gambel's Quail *(Callipepla gambelii = Lophortyx gambeli)*; it was never a Panhandle resident and is found in Texas today along the Rio Grande in the Trans-Pecos (T. O. S., *Checklist of Birds,* 37-38). Past attempts to introduce the Gambel's Quail have failed (Hawkins, "Bird Life," 127).

my left, with her usual cries and bodily agony. After going a few steps, and finding her stale decoy a failure, she continued a pace or two, and, observing me still keep on directly ahead, she altered her tune in a second. Forgetting the pain she possessed a moment before, she changed her notes to a series of the sharpest calls that a Quail could utter, evidently signals to her partner, wherever he was.

The old gentleman, in obedience to the sharp remarks of his dame, promptly set forth and dashed out from before me, with the lovely little chicks running out from the grass beneath. The mother watched them with intense anxiety from the left, and as the cock ran off, calling them to follow, she added a few more notes, quick and decided, evidently remarks directed to the lagging little ones, and intended to hurry them on, and then cut across behind me and joined her family, safe from danger, with some haste and doubtless a great deal of satisfaction.

During our marches, the Quail met showed little wariness and generally allowed us to get very near, and it was only when a horse was turned aside and came directly toward or among them that the covey rose and flew to cover.cc

Neither the Scaled Partridge or Blue Quail *(Callipepla squamata)*, the curiously-striped Massena Partridge *(Cyrtonya massena)*, nor the beautiful Arizona Quail or Gambel's Partridge *(Lophortyx gambeli)*, for all of which Texas is a habitat, were observed in any part of the section visited. Gambel's Partridge, generally called by the ranchmen "Plumed Quail," I observed in great numbers last February at Fort Selden, N. Mex., latitude 32⁰ 25', and thence in traveling south. Returning, over a month later, I did not observe any north of that point. Immediately above Selden, at whose edge it lies, stretches to the north the Jornado del Muerto (Journey of Death), a great treeless desert of ninety miles, without water save that to be purchased at a well sunk midway upon the line of travel; bordered on its west side by two steep volcanic mountain-ranges, Sierra del Caballo and Sierra Fra Cristóbal, the two the same range but for a narrow gorge or cañon between, an effectual barrier along the Rio Grande, preventing a road by its inaccessible banks; upon the east extends like a range, the San Andreas Mountains, continued under the name of Sierra Soledad, the whole a long, level plain, shut in by two great impassable rocky walls, relieved only by a sight of the Rio Grande at Paraje — well named in olden times "The Rest" — latitude 33⁰ 33', on its northern limit. No more effectual obstruction to the migration of these birds could be presented. In extreme Eastern New Mexico, however, the valley of the Pecos may render their migration not only possible, but very probable.

Nests of eggs freshly laid were found May 15 along McClellan Creek, etc.

TABLE 45

Number of Collection.	Sex.	Locality.	Date.	Collector.	Collector's Name.	Length.	Extent.	Wing.	Tail.	Remarks.
58	♂ ad.	Mulberry Creek	June 17	McCauley		231	9.6	—	4.6	2.6	
59	♀ ad.	do	June 17	do		232	9.5	—	4.5	2.6	

CHARADRIIDAE.

CHARADRIUS FULVUS VIRGINICUS, (Borck.) Coues. — *Golden Plover.*[74]

Whilst abundant in March along the Upper Rio Grande region of Texas, bordered by New and Old Mexico, none of this species had, when we were traveling south early in May through Kansas, Indian Territory, and Texas to the Red River, as yet found their way thither or been noticed in that region. The days, especially mornings, were often cold, and northers were not infrequent. On our return, in the latter part of June, this fine game bird had, like the buffalo, come north with the increasing heat, and were abundant on the route, apparently keeping up their journey. As we drove by them, if near the road, they would show no shyness whatever.

AEGIALITIS VOCIFERA, (L.) Cass. — *Killdeer Plover.*[75]

Very abundant in all sections, including alkaline, throughout our entire trip. In following up any sunken stream, if but a small bit of water was visible, alkali or otherwise, there was always heard the oft-repeated monotonous notes of this Wader.

In some of the smallest creeks running through sandy bottoms, tributaries of the Mulberry, etc., no water, and, save a moist surface, no indication of it, could be found in the afternoons from the great heat during the days; visiting them in the early morning, a good-sized stream would be found in its bed. Hereabouts and abundant were the Killdeer, in batches of twos and threes, and at times alone, running through the grass or along the banks.

TABLE 46

Number of Collection.	Sex.	Locality.	Date.	Collector.	Collector's Name.	Length.	Extent.	Wing.	Tail.	Remarks.
31	♀ ad.	Mulberry Creek	June 15	McCauley		204	10.75	20.0	6.5	4.25	Bill .86;
37	♀ —	White Fish Creek	June 19	Ruby		—	— —	— —	— —	— —	tarsus 1.36.
70	♂ ad.	Sweetwater Creek	June 21	McCauley		243	10.80	20.5	6.6	4.30	Tarsus 1.40.

[74]Lesser Golden-Plover. *Pluvialis dominica* (Müller). The age in which this handsome shorebird literally swarmed across the continent in migration was evidently almost over when McCauley made his observations. The surprising thing was his not finding any on the outward journey and then finding them common on returning in late June. Today it is a rare migrant, not recorded every year, with spring dates of 22 April — 25 May (Texas Panhandle Audubon Society). The only summer sighting on record is of an injured bird observed on a playa lake in northwestern Armstrong County on 7 July 1985 (personal records).

[75]Killdeer. *Charadrius vociferus* Linnaeus. This species has adapted well to human

The eggs were of the usual pyriform shape, and color, and averaged 1.53 by 1.09 inches. The birds in two cases observed, instead of laying their eggs directly in the sand, had selected for their "nest" buffalo "chip" (as the plainsmen call the masses of dried manure), conveniently near the water.

TABLE 47

Number of Collection.	Locality.	Date.	Collector.	Nests.	Eggs.	Remarks.
15	Battle Creek	June 13	Ruby	1	2	Embryo, very far advanced.
18	Mulberry Creek tributary	June 14	do	1	2	

EUDROMIAS MONTANUS, (Towns.) Harting. — *Mountain Plover.*[76]

A number noted between Camp Supply, Indian Territory, and Fort Dodge, Kansas, upon the fine prairie land, where were also frequently seen the Long-billed Curlew and the Burrowing Owl, as usual in prairie-dog towns.

SCOLOPACIDAE.

GALLINAGO WILSONI, (Temm.) Bp. — *American or Wilson's Snipe.*[77]

Observed along streams between Camp Supply, Indian Territory, and Fort Elliott, Texas.

TRINGA MINUTILLA, V. — *Least Sandpiper or Peep.*[78]

A very few observed *en route* whilst passing through the southern part of the Indian Territory, near Fort Elliott.

TOTANUS SOLITARIUS, (Wils.). — *Solitary Tattler.*[79]

Occasionally observed along water-courses, as the Canadian, etc.

settlement and is still common today throughout the area. It has adapted so well that it has been known to nest on the flat tops of buildings in Amarillo.

[76]Mountain Plover. *Charadrius montanus* Townsend. The mountain plover is still today a common migrant in the Panhandle but more so through the western half where it was probably a nesting species in McCauley's day (Walter D. Graul and Lois E. Webster, "Breeding Status of the Mountain Plover," *Condor* 78 (1976): 265-267). Today nesting is unconfirmed, with scattered summer sightings confined to Dallam and Hartley counties.

[77]Common Snipe. *Gallinago gallinago* (Linnaeus). Today this is an uncommon to common migrant with occasional sightings in winter. McCauley must have observed the birds on his outward journey (3-6 May) as it has not been recorded in that area past 17 May (Sutton, *Oklahoma Birds,* 182).

[78]Least Sandpiper. *Calidris minutilla* (Vieillot). Today this bird is a common to abundant migrant, as it probably was in McCauley's day. He speaks of seeing only a few, but large empoundments today have exposed mudflats where the birds congregate to feed and rest.

[79]Solitary Sandpiper. *Tringa solitaria* Wilson. As its name implies, it is usually found singly or in very small groups.

ACTITURUS BARTRAMIUS, (Wils.) Bp. — *Bartramian Sandpiper* or *Upland Plover.* [80]

Frequently observed on the prairie-land and near the streams, upon returning in latter part of June. Very friendly, allowing an ambulance to pass on the road within a few yards.

NUMENIUS LONGIROSTRIS, (Wils.). — *Long-billed Curlew.* [81]

Frequent, and perhaps of as general distribution as any other species throughout the section traversed. First seen upon the prairie-lands of Kansas and the Indian Territory; its range and habitat extended over all the places visited, save in cañons themselves and in the immediate vicinity of alkali water, where I do not recall having observed it. It was found in the same abundance several miles from water, on the Staked Plain, as upon the prairie or rolling-land lying about the lower parts of the creeks. In going south early in May, the birds were very shy, and could only be approached within range of a shot-gun by driving near in an ambulance, concealing your intention, as you try to "fool" a Hawk. In June, nidification was in progress, and frequently, in riding along, the bird would wait till within twenty-five yards before rising, mounted or afoot making little difference. In early May, they were in flocks of from three or four to ten or twelve; but in June, in smaller numbers, not half a dozen being seen together. Their vocal powers, at no time weak, are apparently strengthened during their hatching; then, as a shrieker, the mother proves herself an immense success. On her nest being approached, she waits until within forty yards perhaps, often less, rises up, and, circling about the spot, sends forth those touching notes so well calculated to induce one to leave to get rid of them. Their immediate effect, however, is the sympathy she seeks. At once appear a few more intimate friends, doubtless to join her in the chorus, each attempting louder calls and harsher than the rest, all circling about as if desirous of attacking the intruder with their long, ungraceful bills. The curlew pandemonium is continued with energy until the invader has gone from the vicinity and there is no sign of his return.

For the extreme delicacy of its flesh, this is to the sportsman making a fall trip through Western Texas one of the highest prized of the game birds.[dd]

[80]Upland Sandpiper. *Bartramia longicauda* (Bechstein). This species was decimated by hunters in the nineteenth century. It has been eliminated from the Panhandle as a breeding species, although recent scattered summer sightings indicate possible nesting.

[81]Long-billed Curlew. *Numenius americanus* Bechstein. Known today as a nesting species only in the northwestern sector of the Panhandle, in all other areas it is a common migrant.

TANTALIDAE.

TANTALUS LOCULATOR, L. — *Wood Ibis.*[82]

This large and notable bird has ventured to take up his dwelling in the Staked Plain, one having been observed on the Palo Duro, a few miles below its head; some days later, two others were met with near the upper part of the Tierra Blanca. As he has informed me, this species was previously observed by my friend, Dr. H. S. Turrill, assistant surgeon United States Army, when crossing the Staked Plain with a column of the Eighth Cavalry, under General Gregg, United States Army, in 1872.[ee] As usual, those seen were very shy. The one upon the Palo Duro, a magnificent bird, rose from the thick undergrowth bordering the stream, less than a hundred yards away, and took refuge upon the other bank below. The stream, unfortunately, being impassable from recent rains, I was prevented from attempting to follow and secure him.

ARDEIDAE.

ARDEA HERODIAS, L. — *Great Blue Heron.*[83]

Frequenting the Canadian, lower part of McClellan Creek, and below its mouth, on North Fork of Red River, etc. Here the vegetation changes to a denser, a ranker character; swampy places occur; the passage of the creeks or rivers by wagon-train or horseback is often a matter of difficulty, and the vicinity of the streams assumes in great part a sub-tropical aspect.

ARDEA CANDIDISSIMA, Jacquin. — *Little White Egret or Snowy Heron.*[84]

Occurring in same localities as *A. herodias.*

ARDEA CAERULEA, L. — *Little Blue Heron.*[85]

Occasional; same range as previous species.

---

[82]Wood Stork. *Mycteria americana* Linnaeus. These sightings are among the more remarkable McCauley recorded and represent the only known reference to the species in the Texas Panhandle. Today it is known only as a post-breeding visitor to the state and then casually no nearer than Denton, Tarrant, and Concho counties (T. O. S., *Checklist of Birds,* 20). It should be noted that here, as in other passages, McCauley describes streamside and surrounding habitats that differ markedly from what can be found today. Such changes are vividly depicted by Carlson in comparing the Canadian River of 1874 to what it is today (Paul H. Carlson, "Panhandle Pastores: Early Sheepherding in the Texas Panhandle," *Panhandle-Plains Historical Review* 53 (1980): 1). Such habitat changes have a direct bearing on bird distributions.

[83]Great Blue Heron. *Ardea herodias* Linnaeus. This species is still fairly common in the areas described, with scattered colonies of nesting birds. The bulky nests are always placed in the upper branches of tall cottonwood trees.

[84]Snowy Egret. *Egretta thula* (Molina). Today this bird is a rare transient.

[85]Little Blue Heron. *Egretta caerulea* (Linnaeus). Today it is a rare transient.

GRUIDAE.

GRUS CANADENSIS, (L.) Temm. — *Brown* or *Sandhill Crane.*[86]

A few noted near water-courses; more common near the Canadian. Nowhere seen in that abundance in which I observed them last April along the Rio Grande, in Central New Mexico, near Belen, etc.

RALLIDAE.

RALLUS VIRGINIANUS, L. — *Virginia Rail.*[87]

A very few found at swampy places on lower part of McClellan Creek.

FULICA AMERICANA, Gm. — *American Coot* or *Mud Hen.*[88]

Occasionally noted at a few points where there were swamps or large reedy pools of water.[ff]

ANATIDAE.

ANSER HYPERBOREUS, Pall. — *Snow Goose.*[89]

Two fine adult specimens seen on the upper Tierra Blanca, where there are strips of wide marshy pools along the stream. They undoubtedly frequent some of the lower parts of creeks and the Canadian, but were not noticed in passing along. None of the ordinary Wild Geese *(B. canadensis)* were seen in any section visited.

This latter species I observed last February, in large numbers, in the Rio Grande region, at Albuquerque, New Mexico, and below, in April, in about the same sized flocks, but ranging more extensively from Fort Craig north to Algodones, etc.

86Sandhill Crane. *Grus canadensis* (Linnaeus). The remarkable thing about this entry is the time of year in which the species was seen. It is known today as a migrant and winter resident, with its northward passage in spring completed by late March. At the time of year in which McCauley observed them, they are already on their nesting grounds far to the north.

87Virginia Rail. *Rallus limicola* Vieillot. Subsequent to McCauley's observations, there were very few reports of this species in the Panhandle until the construction of Sanford Dam in Hutchinson County and the filling of Lake Meredith. In the early 1970's, wintering birds were discovered in the cattail swamp that developed downstream from the dam, and the species is now present the year around.

88American Coot. *Fulica americana* Gmelin. The coot is still to be found in these areas.

89Snow Goose. *Chen caerulescens* (linnaeus). The snow goose is a migrant and winter resident that is today rarely reported as late as May. Single birds are occasionally seen later, but they are probably ill or injured birds, as may have been the case with McCauley's birds. The fact that he did not see the Canada goose *(Branta canadensis)* is not surprising as wintering birds have left the area by early March.

ANAS BOSCHALS, L. — *Mallard.*90

Abundantly found on all the lower parts of water-courses and at suitable places above.

DAFILA ACUTA, (L.) Jenyns. — *Pintail* or *Sprigtail.*91

Not uncommon on Canadian and other waters.

QUERQUEDULA CAROLINENSIS, (Gm.). — *Green-winged Teal.*92

Frequently seen in about the same localities as *A. boschals.*

QUERQUEDULA DISCORS, (L.) Steph. — *Blue-winged Teal.*93

Frequenting same sections as *Q. carolinensis,* and more abundant than any other of the *Anatidae.* Very plentiful on the upper part of Red River, where the formation of pools brings many flocks of this and kindred species into the cañon made by the stream.

In plazas or villages of Old Mexico, where agriculture is promoted solely by irrigation, the ditches are often enlarged and dammed up, serving as a reservoir for the town. Passing through on the coach I have frequently noted flocks of this and kindred species, swimming about in the most friendly manner, having become so nearly tamed by long immunity from danger that they do not mind the passer-by going within less than even a dozen yards. The villagers come and go for water and the dirty children play about its edge without being heeded, the ducks knowing undoubtedly that natives with shot-guns are to be looked for less often than those other visits so "few and far between."

TABLE 48

Number of Collection.	Sex.	Locality.	Date.	Collector.	Collector's Name.	Length.	Extent.	Wing.	Tail.	Remarks.
1	♀ ad.	Sweetwater Creek	May 12	McCauley		176	15.5	—	7.4	3	Tarsus 1.3; bill 1.6.

90Mallard. *Anas platyrhynchos* Linnaeus. Today this bird is abundant as a migrant and winter resident, and it is the most common breeding duck in the Panhandle (Max S. Traweek, Jr., *Texas Waterfowl: Waterfowl Production Survey,* Federal Aid Project No. W-106-R-5, Final Report [Austin: Texas Parks and Wildlife Department, 1978], 17 pp. [mimeo]).

91Northern Pintail. *Anas acuta* Linnaeus. The pintail is still common to abundant, with nesting (Ibid.).

92Green-winged Teal. *Anas crecca* Linnaeus. A common to abundant migrant and winter resident, these late birds of McCauley's were probably not nesting, although he does not say so. Today small numbers can be found in late spring and early summer, but they are usually groups of non-nesting males. A pair with four ducklings were observed at Lake Meredith, in Hutchinson County, on 15 June 1975, the only known nesting in the area (Frances Williams [compiler] "Southern Great Plains," *American Birds* 29 (1975): 1000).

93Blue-winged Teal. *Anas discors* Linnaeus. The blue-winged teal is still a common to abundant migrant and is second only to the mallard as a nester. (M.S. Traweek, Jr., *Texas Waterfowl*).

QUERQUEDULA CYANOPTERA, (V.) Cass. — *Cinnamon Teal*.[94]

A number of the species observed in similar localities as *Q. discors*.

SPATULA CLYPEATA, (L.) Boie. — *Shoveler*.[95]

A few noted on the Canadian and the lower part of McClellan Creek.

AIX SPONSA, (L.) Boie. — *Summer or Wood Duck*.[96]

Frequently observed in various streams, cañon localities, and elsewhere. Met with by one of our parties upon the hills bordering the Sweetwater, a mile or so from water, wading about through the prairie-grass as contentedly as if it belonged to the Plover family.

FULIGULA MARILA, (L.) Steph. — *Greater Blackhead*.[97]

Frequenting the Canadian and Lower McClellan Creek.

FULIGULA VALLISNERIA, (Wils.) Steph. — *Canvasback*.[98]

Whilst riding up Red River Cañon, May 24, I suddenly came upon a large reedy pool of the stream, from over which rose a dozen Ducks of various kinds, and among them two of this species, not met with elsewhere.

MERGUS MERGANSER, L. — *Merganser or Fish Duck*.[99]

A few specimens noted frequenting the Canadian; none observed elsewhere.

PELECANIDAE.

PELECANUS TRACHYRHYNCHUS, Lath. — *White Pelican*.[100]

Some of the localities visited form part of the habitat for this species. At the crossing of the Cimarron (Kansas), a few miles north of the line of the Indian Territory, a fine specimen was shot by one of our escort.

[94]Cinnamon Teal. *Anas cyanoptera* Vieillot. This bird is a common migrant with scattered nesting (Ibid.).

[95]Northern Shoveler. *Anas clypeata* Linnaeus. This bird is a common to abundant migrant and wintering resident, but it is not known as a breeder.

[96]Wood Duck. *Aix sponsa* (Linnaeus). The wood duck is not to be as frequently observed today. Scattered nesting occurs in the eastern Panhandle, and of late years it appears to have increased its range and numbers.

[97]Greater Scaup. *Aythya marila* (Linnaeus). It is extremely rare to see this species in the Panhandle at any time. Did McCauley confuse it with the more common lesser scaup *(A. affinis)*, which he does not mention? Without birds in hand it is very difficult to tell them apart, particularly without the aid of a binocular.

[98]Canvasback. *Aythya valisineria* (Wilson). This is late in the year to be finding canvasbacks. It is rarely reported today past April.

[99]Common Merganser. *Mergus merganser* Linnaeus. One would not find mergansers on the Canadian today because of changes in the nature of the river. It is no longer a river ". . . hardly more than twenty feet wide . . . with . . . no sand bars . . . and deep with clear, living water" (Carlson, "Panhandle Pastores"). The merganser is a diving duck, fond of deep waters which the Canadian River no longer provides, and it is recorded rarely today past April.

[100]American White Pelican. *Pelecanus erythrorhynchos* Gmelin. This is a migrant with an occasional spring or summer sighting today of non-nesting birds.

LARIDAE.

STERNA SUPERCILIARIS ANTILLARUM, (Less.) Coues. — *Least Tern.*[101]
Occasionally a few were noted on the Canadian.

PODICIPIDAE.

PODILYMBUS PODICEPS, (L.) Lawr. — *Pied-billed Dabchick or Dipper.*[102]
Occasional upon the Canadian.

[NOTE: The general drift of this list reminds one of that of Dr. S. W.
Woodhouse (Sitgreaves's Exploration of the Zuni, &c.),[gg] though the latter contains various species from further southwest not represented
in the region explored by Lieutenant McCauley. The ornithology of the
country traversed by the latter is interesting from the number of species
more or less perfectly characteristic of the Eastern province, which there
meet with Western species, producing some novel combinations. I have
examined but very few of the specimens collected by Lieutenant
McCauley; presuming, however, upon his accuracy of identification
throughout, we have the following unusual juxtapositions of species: —
Eastern. — *Protonotaria citraea, Helmitherus vermivorus, Dendraeca
dominica, Pyranga aestiva, Euspiza americana, Cyanospiza ciris, C. Cyanea,
Cardinalis virginianus, Icterus spurius, I. baltimore, Myiarchus crinitus,
Ortyx virginiana, Melagris americana.*
   Western. — *Catherpes conspersus, Passerculus bairdi, Peucaea cassini,
Spizella breweri, Chondestes grammaca, Calamospiza bicolor, Goniaphea
melanocephala, Pyrrhuloxia sinuata, Icterus bullocki, Corrus cryptoleucus,
Milvulus forficatus, Tyrannus verticalis, Myiarchus cinerascens, Sayorius
sayus, Antrostomus nuttalli, Geococcyx californianus, Picus scalaris, Speotyto
hypogaea, Falco mexicanus.* — Ed.]

101Least Tern. *Sterna antillarum* (Lesson). In 1985 the least tern was placed
on the Endangered Species list (50 *Federal Register* 21792, 28 May 1985 [effective
27 June 1985]). Prior to this classification, the Texas Parks and Wildlife Department conducted aerial and ground surveys along the major waterways of the
Panhandle to determine the locations of any nesting colonies (Bruce C. Thomp-
son, *Nongame Wildlife Investigations: Interior Least Tern Distribution and Taxonomy,*
Job No. 54 [Austin, July 1985, Texas Parks and Wildlife Department], 11 pp,
[mimeo]; Diane McCament, *Nongame Wildlife Investigations: Interior Least Tern
Distribution and Taxonomy,* Job No. 54 [Austin, November 1985, Texas Parks and
Wildlife Department], 11 pp. [mimeo]). These surveys disclosed small nesting
colonies on the Canadian River in eastern Hemphill County and on the Prairie
Dog Town Fork of Red River in central Childress and northcentral Hall counties. McCauley's brief mention of seeing a few on the Canadian River is the
area today where it can most often be observed.

102Pied-billed Grebe. *Podilymbus podiceps* (Linnaeus). As in the case of the
other diving waterfowl in this report, this grebe is rarely seen on the Canadian
River today but can be found on empoundments and playa lakes where the
water is deeper and to its liking.

HISTORICAL NOTES

aThe manuscript of the offical report for the 1876 Survey of the Headwaters of the Red River may be found in U. S., Department of War, Army, Division of the Missouri, Correspondence of General Records Division Exclusive of Accounts and Returns, Letters Received 1871-86, General Records File 2187 (1877), National Archives, Washington, D. C. It was published in a slightly altered form in E. H. Ruffner, "Annual Report of Lieutenant E. H. Ruffner, Corps of Engineers, for the Fiscal Year Ending June 30, 1877," U. S., Department of War, *Report of the Secretary of War,* vol. 2, part 2, in U. S., Congress, 45th Cong., 2nd Sess., House Executive Document 1, part 2 (Washington, D. C.: Government Printing Office, 1877), 1399-1438. The manuscript official report was edited and published in T. Lindsay Baker, ed., *The Survey of the Headwaters of the Red River, 1876, Panhandle-Plains Historical Review* 57 (Canyon, TX: Panhandle-Plains Historical Society, 1985), 7-51.

bGeorge W. Cullum, ed., *Biographical Register of the Officers and Graduates of the U. S. Military Academy at West Point, N. Y. [,] from its Establishment in 1802, to 1890,* III (Boston: Houghton, Mifflin and Company, 1891), 152. McCauley remained for over three decades an officer in the U. S. Army, mostly in the quartermaster corps, seeing service in Pennsylvania, New York, Indiana, Colorado, Wyoming, and Utah. During the Philippine Insurrection he was stationed at Cebu, Iloilo, and Manila. After long service he retired at his own request on 31 October 1900, residing at Highland Park, Illinois. On 20 December 1913 he died in Chicago at the age of sixty-six (Ibid.; Charles Braden, ed., *Biographical Register of the Officers and Graduates of the U. S. Military Academy at West Point, New York[,] Since Its Establishment in 1802,* supplement vol. 5 [Saginaw, MI: Seemann & Peters, Printers, 1910], 169; Wirt Robinson, ed., *Biographical Register of the Officers and Graduates of the U. S. Military Academy at West Point, New York[,] Since Its Establishment,* supplement vol. VI-A [Saginaw, MI: Seemann & Peters, Printers, 1920], 150).

cIbid.; Wallace E. Sabin, Acting Asst. Surgeon, Form of Certificate for Absence on Account of Sickness, 2nd. Lieut. C. A. H. McCauley, of the Third Regiment of Artillery, 21 May 1876, in U. S., Department of War, Army, Compiled Military Service Record for Charles Adam Hoke McCauley, National Archives, Washington, D. C., hereafter cited as McCauley Compiled Military Service Record; Timothy E. Wilcox, Asst. Surg., Fort Leavenworth, Kansas, to Lt. Chas. A. H. McCauley, Fort Leavenworth, Kansas, 7 July 1876, in McCauley Compiled Military Service Record.

dC. A. H. McCauley, Santa Fe, New Mexico, to Adjutant General, U. S. Army, Washington, D. C., 15 April 1876; C. A. H. McCauley, Camp Ruffner, Cañon Red River, Texas, to Adjutant General, U. S. A[rmy], Washington, D. C., 21 May 1876; C. A. H. McCauley, Fort Leavenworth, Ka[nsa]s, to Adjutant General, U. S. A[rmy], Washington, D. C., 7 July 1876, all of the above in McCauley Compiled Military Service Record.

eC. A. H. McCauley, Fort Craig, New Mexico, to Dear Father [C. F. McCauley, Reading, Pennsylvania], 3 April 1876; C. F. McCauley, Reading, P[ennsylvani]a, to the Hon. Alphonso Taft, Secretary of War, [Washington, D. C.], 17 April 1876, both of the above in McCauley Compiled Military Service Record.

fE. H. Ruffner, Fort Leavenworth, Ka[nsa]s, to Dear Mr. McCauley, Fort Bliss, Texas, 10 February 1876, in McCauley Compiled Military Service Record.

gIbid.; Carl Julius Adolph Hunnius, "Survey of the Sources of the Red River
April 25th to June 30th[,] 1876," Carl Julius Adolph Hunnius Collection, Kansas
Collection, Kenneth Spencer Research Library, University of Kansas, Lawrence,
Kansas, available in print in Baker, ed., *Survey of the Headwaters,* 59.

hRuffner in Baker, ed., *Survey of the Headwaters,* 14.

iCullum, *Biographical Register,* 152; C. A. H. McCauley, "Notes on the Ornithology of the Region about the Source of the Red River of Texas, from Observations Made during the Exploration Conducted by Lieut. E. H. Ruffner, Corps
of Engineers, U. S. A.," *Bulletin of the United States Geological and Geographical
Survey of the Territories,* III, No. 2 (Washington, D. C.: G. P. O., 1877), 655-695.
For biographical data on Dr. Elliott Coues, see *The National Cyclopaedia of American Biography,* V (New York: James T. White & Company, 1907), 240-241.

jRuffner in Baker, ed., *Survey of the Headwaters,* 14.

kFor the reader's convenience in following the narrative, a general map of
the Red River Survey of 1876 has been included; the seventeen submaps to
which the general map refers may be found in Volume 58 of the *Panhandle-Plains
Historical Review* (1985).

lRuffner in Baker, ed., *Survey of the Headwaters,* 12-13.

mHunnius in Baker, ed., *Survey of the Headwaters,* 71.

nRandolph B. Marcy and George B. McClellan, *Exploration of the Red River
of Louisiana, in the Year 1852,* U. S. Congress, 33rd Cong., 1st Sess., House Executive Document (Washington, D. C.: A. O. P. Nicholson, Public Printer, 1854).

oThe crossing of the plains noted here was a scout by Colonel John Irvin
Gregg with 214 enlisted men and 11 officers from Fort Bascom, New Mexico,
to the head of Tierra Blanca Creek in the summer of 1872 (Charles L. Kenner,
A History of New Mexican-Plains Indian Relations [Norman, OK: University of
Oklahoma Press, 1969], 197-199).

pElliott Coues, *Key to North American Birds* (Boston: Estes and Lauriat, 1872).

qFrancis B. Heitman, *Historical Register and Dictionary of the United States
Army, from Its Organization, September 29, 1789, to March 2, 1903,* 2 vols. (Washington, D. C.: G. P. O., 1903), 1034.

rElliott Coues, *A Check List of North American Birds* (Salem, [Mass.]:
Naturalists' Agency, 1873).

sElliott Coues, *Birds of the Northwest: A Hand-Book of the Ornithology of the
Region Drained by the Missouri River and Its Tributaries,* U. S., Geological and
Geographical Survey of the Territories, Miscellaneous Publications No. 3 (Wash-
ington, D. C.: G. P. O., 1874).

tFrancis Huntington Snow, *A Catalogue of the Birds of Kansas Contributed to
the Kansas Academy of Science* (Lawrence, KS: Kansas Academy of Science, 1873).

uDraftsman Adolph Hunnius shared the opinion of others on the expedition
that it was unfortunate for the men to have to kill the Scissortailed Flycatchers
in order for McCauley to secure their skins as specimens. On 16 May 1876
he wrote in his diary, "about dark Lt. [Frank D.] Baldwin shot two so-called
Scissorbirds, which have their name of the scissor-like tail. it is a very pretty
looking bird and a pity to shoot them" (Hunnius in Baker, ed., *Survey of the
Headwaters,* 72).

vHunnius found three apparent Poorwill eggs on 5 May 1876 near the Washita
River, but they are not listed with the seven in the table probably because he
returned them to their nest: "By walking near our camp found three eggs laying
on the ground no nest, only a little hole scratched. took them to Lt. Ruffner,
where I was informed that they were of the Whip-poor-will, so I carried them

back from the place I took it. The eggs was very sharply pointed and the other end very rounded with irregular dark brown speckles [but] at [the] point nearly none" (Hunnius in Baker, ed., *Survey of the Headwaters,* 62).

wThe low-flying Nighthawks occasionally startled the expedition participants. On 22 May 1876 Adolph Hunnius noted in his diary, "During the evening shortly after sunset the bullbat birds were around the rocks very thick. they will go and fly quite near a person. they scared me with their sharp cry several times" (Hunnius in Baker, ed., *Survey of the Headwaters,* 77).

xAlthough Adolph Hunnius was not one of the party that secured the hawk chicks, he was present when they were brought into camp on 5 June 1876: "Lt. [Frank D.] Baldwin and party came in late and brought . . . 3 young hawks . . . taken alive from a nest in a hole on the big rocky wall near camp." The parents of the chicks were probably the birds Hunnius had observed two days earlier on 3 June: "by going down in the Cañon I came near a place where a hawk had his nest and the old ones went for me, with shrill cries and angry flapping of wings" (Hunnius in Baker, ed., *Survey of the Headwaters,* 85, 87).

yAccording to Hunnius, Ruffner rather than McCauley claimed credit for taking the specimen of the Swainson's Hawk. On 26 May 1876, the day it was secured, the draftsman wrote, "Lt. Ruffner showed me a splendid Hawk he killed" (Hunnius in Baker, ed., *Survey of the Headwaters,* 80).

zOn several occasions Hunnius wrote in his diary about the captive eagle chicks. On 17 June 1876 he penned, "Dr. Mendenhall and Mr. Sullivan had been out in the breaks of the Cañon and found in a tree the nest of an Eagle. They brought both young ones in. Mr. Sullivan presented his to Sergt. Lichtenberg, who put his to Dr. Mendenhall[']s box and takes care of those animals. They are very young, but of large size." The next day he noted, "The two old Eagles have been pretty near all afternoon over our Camp, watching their young ones, sitting in a box in front of our tent." The eagle chicks survived the trip back to civilization, Hunnius noting in Dodge City, Kansas, on 30 June 1876 that Sergeant Lichtenberg "got his eagles all right and takes care of the Mercurial Barometer" (Hunnius in Baker, ed., *Survey of the Headwaters,* 99, 101, 111).

aaTurkeys were among the most popular birds among the expedition members because of their fine edible qualities. On 3 May 1876, the first night out from Camp Supply on the trail to Fort Elliott, Adolph Hunnius described the method that one of the civilian teamsters employed for hunting turkeys: "After supper . . . Mr. Sullivan said to me to be quiet and he would bring [in] a wild turkey. he was not more than ½ hour gone when he brought one. Several went to do the same but without success. He said they were only good to shoot at in a moon[lit] night as they roost close on a tree and you have to get the turkey between the moon and the gun or else you will hit nothing." The next day Hunnius noted, "after 2 P. M. crossed North Commission Creek where there is much and fine timber, & celebrated turkey roost as I was told[;] sometimes one can see them here by thousands." A few days later, on 12 May 1876, the draftsman penned in his journal: "Mr. Sullivan brought a turkey gobbler in he killed, a splendid shot, hit the head. Helped him in dressing the bird. he gave me a so-called turkey caller[,] a bone out of the wing[,] and the beard." On yet another day, 17 May 1876, Hunnius described the canyon of Mulberry Creek, reporting finding "in the bottom much wild Turkeys" (Hunnius in Baker, ed., *Survey of the Headwaters,* 60-61, 67, 73).

bbHunnius also observed Prairie-Chickens during the early part of the trip to Texas. On the first day out from Dodge City, 27 April 1876, he commented that "3 prairie chickens were killed after some skirmish. they let the ambulance right up to them but as soon [as] they saw a person they would take wing."

Then on 4 May 1876, after leaving camp on Wolf Creek, he noted, "saw some prairie chickens, antelopes" (Hunnius in Baker, ed., *Survey of the Headwaters*, 54, 61).

ccThe Bobwhites similarly showed little fear when approached by draftsman Hunnius. On 9 May 1876 he encountered many of them on a horseback ride near Fort Elliott: "On the way back from that place [the Upper Town] we saw a great many Quails which were quite tame just running a few feet from our horses" (Hunnius in Baker, ed., *Survey of the Headwaters*, 65).

ddIt may have been a Long-billed Curlew that Hunnius observed between Battle Creek and Mulberry Creek on 14 June 1876 when he wrote, "Saw some long billed snipe" (Hunnius in Baker, ed., *Survey of the Headwaters*, 96).

eeThis expedition was the one in 1872 led by Colonel John Irvin Gregg already cited. Kenner, *Plains Indian Relations*, 197-199.

ffWhile in camp at Scare Spring in Tule Canyon, Hunnius noted "Some ducks and mud hens came to the creek" (Hunnius in Baker, ed., *Survey of the Headwaters*, 92).

ggL[orenzo] Stitgreaves, *Report of an Expedition down the Zuñi and Colorado Rivers*, U. S. Congress, 32nd Cong., 2nd Sess., Senate Executive Document No. 59 (Washington, D. C.: Robert Armstrong, Public Printer, 1853).

INDEX

tridge, 204; Scissor-tailed Flycatcher, 67–68, 166, 179–81, 182; 214*n* v; Scissor-tails, 179–81; Short-eared Owl, 191; Shoveler, 211; Snipe, 92 (*see also* birds, individual varieties); Snow Goose, 209; Snowy Egret, 208*n* 84; Snowy Heron, 208; Solitary Sandpiper, 206*n* 79; Solitary Tattler, 206; Solitary Vireo, 168; Southern Pinnated Grouse, 202–203; Southwestern Lark, 159, 163–64; Sparrow, 196 (*see also* birds, individual varieties); Sparrow Hawk, 180, 182, 196–97; Sprigtail, 210; Summer Duck, 211; Summer Redbird, 167; Summer Tanager, 167; Summer Warbler, 165; Swainson's Buzzard, 197–98; Swainson's Hawk, 197*n* 63, 215*n* y; Swallow (*see* birds, individual varieties); Swallow-tailed Flycatcher, 179–81; Swallow-tailed Kite, 193; Texas Cardinal, 174, 180; Texas Woodpecker, 190; Thrush, 166 (*see also* birds, individual varieties); Turkey, 56, 57, 58, 63, 69, 95, 215*n* aa (*see also* birds, Common Wild Turkey); Turkey Buzzard, 200; Turkey Vulture, 200; Upland Plover, 207; Upland Sandpiper, 207; Vireo (*see* birds, specific varieties); Virginia Nightingale, 174; Virginia Partridge, 203–205; Virginia Rail, 209; Warbler, 166 (*see also* birds, individual varieties); Warbling Vireo, 168; Western Field Lark, 176–77; Western Kingbird, 182*n* 44; Western Meadowlark, 176*n* 34; Western Nighthawk, 159; Whippoorwill (*see* birds, Nuttall's Whippoorwill); White-headed Eagle, 199; White-necked Raven, 179; White Pelican, 211; White-throated Wren, 163; White-winged Blackbird, 172; White-winged Dove, 201; Wild Turkey, 201*n* 71; Wilson's Snipe, 206; Wilson's Warbler, 166*n* 10; Wood

Duck, 211; Wood Ibis, 208; Wood Stork, 208*n* 82; Worm-eating Warbler, 164; Yellow-billed Cuckoo, 189–90; Yellowbird, 168; Yellow-breasted Chat, 166*n* 11; Yellow-headed Blackbird, 175–76; Yellow-rumped Warbler, 166*n* 10; Yellow-throated Warbler, 165; Yellow Warbler, 165. *See also* ornithological report

Bishop, Lt. (officer at Camp Supply, Okla.), 54

Blake, Charles A., 30

Bluff Creek, Kans.: as camping place, 50, 104; geology at, 39; mentioned, 38, 77; ornithological specimens collected at, 193

Bluff Creek Mail Station, Kans., 104

bones, 7; as survey markers, 60 (*see also* buffalo, bones from)

Bonita Creek (Arroya Bonita), Tex.: as point on stadia-line survey to Canadian River, Tex., 16, 17, 112*n* 35

Boot Hill cemetery, Dodge City, Kans., 106

botanical report, 21–27; notes on, kept by Woodruff, 5–6

botanical specimens. *See* specimens, botanical

bottles: for flavoring extract, 81; for preserving specimens, 29, 58, 65, 71, 74, 89, 100; for whisky, 61

Bronnecker, Mr. (individual at Dodge City, Kans.), 49–50

Brownsville, Tex., birds observed at, 188

buffalo: bones from, 7, 172 (*see also* bones); calves, 99; carcasses of, 178, 199*n* 66, 200; drink water from pools on McClellan Creek, Tex., 191; huge herd of, 103; hunted for food, 10, 70, 78, 80, 81, 82, 84, 85, 87, 90–91, 94; hunted for hides, xv, 7, 11, 97, 99 (*see also* buffalo hunters); hunted for sport, 99; observed by expedition members, xv, 67, 82, 88, 92, 94, 97, 99, 100, 101, 103, 205; tallow rendered from, 84, 89; trails from, 96